IN THE
NEW ENGLAND
FASHION

IN THE NEW ENGLAND FASHION

RESHAPING WOMEN'S LIVES

IN THE NINETEENTH CENTURY

Catherine E. Kelly

CORNELL UNIVERSITY PRESS

ITHACA AND LONDON

GRATEFUL ACKNOWLEDGMENT IS MADE TO THE CASE WESTERN RESERVE UNIVERSITY
DEPARTMENT OF HISTORY FOR ITS GENEROUS SUPPORT FOR THE COVER ILLUSTRATION.

First published 1999 by Cornell University Press

Printed in the United States of America

LIBRARY OF CONGRESS CATALOGING-IN-PUBLICATION DATA

Kelly, Catherine E.
    In the New England fashion : reshaping women's lives in the
nineteenth century / Catherine E. Kelly.
       p. cm.
    Includes index.
    ISBN 0-8014-3076-3 (cloth : alk. paper)
    1. Women—New England—History.   2. Rural women—New
England—History.   3. Middle class—New England—History.   I. Title.
    HQ1438.N35 K45 1999
    305.4'0974—dc21   98-36485

For my parents
Helen Burns Kelly
Charles A. Kelly, Jr.

Contents

Acknowledgments   ix

Abbreviations   xiii

CHAPTER 1 "It seems like a little paradise compared with
           the city"   1

CHAPTER 2 "All the work of the family"   19

CHAPTER 3 "Never was a separation so painful"   64

CHAPTER 4 "With joy I bear his name and pay the duties
           which his virtue claims"   93

CHAPTER 5 "Old people never believe in Love"   127

CHAPTER 6 "Simple ideals of living"   162

CHAPTER 7 "All the artificial barriers which society sometimes
           erects, appeared to be thrown down"   188

CHAPTER 8 "Joining anon in fashion's noisy din"   214

CHAPTER 9 "An elevated tone to the whole town"   242

Index   253

Acknowledgments

Writing a book often feels like a solitary, thankless task. Writing acknowledgments puts things in perspective.

A number of institutions provided financial support for this book and the dissertation that preceded it. The Case Western Reserve University W. P. Jones Presidential Faculty Development Fund, the American Antiquarian Society, the University of Rochester Susan B. Anthony Womens Studies Center, and the University of Rochester Department of History offered generous support for research; fellowships from the University of Rochester also supported my graduate education. My writing has been supported at various stages by a dissertation fellowship from the Spencer Foundation and a postdoctoral fellowship at Case Western Reserve University. A grant from the Case Western Reserve University W. P. Jones Presidential Faculty Development Fund subsidized the illustrations for this book. John Bassett, Dean of the College of Arts and Sciences at Case Western Reserve University, has graciously encouraged and supported the research and writing of this book.

The process of bookmaking has left me with a number of debts. I have depended on the generosity and patience of librarians and archivists at the American Antiquarian Society; the Schlesinger Library; the Houghton Library, Harvard University; the Massachusetts Historical Society; the Robert Frost Memorial Library at Amherst College; the Jones Library, Inc.; Sophia Smith Collection; Historic Northampton; Forbes Library; the Pocumtuck Valley Memorial Association; Springfield City Library; the Historical Society of Cheshire County; the Baker Library at Dartmouth College; the New Hampshire Historical Society; the Vermont Historical Society; and the University of Vermont Library. Special thanks are due Daria D'Arienzo, Amherst College Archives and Special Collections; and Susan Lisk, Porter-Phelps-Huntington Foundation, Inc. And I am deeply grateful for the assistance of librarians at the Rush Rhees Library, University of Rochester, and the Kelvin D. Smith Library, Case Western Reserve University. Bryna Leeder, Mary Beale, and Sue Fortier opened their homes to me during research trips to Massachusetts and New Hampshire. At the end of the project, Andrea Westcot, Joe Heinen, and Steve Hach offered terrific research assistance. Peter Agree, my editor at Cornell University Press, believed that my dissertation would yield a book long before I did. I am grateful both for his unfailing support and for the close attention that other Cornell staff members have devoted to the project; thanks are due Barbara Sutton and most especially Nancy J. Winemiller.

Like all scholars, I have benefited much from other people's learning. I owe much to my teachers at the University of California, Santa Barbara, especially Patricia Cline Cohen, who gave me my first formal training in women's history. At the University of Rochester, May Young and Eugene Genovese introduced me to the early nineteenth century. My dissertation advisor, Christopher Lasch, demonstrated the potential for an engaged cultural and intellectual history. His work as a scholar and teacher set standards that I might never meet but still claim as my own. In the past ten years, I have visited portions of this book on scholars at conferences, in seminars and colloquia, and over dinner. In return, I have benefited from the judicious criticism and lively conversation of Molly Berger, Jeanne Boydston, Richard Bushman, Seth Fein, Betsey Fox-Genovese, Jean Friedman, Michael Grossberg, David Hammack, David Hochfelder, Traci Hodgson, David Jaffee, Mary Kelley, Carol Lasser, Ken Ledford, Jonathan Prude, Carroll Pursell, Randy Roth, Jonathan Sadowsky, Alan Taylor, and members of the Case Western Reserve University History works-in-progress group. Christopher Clark gave the final manuscript a careful, timely, and incisive reading.

I am especially indebted to Alan Rocke, my department chair, whose support for my scholarship has been matched only by his commitment to my academic career. Every junior professor should have a chair like him; it is a shame that so few do. I have also been graced with two extraordinary mentors, Lynn Gordon and Angela Woollacott, who have given me support, counsel, humor, and friendship in equal measure and beyond all reasonable expectation; I cannot imagine either my career or my life without them.

My deepest debts are to my family—real and fictive. Dave Hochfelder has been a generous friend. Tod Kelly, Niki Steckler, Aidan Steckler Kelly, and Perrin Love have long given me their enthusiastic support. Rich Hamerla entered my life around the time that this book was leaving it, improving both in immeasurable, if intangible, ways. Susanna Holm, Beth McGee, and Michelle Togut, the sisters I never had growing up, have done what all good sisters do. As I wrote about the dilemmas and the richness of women's lives, these three were never far from my mind. Together with my mother, Beverly Burns Love and Barbara Straub Denton provided me with a childhood rich in women's stories and family narratives; the first women's history I learned, I learned from them. For as long as I can remember, my father and mother have encouraged me to speak my mind, especially when it differed from theirs. This book is surely the fruit of that early training. Just as surely, this book is for them, with love.

Abbreviations

AAS   American Antiquarian Society, Worcester, Massachusetts

ACASC Amherst College Archives and Special Collections, Amherst, Massachusetts

CVHM Genealogy and Local History Library, Connecticut Valley Historical Museum, Springfield, Massachusetts

DCL   Dartmouth College Library, Hanover, New Hampshire

FL   Forbes Library, Northampton, Massachusetts

HCL   Houghton Library, Harvard University, Cambridge, Massachusetts

HSCC   Historical Society of Cheshire County, Keene, New Hampshire

JL   The Jones Library, Inc., Amherst, Massachusetts

MHS   Massachusetts Historical Society, Boston

NHS   Northampton Historical Society, Northampton, Massachusetts

NHHS   New Hampshire Historical Society, Concord

PPHFP Porter-Phelps-Huntington Family Papers, on deposit at Amherst College Archives and Special Collections, Amherst, Massachusetts

PVMA Pocumtuck Valley Memorial Association, Deerfield, Massachusetts

SL   Schlesinger Library, Radcliffe College, Cambridge, Massachusetts

SSC   Sophia Smith Collection, Smith College, Northampton, Massachusetts

UVM   Special Collections, University of Vermont Library, Burlington

VHS   Vermont Historical Society, Montpelier

IN THE
NEW ENGLAND
FASHION

1

"It seems like a little paradise compared with the city"

"It is pleasant to go and visit a city, but I never desire to live in one," concluded Sabra Clark Snell following a visit to New York City near the end of the antebellum period. "There is too much <u>noise</u> and <u>confusion</u>, <u>dirt</u> and <u>dust</u> for me." Writing to her sister-in-law from the comfort of her home in Amherst, Massachusetts, Snell regarded her life as the wife of a small-town college professor with considerable satisfaction. With equal parts pride and relief, she declared that "<u>my dear home</u> is more pleasant this summer than it ever was it seems like a little paradise compared with the city."[1] Measuring her home, and her hometown, against the chaos of the nation's largest city, Snell clearly favored Amherst, crediting it with cleanliness, order, stability, and security—the traditional virtues of the New England village.

Harriett Goodell, a teenage contemporary of Mrs. Snell, agreed that Amherst was indeed secure. But where Snell considered her home a refuge from the disruptions of modern life, Goodell dismissed it as a provincial backwater. As a girl, Harriett corresponded regularly with her New York City cousin, Angelo Goodell. The two shared their daily lives and common interests, describing the weather, their lessons and outings, and the peculiar and occasionally inexplicable behavior of adults. In 1854, however, Angelo's request for "Amherst news" brought a sharp retort from Harriett, usually the most amiable and con-

[1]Sabra Cobb Clark Snell to Sarah Snell, n.d., Box 2 folder 27, Snell Family Papers, ACASC.

1

ventional of correspondents. Railing against the emptiness of rural life in general and the stagnation of Amherst life in particular, she observed that in Amherst "we have no such thing as News. It would make the worthy citizens of this most worthy town 'gape with wonder and amazement' should they hear of any thing new." To Harriett's way of thinking, a stubborn parochialism kept her town "much behind the times," bereft of the "advantages for receiving much that is new and interesting." Where the city's "noise" and "confusion" disoriented Sabra Clark Snell, Harriett Goodell was exhilarated by the prospect of "vast multitudes . . . experiencing constant changes." She chafed at the complacency of her kin and neighbors, who could "remain at home quiet & contented" while the world passed them by. But if Harriett condemned Amherst's provincialism, she could not escape it; for all her sophistication, she remained Angelo's "rustic cousin," his "country cousin." Even the most ambitious girl could not expect to transcend such parochial surroundings.[2]

The differences between these two accounts of provincial life owe much to the differences between the writers themselves. Middle-aged Sabra Clark Snell had achieved an established position within her community; in antebellum Amherst, to be the wife of a respected professor was no small thing. Most likely, she had long since made peace with whatever reservations she might have entertained about her life's possibilities. The serenity of her own life and position perfectly mirrored the stillness she perceived in Amherst's streets and gardens. Harriett Goodell, on the other hand, was full of adolescent impatience and a sense of unrealized potential. Projecting her desires for excitement and autonomy onto the urban landscape, she conflated the country town with the confinements of middle-class girlhood.

Differing in age, in temperament, and in their estimation of their community, Sabra Clark Snell and Harriett Goodell nevertheless possessed a common understanding of the relation between town and country. Both women envisioned the city as the center of national life and the engine of national progress, casting the country as a static retreat from the corruptions, confusion, and tumult of urban life. Drawing on the conventions of sentimental literature, they envisioned rural New England as an extension of the domestic circle. Like the middle-class home, the countryside had become a haven from the world of economic production. The shops and factories that propelled and symbolized the development of rural capitalism vanished from small-town streets; marketable crops and livestock disappeared from the sur-

[2]Harriett Goodell to Angelo Goodell, 13 January 1854, Goodell Papers, JL.

rounding fields; labor and commerce were leached from the substance of community life. Collapsing ruralness into domesticity, Snell and Goodell reduced the countryside to a genteel landscape. These geographic and social boundaries also helped define the boundaries of self, delineating a distinctive range of opportunities and limitations. In the eyes of Snell and Goodell, rural New England and rural New Englanders stood apart from the vices and rewards of nineteenth-century market society. For good or ill, Amherst and towns like it had become places where nothing happened, places that escaped time and history.[3]

Continuity and Change in the Countryside

Of course, no place and no people can escape historical change. But Snell and Goodell, along with their parents and grandparents, confronted greater change than many. In the first half of the nineteenth century, rural New England witnessed a thoroughgoing social transformation as the household economy gave way to a market society. Broadly put, that household economy had been distinguished by face-to-face transactions between neighbors and kin, noncash payment for goods and services, and an ethos of restraint in the collection of debt, all of which were aimed at preserving the independence of rural households. Although rural communities hardly escaped inequalities of wealth and power, there were distinct limits on men's ability to accumulate considerable wealth and to translate that wealth into political power. Between 1820 and 1840, local and regional pressure combined to erode this household economy. The growth of urban markets increased the need for farm produce as well as the opportunities for families to earn extra income through outwork. At the same

[3]The literature on the sentimentalization of rural New England is enormous. My thinking on the connections between the New England ideal in particular and nineteenth-century bourgeois culture has been influenced especially by Joseph S. Wood, *The New England Village* (Baltimore: Johns Hopkins University Press, 1997); Stephen Nissenbaum, "New England as Region and Nation," in *All over the Map: Rethinking American Regions*, ed. Edward L. Ayers et. al. (Baltimore: Johns Hopkins University Press, 1996); Robert A. Gross, "The Confidence Man and the Preacher: The Cultural Politics of Shay's Rebellion," in *In Debt to Shays: The Bicentennial of an Agrarian Rebellion*, ed. Robert A. Gross (Charlottesville: University of Virginia Press, 1993), 297–324; Lawrence Buell, "American Pastoral Ideology Reappraised," *American Literary History* 1 (1989): 1–29, and *New England Literary Culture: From Revolution to Renaissance* (New York: Cambridge University Press, 1986); Sarah Burns, *Pastoral Inventions: Rural Life in Nineteenth-Century Art and Culture* (Philadelphia: Temple University Press, 1989); and John R. Stilgoe, *Borderland: Origins of the American Suburb, 1820–1939* (New Haven, Conn.: Yale University Press, 1988).

time, a steady population increase led to a land shortage, compelling families to farm their land more intensively and forcing them to seek out new "careers" for their sons and to use the labor of their women in new ways. As farmers deepened their involvement with and their dependence on regional and national markets, their wives and daughters abandoned spinning and weaving to purchase the commercially manufactured cloth that rolled out of New England's textile mills. Merchants and manufacturers increased the scope and pace of business, carving out new positions of economic and political influence. Local exchange increasingly conformed to the rules and ethics of the market, which had previously applied only to long-distance trade and very large purchases, such as land. Rather than relying on outright trade or long-term, flexible credit, basic purchases began to require cash. Many men and women turned to wage and outwork simply to make ends meet, while others amassed fortunes that would have been unthinkable to earlier generations.[4]

To be sure, the regional economy remained dominated by agriculture. But the commercialization of agriculture, the advent of industrial production, the gradual evolution of the provincial household from a center of production to a center of consumption, and the increasing

---

[4]On the development of rural capitalism in New England, see James A. Henretta, "Families and Farms: *Mentalite'* in Pre-Industrial America," *William and Mary Quarterly*, 3d ser., 35 (1978): 3–32; Henretta, "The Transition to Capitalism in Early America," in *The Origins of American Capitalism: Collected Essays* (Boston: Northeastern University Press, 1991), 256–95; Winifred B. Rothenberg, "The Market and Massachusetts Farmers, 1750–1855," *Journal of Economic History* 41 (June 1981): 283–314 (along with the following exchanges: Rona S. Weiss, "The Market and Massachusetts Farmers, 1750–1850: Comment"; Rothenberg, "The Market and Massachusetts Farmers: Reply," both in *Journal of Economic History* 43 [1983]; 475–80); Michael A. Bernstein and Sean Wilentz, "Marketing, Commerce, and Capitalism in Rural Massachusetts," and Rothenberg "Markets, Values, Capitalism: A Discourse on Method," both in *Journal of Economic History* 44 (1984): 171–73; Rothenberg, *From Market-places to a Market Economy: The Transformation of Rural Massachusetts, 1750–1850* (Chicago: University of Chicago Press, 1992); Jonathan Prude, *The Coming of the Industrial Order: Town and Factory Life in Rural Massachusetts* (New York: Cambridge University Press, 1983); Hal S. Barron, *Those Who Stayed Behind: Rural Society in Nineteenth-Century New England* (New York: Cambridge University Press, 1984); Gregory H. Nobles, "Commerce and Community: A Case Study of the Rural Broom-making Business in Antebellum Massachusetts," *Journal of the Early Republic* 4 (1984): 287–308; Nancy R. Folbre, "The Wealth of Patriarchs: Deerfield, Massachusetts, 1760–1840," *Journal of Interdisciplinary History* 16 (1985): 199–220; Steven Hahn and Jonathan Prude, eds., *The Countryside in the Age of Capitalist Transformation: Essays in the Social History of Rural America* (Chapel Hill: University of North Carolina Press, 1985); Daniel Vickers, "Competency and Competition: Economic Culture in Early America," *William and Mary Quarterly*, 3d ser., 47 (1990): 3–29; and Christopher Clark, *The Roots of Rural Capitalism: Western Massachusetts, 1780–1860* (Ithaca, N.Y.: Cornell University Press, 1990).

commercial and cultural ties between the North's urban centers and its hinterland all signaled the emergence of rural capitalism, which disrupted and eventually destroyed the older household economy. If many families continued to stake their lives and their livelihoods on independent farms, the economic, social, and cultural contexts of farming and of rural life in general had changed considerably. Looking back on this period from the close of the nineteenth century, historian Frances Underwood observed that "there are few instances in history of a transformation more complete than has been seen in Massachusetts." And Underwood's point can be easily extended to much of rural New England.[5]

Given the magnitude this change, how are we to make sense of the comments of Sabra Clark Snell and Harriett Goodell? How—and why—did they and women like them see unwavering continuity where others have seen sweeping change? This book explores how provincial women arrived at this singular understanding of their communities, their neighbors and families, and themselves. It takes seriously both the overwhelming evidence of social and economic change and women's attempts to makes sense of the interplay of change and continuity in their daily lives. In what ways did women's sense of cultural persistence reinforce or counter experience? How did it shape their identities as wives and daughters, as friends and neighbors, as mistresses of households and members of communities? And what can their worldviews and experiences tell us about the development of rural capitalism, about the ways in which women and men both experienced and shaped the Great Transformation?

If women like Sabra Clark Snell and Harriett Goodell could claim membership in rural communities, they could also claim membership in a new, provincial middle class. Just as the Great Transformation led growing numbers of men to despair of ever owning a farm or shop, it allowed others to take advantage of new opportunities for wealth and power. The diversification of local economies, the expansion of credit, and the growth of markets simultaneously created new occupations and transformed older ones. Increasing numbers of merchants, lawyers, clerks, men-of-letters, and ministers built careers within rural towns. Over the course of the antebellum era, these "professionals" and their families allied themselves with artisans-cum-manufacturers and prosperous farmers, with those who shared both their faith in this process of economic transformation and their ability to maneuver within it. As

[5]Francis H. Underwood, *Quabbin: The Story of a Small Town with Outlooks on Puritan Life*, quoted in Clark, *Roots of Rural Capitalism*, 7.

we shall see, these women and men helped reshape the provincial economy. But they as they negotiated between the household economy and market society, between continuity and change, they also decisively recast provincial society and culture.

To explore these issues is to explore the tension between lives that testified, however ambiguously, to change and beliefs that bespoke a commitment, however conflicted, to tradition. It is also to blur the distinctions between social and intellectual history, between the history of persons and behavior on the one hand and intellect and imagination on the other.[6] The women who form the core of this study left behind an especially rich written record. They counted themselves as the beneficiaries of a New England tradition that prized literacy both as the means to salvation and as the cornerstone of the republic. They also laid claim to a broader transatlantic culture that privileged literary accomplishment as a badge of gentility. Provincial women *wrote*. They wrote for themselves and their loved ones; occasionally, they published for a larger community of anonymous readers. Some women, blessed with leisure, a passion for words, or some combination of the two, wrote on a weekly, if not daily, basis. Others, burdened by household cares or plagued by an aversion to writing, took up their pens far less frequently. While the diaries, letters, and imaginative writings of gifted writers provide especially expressive and compelling descriptions of individual experience, the same themes and experiences appear in more prosaic accounts. Taken together, these documents trace the broad and changing outlines of provincial women's lives, their collective experience of change and continuity.

Such sources have long been the special preserve of social historians, who have read them as accounts of women's behavior, as records of what they did, how often they did it, and in whose company. But these documents are not simply unmediated reflections of experience. The most intimate or haphazard diary is more than a repository of the day's events. It is also a text shaped as much by historically specific literary conventions as by the life and literary talents of a particular individual. The carefully shaped script and elegant turns of phrase, along with the

[6] I use *intellectual history* rather than *cultural history* (or *cultural studies*) to describe my project for several reasons. The first is simply to appropriate the notion of intellectual history for historical subjects who are typically excluded from the ranks of thinkers. For too long, intellectual life has been cast as the exclusive preserve of elite white males, leaving the rest of us to have "experiences." *Intellectual history* also underscores women's and men's conscious attempts to grapple with the surrounding world, both individually and collectively, through both intellect and imagination.

ubiquitous apologies for lapses in composition and penmanship, testify to the craft that women brought to their writing. In both its public and private forms, writing allowed women to articulate their experiences just as it allowed them to articulate the meaning of those experiences. But it also allowed them to define themselves as thinkers whose conscious and unconscious decisions about subject matter and language testify to their intellectual engagement with the world around them. Letters and diaries, friendship books and commonplace books, schoolgirl essays and published poetry marked women as writers, as readers, as participants in a community of letters. Read this way, these sources offer an intellectual history of people who were not intellectuals in any canonical sense. Yet as rich as these sources are, they lose most of their meaning abstracted from the social contexts and material realities of women's lives. Indeed, much of the power of these documents lies precisely in their defiance of the fine distinctions between social and intellectual history. Put another way, these documents served multiple purposes in the lives and minds of their creators; they can certainly withstand multiple readings at the hands of historians.[7]

A close reading of the ways in which provincial women constructed urban change and rural continuity reveals more than the sentimentalization of the countryside. Like other observers, before and since, New Englanders used the familiar opposition between city and country as kind of shorthand, calling to mind a complex and sometimes contradictory constellation of values and practices. But if the broad outlines of this comparison extend back to the classical era, its precise formulations and significance are historically specific.[8] When antebellum New Englanders contrasted city and country, they simultaneously participated in a venerable tradition and in the Great Transformation. This was not simply an intellectual exercise, a game of highfalutin ideas

[7]I am hardly alone in grappling with the connections between intellectual history and social history. Relevant discussions include John E. Toews, "Intellectual History after the Linguistic Turn: The Autonomy of Meaning and the Irreducibility of Experience," *American Historical Review* 92 (1987): 879–907; David Mayfield and Susan Thorne, "Social history and its discontents: Gareth Stedman Jones and the Politics of Language," *Social History* 17 (1992): 165–88; James Vernon, "Who's Afraid of the 'Linguistic Turn'? The Politics of Social History and its Discontents," *Social History* 19 (1994): 81–97; and Patrick Joyce, "The End of Social History?" *Social History* 20 (1995): 73–91. For a feminist approach to these issues, see Joan Wallach Scott, "The Evidence of Experience," *Critical Inquiry* 17 (1991): 773–95, and her *Gender and the Politics of History* (New York: Columbia University Press, 1988).

[8]Raymond Williams, *The Country and the City* (New York: Oxford University Press, 1973). Lawrence Buell, "American Pastoral Ideology Reappraised," offers an insightful analysis of the pastoral in the American literary tradition.

played at a remove from reality. Nor was it the result of an unconscious process in which imagination functioned as a mirror held up to reality. The full range of meanings bound up with "city" and "country" emerged from the intersection of imagination, ideology, and experience. These meanings signify more than the creation of a pastoral fantasy. Narratives about town and country, and particularly about the special nature of rural life, marked the uneasy intersection of tradition and transformation that characterized capitalist development. The meanings embedded in these narratives both reflected and helped constitute new identities of gender and class. Taken together, these meanings, and the process through which women and men created them, point toward the creation of a provincial middle class.

As provincial women and men mapped the geographic, social, and cultural distance between town and country, they elaborated distinctions between change and continuity, between the new and the old. But they also elaborated the differences between two seemingly antithetical ways of life. The difference between town and country was the difference between aristocratic pretension and republican simplicity; between streets crowded with hostile strangers and neighborly greetings from people whose kin had been known for generations; between the abstract rights of the individual and the organic claims of the community. More to the point, the difference between town and country was the difference between market society and household economy. In a market society, degraded and dependent men sold their labor power to handful of merchants and manufacturers in return for wages. Children ignored the good counsel of their parents and shunned them in old age. Women, rich and poor, abandoned industrious housewifery to become the parasitic slaves of fashion. In the household economy, the families of independent freeholders labored together to increase their wealth while preserving their independence from the market.

To illustrate the difference between household economy and market society, New Englanders turned time and again to stories, narratives, and examples that centered on households and the gender and social relations that obtained in them. It was in the daily experience of self, family, and community that the alarming implications of change became visible. As the pronouncements of Sabra Clark Snell and Harriet Goodell suggest, New Englanders generally imagined that the provincial experience of self and community was both organic and eternal. But this sense of timeless tradition was itself a construction, and an especially unstable and contested one at that.

Through the mid-1830s, provincial women and men drew on individual memory and rural culture to elaborate a constellation of values and practices that they ascribed to the household economy, emphasizing the corporate dimensions of provincial culture and the mutual obligations that bound neighbors and kin. Notwithstanding their growing participation in a market economy and their deepening commitment to a market society, this vision of a traditional household economy revealed serious reservations about bourgeois social and gender relations. The persistent juxtaposition of rural virtue to urban vice served as a cautionary defense against the encroachments of market society; after all, who wouldn't choose the life of the stalwart yeoman over the precarious existence of the propertyless wage earner?

This vision of a harmonious country society founded on independent households became far more attenuated and contested around 1840. In part, this was generational. The construction of a "traditional" household economy drew on memories and practices that were increasingly removed from the lives of a younger generation of women and men. But these tensions were not only generational. The renegotiation of gender systems was central to the development of rural capitalism. In provincial communities, New Englanders attempted to advance their (gendered) interests by recasting traditional values, practices, and prerogatives to accord with their own interests, which often conflicted. Redefining woman-and manhood, and the roles through which those identities were realized, provincial women and men increasingly found themselves at odds. Women who looked to the canon of domesticity to bolster their authority within their households and communities found their men all too reluctant to relinquish patriarchal authority. The same domestic rituals and neighborly gatherings that had been celebrated as central to the organic harmony of provincial communities became occasions for conflict; the rhythms of household production and consumption, tea parties and rustic balls, and even courtship became contested terrain.

Ironically, provincial New Englanders' juxtaposition of town and country ultimately smoothed the transition to capitalism. Discourses about rural society in general and the household economy in particular initially revealed reservations about market society and later divided the emerging middle class along generational and gender lines. But these same discourses ultimately proved critical to middle-class hegemony, for the provincial middle class constructed itself by negotiating between the intersecting imperatives of the household economy and market society. Despite all that separated household economy from bourgeois domesticity, both were predicated on the household's detachment from the market.[9] In the household economy, rural families labored to keep their households, and especially their men, free from the market's snare. The twin pillars of nineteenth-century bourgeois culture, individualism and domesticity, were grounded in the construction of the home as a necessary refuge from the violence of commerce. If the celebrated competence of the household economy depended on its independence from the market, antebellum middle-class culture depended on the flight from the market. This ideological convergence, this shared value, was hardly accidental. Antebellum bourgeois culture derived much of its special character—its nostalgic celebration of simplicity and authenticity, its contradictory assessment of the market, and especially its anxious preoccupation with the tropes and conventions of domesticity—from the experiences and expectations of men and women who were grappling with the erosion of the household economy.

This convergence provided a crucial bridge between the household economy of the 1820s and 1830s and the market society that emerged after 1840. It allowed provincial New Englanders to recast the values and practices of the household economy in ways that brought them closer to the bourgeois ideal even as they insisted on their claims to continuity with the past. Locating the evils and excess of market society in the parlors of an urban middle class, provincial men and women deflected attention away from their increasing involvement in market society and their deepening commitment to bourgeois culture. In effect, they created a bourgeois culture that owed less to urban middle-class style than to its disavowal. From the 1840s, provincial New Englanders manipulated an increasingly hollow notion of the traditional household economy to position themselves uneasily between their poorer neighbors and their urban counterparts. Juxtaposing the virtues of their households and their culture against the fashionable commotion they ascribed to bourgeois society, they obscured the growing distance that separated even members of the provincial middle class from their poorer farming and laboring neighbors. At the same time, they embraced bourgeois culture and bourgeois class relations in more subtle ways. Appropriating for themselves the virtues of the yeoman, his wife and the household economy, they dismissed

[9]On the significance of "independence" for rural households, see Henretta, "Families and Farms"; Merrill, "Cash Is Good to Eat"; Prude, *Coming of the Industrial Order*; and Clark, *Roots of Rural Capitalism*. On domesticity as a flight from the market for both men and women, see Gillian Brown, *Domestic Individualism: Imagining Self in Nineteenth-Century America* (Berkeley: University of California Press, 1990).

their neighbors as backward oafs or picturesque rustics. Abstracted from their material underpinnings, the beliefs and conventions that had characterized the household economy could further the interests of an emerging middle class. From this perspective, the testimony of women like Sabra Clark Snell and Harriet Goodell stands at the center of a discourse and a social process that initially worked to resist, then to complicate, and finally to mask the encroachments of a market society.

Capitalism, Gender, and Culture

Examined in the linked contexts of daily life and intellectual engagement, provincial women's narratives of self, family, and community point toward issues that have become central to historians' efforts to understand both the development of rural capitalism and the broader transformation of the antebellum North: the reshaping of rural class relations, the origins of the northern middle class, and the critical role played by gender and culture in each. Although the experiences and stories of such women belie their insistence on the traditionalism of rural life, they hardly recapitulate the narrative of social transformation described by Frances Underwood and subsequent historians.

For many years, American historians interested in the social and economic transformation of the antebellum North echoed the pronouncements of Sabra Clark Snell and Harriett Goodell. Like Amherst, the countryside was a place where little of real importance happened. Industrialization, commercialization, changes in social structure and family life, and the flow of migration and immigration were generally analyzed through the prism of urbanization, even though the overwhelming majority of nineteenth-century Americans made their lives in rural rather than urban areas. Social change was synonymous with city scenes. When most historians noticed the countryside at all, it was only to emphasize its distance from urban centers, its protection from the forces of social and economic change, its resistance to cultural progress. Even rural historians with an obvious stake in demonstrating the significance of the countryside tended to cast it as a pale reflection of dynamic urban centers. The hinterland might have supplied the workers who became mill hands, the streams of men and women who swelled urban populations, and the food that fueled them all. It even provided the backdrop for the rapid expansion of boomtowns like Rochester and Utica, in New York. Yet for the most part, rural men and women remained aloof from these dramas, waiting passively for the forces of change to seep out from the city.[10]

In the past fifteen years, debates over the transition to and development of American capitalism have moved the rural North much closer to the center of historical inquiry. Questions about when, and how, Americans became capitalists (and by extension about the character and meaning of the American past) have come to turn on questions about the nature of rural life. Was the countryside contested terrain, offering resistance to the economic practices and the social relations that constitute a market society? Or was it at the front lines of capitalist development? In these exchanges, "market" historians, drawing on neoclassical economic theory and using quantitative evidence to demonstrate the importance of markets and profits in shaping farmers' behavior, faced off against "social" historians, who examined household production, family strategies, and community mores to question the extent of market influences in determining behavior. If the lively—and occasionally rancorous—debates that followed sometimes culminated in intellectual gridlock, they also brought a new richness to our understanding of rural lives and communities in the eighteenth and nineteenth centuries.[11]

Historians have recently assumed the delicate task of piecing together insights from these two camps. As the new rural synthesis is making clear, if the northern countryside did not mark the frontier of Western capitalism, neither was it exempt from the influence of a growing world market. From the eighteenth century, northern farmers

[10]Methodologies and questions generated by the new social history underscored the close association between socioeconomic change and urbanization. See, among many, Stuart M. Blumin, *The Emergence of the Middle Class: Social Experience in the American City, 1760–1900* (New York: Cambridge University Press, 1989); Mary P. Ryan *Cradle of the Middle Class: The Family in Oneida County, New York, 1790–1865* (New York: Cambridge University Press, 1983); and Paul E. Johnson, *A Shopkeeper's Millennium: Society and Revivals in Rochester, New York, 1815–1837* (New York: Hill & Wang, 1978).

[11]The differences between "market" and "social" interpretations were first described by Alan Kulikoff, "The Transition to Capitalism in Rural America," *William and Mary Quarterly*, 3d ser., 46 (1989): 120–44. For overviews of recent literature on the development of rural capitalism, see Jeanne Boydston, "Women's Market Labor and the Transition to Capitalism in the United States," *Journal of the Early Republic* 16 (1996): 183–206; Michael Merrill, "Putting Capitalism in Its Place: A Review of Recent Literature," *William and Mary Quarterly*, 3d ser., 52 (1995): 315–26; Gordon Wood, "Inventing American Capitalism," *New York Review of Books*, 9 June 1994, 44–49; Nancy Grey Osterud, "Gender and the Transition to Capitalism in Rural America," *Agricultural History* 67 (1993): 14–29; Christopher Clark, "Rural America and the Transition to Rural Capitalism," *Journal of the Early Republic* 16 (1996): 223–36, and "Economics and Culture: Opening up the Rural History of the Early American Northeast," *American Quarterly* 43 (1991): 279–301; and Kulikoff, "The Transition to Capitalism in Rural America."

increased their production for national and even international markets. After the first quarter of the nineteenth century, this commercial impulse not only increased the connections between farmers and markets but began to reshape relations within rural communities. But if rural capitalism eventually overshadowed the household economy, it was far slower to destroy it. Well into the nineteenth century, the values and practices that characterized the household economy persisted, albeit in truncated form. Ironically, households that sought to preserve their independence from the vagaries of the market and that privileged family security over individual ambition often pursued the very strategies that gave rise to rural capitalism. This story—complicated, contradictory, and multicausal—moves us beyond the static juxtaposition of market against society, illuminating the ways in which markets and societies shape each other.[12]

As social and labor historians have demonstrated, this complicated process of social and economic change ultimately helped forge a permanent, rural working class. After more than ten years of careful, even painstaking inquiry, we now know a good deal about rural industrialization. Scholars have illuminated the creation of the factory villages that employed hundreds of men, women, and children in textile production; the gradual transformation of small, family-owned shops; and the spread of outwork that drew growing numbers of women, especially, into the antebellum labor market. More important, they have shown how these processes emerged out of and slowly transformed not only the rural economy but also rural society. Yet while these studies treat the working class in detail, the middle class is conspicuous in its absence. The emerging working class confronts a shadowy coalition of professionals, merchants, artisans-cum-manufacturers, and prosperous farmers. And, for the most part, these historians have paid scant attention to the ways in which gender contributed to the development of rural capitalism, much less to the ways it shaped class formation. When gender is introduced into these narratives of change, it figures simply as evidence of industrialization rather than as a fundamental part of the process of change. Women appear only when as they perform "productive," market-oriented labor—when they churn butter, braid palm-leaf hats, or weave cloth either within their households or in mills. If we now know that provincial elites consolidated their political and economic power in the two decades before the Civil War, we know very little about the formal and informal processes through

[12]See especially Clark, "Rural America and the Transition to Rural Capitalism," and Kulikoff, "The Transition to Capitalism in Rural America."

which they established the legitimacy of their claims to the linked spheres of political, economic, and cultural power. And we know far less about the internal dynamics of class formation, about the ways in which these men and women made sense of the changing social order.[13]

If historians of rural capitalism are generally reticent about the origins of the provincial middle class, historians whose focus is the emergence of the antebellum middle class have been all but silent. Overwhelmingly, these scholars have embedded their accounts of class formation in tales of city-building. Drawing on the methods of what used to be called "the new social history," they have created a more or less structural model of class formation. They locate the markers of class formation not only in work, primarily in the rise of white-collar jobs, but in residential patterns that simultaneously separated home from work and the homes of the middle class form those of the working class.[14] In particular, they have linked the antebellum middle class to the growth of voluntary associations and to changes in family life and women's special role in each of these developments. Drawing on the work of women's historians, they have placed the creation of a female sphere near the center of middle-class formation. The arrival of the middle class is announced either by the rise of evangelical reform movements that allowed women to take aim at the urban evils of drink, prostitution, and godlessness or by the triumph of new forms of family life that privileged the gentle influence and sentimental authority of mothers over the cold and distant authority of the patriarch. To conceptualize the emerging middle class in this way is to conceptualize the growing city; the very notion of a rural middle class becomes a non sequitur.

It would be foolish to banish the city from our understanding of the origins of the middle class. The evangelically fired reform movements that reshaped northern politics and society in the antebellum years were a predominantly urban phenomenon. Rural women and men sponsored charitable fairs to raise money for missionaries and for colonization; they enrolled in societies to eradicate prostitution; and they signed their share of temperance pledges. But their participation in these efforts was far more sporadic than that of city residents. The class and gender identities of provincial men and, especially, provincial

[13]See, for example, Clark, *Roots of Rural Capitalism*; Jensen, *Loosening the Bonds*; and Thomas Dublin, *Transforming Women's Work: New England Lives in the Industrial Revolution* (Ithaca, N.Y.: Cornell University Press, 1994).

[14]See especially Blumin, *Emergence of the Middle Class*.

women owed relatively little to their membership in voluntary associations.

If the outlines of antebellum reform appear to place the middle class squarely within the confines of the city, the contours of domesticity point to a distinctly provincial dimension of middle-class formation. Domesticity was not simply the result of economic change but was itself a fundamental part of the capitalist transformation of the countryside. The ideology of separate spheres, the (fictive) separation of home and work, and the daily practice of domesticity were inextricably bound up with the decline of the household economy.[15] The dilemmas of girls, wives, mothers, and "spinsters" that were addressed by the endless flow of prescriptive literature and that stood at the center of sentimental fiction arose out of the economic and social dislocations that accompanied the erosion of the household economy. It is no accident that northern novelists from Catharine Sedgwick to Harriet Beecher Stowe to Nathaniel Hawthorne located their dramas of domestic relations in New England's villages, for such "sleepy" towns provided the setting for these twinned domestic and economic dramas not only in the fiction but also in the lives and memories of the writers themselves.[16] Despite all the attention that bourgeois domesticity has received from women's and social historians, it demands to be reexamined in the context of the erosion of the household economy and the capitalist transformation of the countryside. The same insights about the development of rural capitalism that have enriched our understanding of the nineteenth century's market revolution must be brought to bear on our understanding of the origins of the antebellum middle class.

In some measure, historians' (justifiable) preoccupations with labor and urban history have worked to deflect their attention away from the creation of a provincial middle class. But the provincial middle class has remained invisible largely because it confounds the conceptual frameworks that have been used to define that class. Provincial communities resist the standard criteria for middle-class formation: Distinctions between blue and white-collar occupations, class-based residential patterns, the dominance of voluntary associations, and clearly divided spheres for men and women. And, as Allan Kulikoff has demonstrated, the ambiguous class position of farmers in an industri-

---

[15]The best account of this process is Jeanne Boydston, *Home and Work: Housework, Wages, and Ideology in the Early Republic* (New York: Oxford University Press, 1990).

[16]Lawrence Buell makes an argument compatible to this one in *New England Literary Culture.*

alizing economy complicates matters even further.[17] These unsatisfying attempts to conceptualize class formation suggest the need to look beyond social structural explanations of class, to consider the role of culture in shaping class formation as well as the subjective experience of class.

Historians of rural capitalism have been surprisingly slow to grasp that the transformation of the countryside was not simply an economic or social process but a cultural and intellectual one as well.[18] In their telling, the values embodied in the household economy continue to stand in stark opposition to the values of bourgeois culture, even as the economic strategies of the household economy merge with the economic imperatives of a market society. Compared with rural historians, historians of the middle class have lavished attention on culture and gender. Indeed, in their analyses, women and culture are linked constructs. Women marry, rear children, and impose polite table manners on their men; they also read novels and shop. But these studies rarely address the cultural work performed by changes in consumption and sociability, in gender roles and identities. In ways that come dangerously close to recapitulating nineteenth-century bourgeois gender ideology, these historians invoke particular gender roles and cultural constructions as proof that the middle class is fully formed. Put another way, the cultural construction of gender and cultural work in general

[17]Allan Kulikoff, *The Agrarian Origins of American Capitalism* (Charlottesville: University Press of Virginia, 1992).

[18]David Jaffee and Robert A. Gross provide the most important exceptions to this rule. See Jaffee, "Peddlers of Progress and the Transformation of the Rural North, 1760–1860," *Journal of American History* 78 (1991): 511–35; "The Village Enlightenment in New England, 1760–1820," *William and Mary Quarterly*, 3d ser., 47 (1990): 327–46; and "One of the Primitive Sort: Portrait Makers of the Rural North, 1760–1860," in *The Countryside in the Age of Capitalist Transformation*, 103–38. Relevant works by Robert A. Gross include "The Confidence Man and the Preacher"; "Culture and Cultivation: Agriculture and Society in Thoreau's Concord," *Journal of American History* 69 (1982): 42–61; "'The Most Estimable Place in All the World': A Debate on Progress in Nineteenth-Century Concord," *Studies in the American Renaissance* (1978): 1–15; and "Transcendentalism and Urbanism: Concord, Boston, and the Wider World," *Journal of American Studies* 18 (1984): 361–81.

Scholars studying the history of reading and the book have also begun to consider the intellectual transformation of the countryside, although they have not necessarily applied their insights to questions about the development of rural capitalism. See Richard D. Brown, *Knowledge Is Power: The Diffusion of Information in Early America, 1700–1865* (New York: Oxford University Press, 1989); William J. Gilmore, *Reading Becomes a Necessity of Life: Material and Cultural Life in Rural New England, 1780–1835* (Knoxville: University of Tennessee Press, 1989); and Jack Larkin, "The Merriams of Brookfield: Printing in the Economy and Culture of Rural Massachusetts in the Early Nineteenth Century," *Proceedings of the American Antiquarian Society* 96 (1986): 39–73.

may mark the finish line, but these constructions have little to do with the race of middle-class formation itself.

The dynamic intersection of gender, class, and culture has been explored with far more success in recent years by a variety of scholars working within what might be called cultural studies. Taking their cues both from the growing body of cultural history and from literary criticism, especially the new historicism, they have examined cultural productions, especially literary texts, as constituent elements of historical change and relations of power. Notwithstanding significant debates over theory and method, the majority of this work examines class and culture together. And a significant portion of this scholarship also insists on the centrality of gender to contests over class and culture. In large measure, the power of this literature derives from its stubborn juxtaposition of canonical and noncanonical texts, from the surprising convergences between "great novels," medical texts, housekeeping manuals, and architectural illustrations. Provocative in all senses of the word, this growing body of scholarship has reminded historians of the need to examine, contextualize, and deconstruct culture. But if this scholarship has served to locate cultural productions in history writ large, it has left them abstracted from the everyday lives of women and men. For all its successes, cultural studies has helped create a body of literature in which cultural productions speak to other cultural productions with only occasional intervention from the cultural producers themselves.[19]

Thinking about the creation of a provincial middle class—about the intersection of gender, culture, and class formation as part of the rural transition to capitalism—demands that we move beyond the limitations of each of these narratives of change. Provincial women's lives, and the stories they told about their lives, challenge and extend our understanding of the capitalist transformation of the countryside, the origins of the northern middle class, and the relation between cultural representation and social practice. The chapters that follow explore these issues from the perspective of middling and middle-class women in rural Massachusetts, New Hampshire, and Vermont from the late eighteenth century until the eve of the Civil War. Chapters 2 and 3 explore the interplay of change and continuity in provincial women's lives. These chapters examine women's attempts to straddle two often

[19]Two studies of antebellum culture that fulfill the promise of what might be called "cultural studies" are Brown, *Domestic Individualism*, and David Leverenz, *Manhood and the American Renaissance* (Ithaca, N.Y.: Cornell University Press, 1989).

contradictory worlds, for in households and in academies, among kin and among friends, women found themselves negotiating between the values and practices of the household economy and the the values and practices of bourgeois culture. Chapter 4 focuses on the social significance of courtship and marriage within provincial communities and for provincial women. Chapter 5 examines the transformation of love, both as a sentiment and as a practice, among members of the provincial middle class. Taken together, these two chapters explore the ways in which women and men reshaped gender systems as they fashioned a middle class; these chapters also explore the ways in which that gender system created new tensions between middle-class women and men. Chapters 6 and 7 examine sociability and the expansion of a provincial public sphere, exploring the ways in which these gendered practices both articulated a distinctive, provincial middle-class identity and eased class tensions. Chapter 8 traces discourses of fashion, consumption, and social emulation in published and private writings and considers the ways in which those discourses shaped and reflected women's understandings of their communities and the development of rural capitalism. Finally, Chapter 9 explores the ways in which the provincial middle class contributed to the creation of a mythical, sentimentalized New England village.

2

"All the work of the family"

Early in the spring of 1841, Elizabeth Phelps Huntington of Hadley, Massachusetts, worked alongside her two daughters and her new daughter-in-law readying a suite of rooms in the rambling Huntington house for her son, Theodore Huntington, and Elizabeth Sumner Huntington, his bride of one month. With the arrival of new furniture in mid-March, she wrote that the newlyweds "turned their backs upon us and set up an establishment of their own" within Elm Valley, as the house was called. Although the purchased furniture "fitted up the new parlor in very pretty style," the capstone of the renovations came not from a Boston retailer, but from the needles of the Huntington women, in a carpet pieced by Phelps Huntington, her daughters Bethia Huntington and Elizabeth Huntington Fisher, and her daughter-in-law, Elizabeth Sumner Huntington.[1]

The addition of the carpet completed the parlor, signaling that the couple was prepared to receive calls from kin and neighbors. But if the finished carpet announced the arrival of the new couple, the process of making of the carpet symbolized important connections between the women. The pleasure the Huntington women took in their carpet speaks not simply to their pride in their needlework but also to the richness of the relationships they crafted with one another.

The stitches that bound the new carpet bound the four women: sixty-two-year-old Elizabeth Phelps Huntington, mother of eleven children;

[1]Elizabeth Phelps Huntington described the scene and its significance in a letter to her son, Frederic Dan Huntington, 22 March 1841, PPHFP Box 12, Folder 9.

19

middle-aged Elizabeth Huntington Fisher, whose own children had finally reached an age that allowed her to visit from Oswego, New York; Elizabeth Sumner Huntington, whose married life had just begun; and Bethia Huntington, an unmarried woman in her thirties who spent her days within her parents' household. The shared labor at once inaugurated Elizabeth Sumner Huntington into her new family and reinforced the attachments between the other Huntington women. Through their needlework, the four also affirmed their shared identities as women. Differences in age, family of origin, and marital status receded into the background as these "female women, that is three Elizabeths and one Bethia made the carpet for the said parlour."

Elizabeth Phelps Huntington's story seems to illustrate the notion of separate spheres, providing a vivid example of the profound disjunction between male and female cultures that seemed to distinguish nineteenth-century, middle-class society. Numerous historians have observed that as industrialization moved economic production out of the household and into factories, shops, and offices, nineteenth-century Americans increased the spatial and social distance between home and work, sharpening and exaggerating the differences between public and private, male and female. Dividing the world in two, this ideology of separate spheres assigned men to the public world of political and economic competition, the world of money and power. Women, in turn, were left to the private sphere, within households that had become homes, to preside over children and hearths. This same ideology recast the meaning of women's work. With the ascendance of the market, work in particular and productivity in general became synonymous with wages. As households became homes, housework became something other than work. In the bourgeois imagination, the labor of feeding, clothing, cleaning, and nursing evaporated, rematerializing first as women's duty and later as an act of magical transformation: Socks were darned, meals were prepared, and parlors were swept not through women's physical exertions but as a result of women's heightened sensibility—their feminizing, civilizing influence.[2] Less the stuff of experience than ideology, the cult of domesticity increased middle-class women's gender consciousness; in Nancy Cott's elegant

[2]See Jeanne Boydston's invaluable study, *Home and Work: Housework, Wages, and the Ideology of Labor in the Early Republic* (New York: Oxford University Press 1990); see also Nancy Folbre, "The Unproductive Housewife: Her Evolution in Nineteenth-Century Economic Thought," *Signs* 16 (1991): 463–85. For a complementary analysis of literary representations of the transformation of housework, see Gillian Brown, *Domestic Individualism: Imagining Self in Nineteenth-Century America* (Berkeley: University of California Press 1990), 63–95.

formulation, womanhood bound women together even as it bound them down.[3] Elevating domesticity's potential to bind women together over its power to bind them down, many scholars have emphasized the relative autonomy of women's sphere, arguing that nineteenth-century women succeeded in forging a distinct, and distinctly female, culture.[4]

At first glance, Elizabeth Phelps Huntington's account of the new carpet and the relationships it symbolized seems to reveal such a "sphere," defined by women's common responsibilities to their families, measured by the rhythms of the female life cycle, bound by the stitches that produced the carpet, and colored by the special affection women reserved for one another. Yet the scene hardly evidenced a separate sphere, much less an autonomous women's culture. Certainly, Phelps Huntington claimed a place for herself within a dense web of female affiliations, a web woven out of family bonds, women's work, and gender identity. But that web was enmeshed in a much larger network of associations that encircled provincial households and communities.

"Three Elizabeths and one Bethia" might have joined together to

[3]The best account of the emergence of separate spheres and the cult of domesticity remains Nancy F. Cott, *The Bonds of Womanhood: Women's Sphere in New England, 1780–1835* (New Haven, Conn.: Yale University Press, 1977). For a wide-ranging and enlightening account of the ways in which the ideology of separate spheres has shaped the historiography of American women, see Linda K. Kerber, "Separate Spheres, Female Worlds, Woman's Place: The Rhetoric of Women's History," *Journal of American History* 75 (1988): 9–39. See also Nancy A. Hewitt, "Beyond the Search for Sisterhood: American Women's History in the 1980s," *Social History* 10 (1985): 299–321, esp. 300–4. The classic feminist theoretical analysis of the gendered division between public and private remains Michelle Zimbalist Rosaldo, "Women, Culture, and Society: A Theoretical Overview," in *Woman, Culture, and Society*, ed. M. Z. Rosaldo and Louise Lamphere (Stanford, Calif.: Stanford University Press, 1974), 17–42.

[4]Nancy Hewitt summarizes and critiques this literature in "Beyond the Search for Sisterhood." The notion of an autonomous and oppositional women's culture has been most forcefully, extensively, and consistently developed by Carroll Smith-Rosenberg. See especially "The Female World of Love and Ritual: Relations between Women in Nineteenth-Century America," reprinted in her *Disorderly Conduct: Visions of Gender in Victorian America* (New York: Oxford University Press, 1985), 63, 53. The essay originally appeared in *Signs* 1 (Autumn 1975), 1–29; Smith-Rosenberg later defended and elaborated her argument in "Politics and Culture in Women's History: A Symposium," *Feminist Studies* 6 (Spring 1980): 55–64, and in "Hearing Women's Words: A Feminist Reconstruction of History," *Disorderly Conduct*, 11–52, esp. 30–39. For further examples of Smith-Rosenberg's formulation of the autonomy of women's culture, see her *Disorderly Conduct*, especially the chapters "Beauty, the Beast, and Militant Woman," "The Cross and the Pedestal," and "The New Woman as Androgyne"; "Writing History: Language, Class, and Gender," in *Feminist Studies/Critical Studies*, ed. Teresa de Lauretis (Bloomington: Indiana University Press, 1986), 31–54; and "Domesticating 'Virtue': Coquettes and Revolutionaries in Young America," in *Literature and the Body: Essays on Population and Persons*, ed. Elaine Scarry (Baltimore: Johns Hopkins University Press, 1988), 166–84, esp. 176–78.

make a carpet, but they relied on their men, Dan and Theodore Huntington, "the two lords of the creation," for help "to put it down." The menfolks were not valued only for their contributions to the afternoon's work; like the four women, they were intimately bound up with the values and alliances represented by the new carpet. Elizabeth Phelps Huntington noted with special pleasure that the carpet was laid on her son Theodore's birthday. To honor her husband, Elizabeth Sumner Huntington "insisted" that the entire Huntington family gather for tea in her new parlor. This impromptu party fused women's culture and family networks, joining kin across gender and generation and binding those who were Huntingtons by birth with those who joined the family through marriage. In Phelps Huntington's imagination, the parlor's inauguration also joined the living to the dead. She recalled that the room that would serve as Theodore's parlor had been occupied by her own mother and father "from the time of their marriage to the time of his death." When her family "consecrat[ed]" the parlor with the "evening sacrifice" and a hymn, summoning the memories of earlier prayers, Phelps Huntington "indulge[d] the thot, that many of the blessings bestow'd on me and my children, were the fruit of earnest and devout prayer offered within those walls."

Making a carpet for her son and daughter-in-law, Elizabeth Phelps Huntington identified herself as one woman among several, one of three Elizabeths and a Bethia. But she also defined herself as a wife, a mother, and a daughter—statuses that depended equally on her connection to male and female kin and that took on a particular meaning within provincial households and towns. Finally, she located herself as a Phelps and a Huntington, linking three generations of an established and influential family within her community. Phelps Huntington's identity was embedded in a complex web of familial relationships. It was performed through women's work, through the piecing of carpet and the preparation of tea. And it was inscribed in the letter she wrote that depicted the afternoon's events and hinted at their meanings. In her description of carpets and parlors, family teas and evening prayers, Phelps Huntington revealed the interplay between family relations and daily labor that structured provincial women's lives and relationships throughout the first half of the nineteenth century. But to say that kinship, work, and the connections between the two remained central to women's gender roles and gender identities is not to say that these things defied the passage of time. Changes in rural economy, society, and culture transformed the structure and meaning of work, family, and gender in subtle but significant ways. And provincial women participated in that process of change, attempting to harness it to advance their own interests and the interests of their kin. Beyond the serenity of the Huntingtons' new parlor—and even within it—changes were at work.

Housework

The middle-class household was transformed from a center of production to a center of consumption throughout the nineteenth century. Indeed, this process was fundamental to the creation of a middle class.[5] But to say that northern men and women gradually abandoned domestic manufactures in favor of commercially produced goods is not to say that women abandoned production for consumption, that they escaped lives of labor for lives of leisure. The overwhelming majority of women, middle class and otherwise, worked long and hard throughout the antebellum period.[6] Provincial women were no exception. The kinds of labor they performed varied over time and among households. But throughout, women's work was bound up with their households' relation to the market. New England families responded to the market penetration of the early nineteenth century by driving themselves to increase their productivity and cut costs. As Christopher Clark has observed, this burden fell disproportionately on women.[7]

During the antebellum period, increasing numbers of women took advantage of opportunities to earn cash. Single women sought out positions in schools and mills. Married women took in boarders. Single and married alike took in piecework; they also produced extra yarn, cloth, butter, and vegetables for the market. Women also eased the leverage that merchants and manufacturers wielded over their families by producing goods for cash or, more frequently, credit. Historians have documented the hundreds of hours that the wives and daughters of New England's yeomen spent churning butter, making buttons, and braiding palm-leaf hats. But these same women produced smaller quantities of an enormous variety of marketable goods. For example, Marion Hopkins of Sunapee, New Hampshire, stitched Bellows wallets in between helping her mother with the washing and spending time at the family shop. Louisa Bradlee found that by painting window hang-

[5]Stuart M. Blumin, *The Emergence of the Middle Class: Social Experience in the American City, 1760–1900* (New York: Cambridge University Press, 1989), 179–91.

[6]The best description of nineteenth-century housework is Boydston, *Home and Work.* See also Susan Strasser, *Never Done: A History of American Housework* (New York: Pantheon Books, 1982).

[7]Christopher Clark, *The Roots of Rural Capitalism: Western Massachusetts, 1780–1860* (Ithaca, N.Y.: Cornell University Press, 1990), esp. 122–55.

ings with "very <u>handsome</u> designs such as Lord Byron's residence, Sir Walter Scott's &c," she could earn around six dollars a week.[8]

Women often took on tasks to save money as well as to earn it, for what women could produce, their families need not purchase. The four Huntington women whose afternoon work party introduced this chapter surely understood that the carpet they pieced reduced their debt to the Boston retailer; from their perspective, the carpet-making party was not simply a manifestation of women's sphere or a symbol of family unity but a part of the household's economic strategy. Dan Huntington and Elizabeth Phelps Huntington used their extensive farm and the labor of their large family not only to reduce their own reliance on the market but also to help their children do so. When their eldest daughter became engaged in 1824, her marriage portion included linens and woolens produced within the Huntington household as well as "the promise of all the flax and wool . . . that she could spin, to be made into fabrics." Years later, her brother "doubt[ed] if the little spinning wheel ever knew a more busy season than that which preceded her wedding." Women's work offset large, one-time expenditures associated with setting up a new household. But it also relieved their families' day-to-day dependence on merchants and manufacturers. As Harriet Aiken declared, "On the 4th of July 1828 our independence was achieved, since on that day did we for the fist time become the owners of <u>a cow</u>! So now I have <u>a dairy</u> . . . & make my own butter."[9] Far from elevating middling women to a sphere of leisure, the development of rural capitalism tied them more closely to a world of work.

[8]Louisa Bradlee to Samuel C. Bartlett, 30 May 1844, Bartlett Family Papers, NHHS. Marion Hopkins Diary 1976–53, 9, 13, 19 September 1853, 1 October 1853, NHHS. For accounts of rural women's market production, see Sally Ann McMurry, *Transforming Rural Life: Dairying Families and Agricultural Change* (Baltimore: Johns Hopkins University Press, 1995); Thomas Dublin, *Transforming Women's Work: New England Lives in the Industrial Revolution* (Ithaca, N.Y.: Cornell University Press, 1994); Clark, *Roots of Rural Capitalism*, 139–50, 179–89; Nancy Grey Osterud, *Bonds of Community: The Lives of Farm Women in Nineteenth Century New York* (Ithaca, N.Y.: Cornell University Press, 1991); and Joan M. Jensen, "Cloth, Butter, and Boarders: Women's Household Production for the Market," *Review of Radical Political Economics* 12 (Summer 1980): 14–24, and *Loosening the Bonds: Mid-Atlantic Farm Women, 1750–1850* (New Haven, Conn.: Yale University Press, 1980). For overviews of rural women's work, see Osterud, "Gender and the Transition to Capitalism in Rural America," *Agricultural History* 67 (Spring 1993): 14–29; and Elizabeth Fox-Genovese, "Women in Agriculture during the Nineteenth Century," in *Agriculture and National Development: Views on the Nineteenth Century* ed. Lou Ferleger (Ames: Iowa State University Press, 1990).

[9]Harriet Adams Aiken to Eliza Minot Adams, 16 July 1828, Adams Family Papers, MS 420, Box 3, Folder 39, DCL. Theodore G. Huntington, "Sketches by Theodore G. Huntington of the Family and Life in Hadley Written in Letters to H. F. Quincy," 57, PPHFP, Box 21, Folder 7.

Whether spinning for a marriage portion, churning butter for credit with a local merchant, or painting window screens for cash, provincial women also found themselves scrambling to meet their other domestic responsibilities. They spent endless hours keeping house. Indeed, much of the work that women did for exchange or for the market was structured to accommodate the demands of housework, which claimed the majority of most women's time. Whatever income-earning opportunities the development of capitalism created, the bulk of most women's labor remained housework—performed in their households and for their kin. Then as now, the rhythms of housework were relentless. But if the pace of housework has fluctuated less than we might expect, the effort required of housekeepers has changed dramatically[10] Antebellum housework was often hard, physical labor. And antebellum women observed that tending to a middling provincial household was far more difficult than tending to an urban one. When Mary Cochran and her three daughters moved from Boston to Northampton, Massachusetts, in 1836, they saw a pronounced deterioration in their standard of living. "It is difficult here to get any variety of provisions, & we cannot always get what we want at the time we want it," wrote one daughter. If the women lacked familiar resources, they also lacked fundamental skills. "Not understanding the art of cooking very well, we do not perhaps make the best use of our means," she admitted. The move necessitated a crash course in domestic economy. Although she was in her late forties, Mary Cochran was "determined to learn everything . . . she goes to work very vigorously about the bread and butter &c. &c. thus far she has been very successful." Some ten years later, on a visit to Princeton, Massachusetts, Maria Wiswell Russell was daunted by her mother-in-law's skills. "I am learning everything I can by looking on," she wrote; mercifully, her endless questions did not put her mother-in-law "out of patience."[11]

If provincial housekeeping generally required women to do more work with fewer resources, the development of rural capitalism also compelled them to do more with less help. Young women who might once have served as household help increasingly looked to teaching, textile mills, and outwork to earn money. By the early 1830s, women living in the vicinity of mills reported that domestic help was rapidly

[10]Ruth Schwartz Cowan, *More Work for Mother: The Ironies of Household Technology from the Open Hearth to the Microwave* (New York: Basic, 1985); JoAnn Vanek, "Time Spent in Housework," *Scientific American* (1974); 116–21.

[11]Maria Wiswell Russell to Thomas Russell, 23 June [ca. 1840s], Charles Russell Papers, MHS. Marianne Cochran to Agnes Cochran Higginson, 1 July 1836; Martha Cochran to Agnes Cochran Higginson, 12 March 1837, Fuller Family Papers, PVMA.

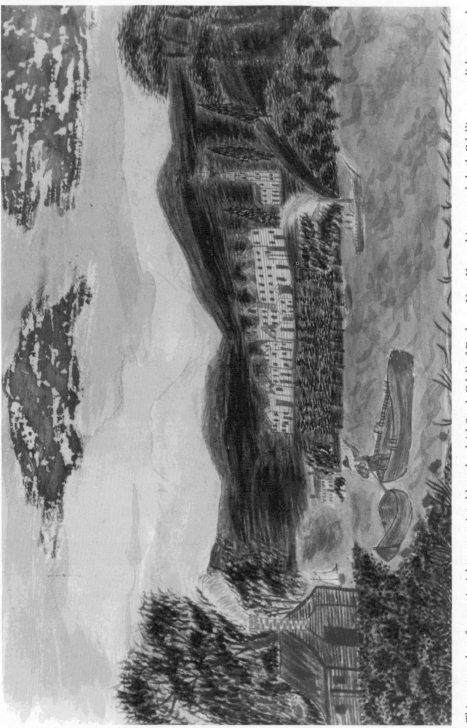

This watercolor of a provincial town, painted by schoolgirl Sarah Odell of Durham, New Hampshire, reveals both Odell's accomplishment and the growing commercialization of the New England countryside. New Hampshire Historical Society #F4663.

disappearing. In 1836, after the creation of a mill village in Chicopee, Massachusetts, Amelia Peabody of nearby Springfield succinctly explained the effects of industrialization on domestic economy:

> Just about the old Chicopee Bridge, adorned with piles of factories, where oceans of Boston money is invested; and where all the farmers find a market for their supplies, which makes our living half as high again as it used to be; and where every pair of hands that the Chicoppee Establishments do not need, can be supplied with work and wages; that makes it impossible to obtain any in families, or to pay them if they could be got. Rich folks pay two dollars a week; poor ones go without, and are better served."[12]

As Peabody and the Cochrans discovered, the strategies that rural families used to regulate their contact with the market forced women to shoulder heavy burdens regardless of whether they produced goods for exchange.

Finding Good Help

If housework occupied an enormous share of women's lives, it played a far less conspicuous role in their accounts of daily life, in their literary representations of themselves. Women rarely wrote at length about cooking, cleaning, or sewing. Although they were far more forthcoming about child-rearing, they privileged the affectional and spiritual dimensions of motherhood over the physical labor that children required. References to housework appear most often in diaries, in terse phrases: Women wrote merely that they "sewed some" or "washed some." One way to apprehend the magnitude and strain of housework is to examine the significance of "help," of servants, in provincial women's lives. Although only a small minority of antebellum women could count on the assistance of live-in servants for any length of time, the majority of middling provincial women depended on the labor of others to maintain their households. Very few families included enough women to allow them to forgo "help" either from hired women or kin who worked in exchange for board, some money, or a few new dresses.[13] Women's comments about hired help or, more

[12]Amelia White Peabody to Mary Jane White, 17 April 1836, Everett-Peabody Family Papers, MHS.

[13]I discuss exchanges of women's labor among kin later in this chapter. Because so much early nineteenth-century paid domestic help was relatively episodic and casual, it is difficult to determine precisely either the numbers of women and men who worked as servants or the numbers of households that employed them. Christopher Clark (*Roots of Rural Cap-*

frequently, about its scarcity, speak to the sheer quantity of labor that women were expected to perform as well as its physical toll. Their comments also point to the distinctive dynamics of provincial class relations within households and between women.

Most examinations of domestic service have taken the plaintive, patronizing cry that "good help is hard to find" as their starting point. Casting the middle-class woman as an increasingly unskilled lady of leisure, they have traced the ways in which widening class divisions and deepening ethnic tensions created friction between mistress and maid. Sometime in the early nineteenth century, historians agree, the reciprocity of "help" declined into the indignities of "service."[14] But the diaries and letters of provincial women complicate this story. Provincial women tended to appreciate good help when they could get it. And virtually all help qualified as "good."

Elizabeth Phelps Huntington certainly understood the value of household help. Preparing to take in two boarders in 1801, she wrote that "we should not have undertaken this business had we not the prospect of good help—a black girl in town, by the name of Chloe, who has formerly kept a family is coming to live with us." The next year, when she was preparing for the birth of her first child, she engaged another African American woman, Clara, who understood "kitchen

---

italism, 106) has estimated that in 1820, within the Connecticut River Valley, around 15 percent of the population worked as live-in servants and that just over half of the valley's households employed at least one live-in servant.

But evidence from diaries, letters, and account books offers ample evidence that if most middling New England families aspired to make do with as little help as possible, most also employed some kind of domestic help on a regular basis. On the scope of northern domestic service during the early republic, see especially Faye E. Dudden, *Serving Women: Household Service in Nineteenth-Century America* (Middletown, Conn.: Wesleyan University Press, 1983), 27–35, 45–50. See also Clark, *Roots of Rural Capitalism*, 105–11; Boydston, *Home and Work*, 79–88; Laurel Thatcher Ulrich, *The Midwife's Tale: The Life of Martha Ballard, Based on Her Diary, 1785–1812* (New York: Vintage, 1991), 82, 220–28, and "Martha Ballard and Her Girls: Women's Work in Eighteenth-Century Maine," in *Work and Labor in Early America* ed. Stephen Innes (Chapel Hill: University of North Carolina Press, 1988), 70–105; Lasser, "The Domestic Balance of Power: Relations between Mistress and Maid in Nineteenth-Century New England," *Labor History* 28 (1987): 5–22; Cott, *Bonds of Womanhood*, 27–30, 48–52; Joan Hedrick, *Harriet Beecher Stowe: A Life* (New York: Oxford University Press, 1994), 110–21; and Mary P. Ryan, *Cradle of the Middle Class: The Family in Oneida County, New York, 1790–1865* (New York: Cambridge University Press, 1981), 206–208. For discussions of farm families' use of domestic service, see also Paul G. E. Clemens and Lucy Simler, "Rural Labor and the Farm Household in Chester County, Pennsylvania, 1750–1820," in Innes, ed., *Work and Labor in Early America*, 106–143; Osterud, *Bonds of Community*, 194–98; and Jensen, *Loosening the Bonds*, 42–46.

[14]This argument was first elaborated by Faye E. Dudden. On the distinctions between "help" and "domestic service," see Dudden, *Serving Women*, 4–8.

work quite well and appeared very neat"; Clara's presence as well as her potential offered proof that "we did not trust the Lord in vain." Three weeks later, Phelps Huntington happily reported that "since Clara has been with me, I have had time to do much of my sewing, and indeed have nearly worked myself out—or rather have done those things that were more immediately necessary . . . I have so little hard work to do these three weeks past that my back is very comfortable and hardly troubles me at all." When Harriet Adams Aiken began house-keeping, she found that in the absence of her family, her only comfort was a "good girl, whom I can depend on at least till Spring." Over-whelmed by work, her "good girl" offered "no small relief to the per-plexities of mine & fatigue of body wh. I have heretofore found in housekeeping."[15]

Novice housekeepers were not the only ones to depend on help. After ten years as mistress of a large household, Amelia Peabody found housework exhausting and the aid of one Hannah Kingsbury indis-pensable. By 1834, she had worked herself sick: Family cares had become an "insupportable burden," and her spirit "fainted at the sight of mending a basket or a dilapidated coat." A much-needed vacation and the sewing of Hannah Kingsbury made her feel the "very reverse." The following year, Peabody hired Kingsbury to live in and sew, explaining that she "really never had any species of help that has relieved me so much." Kingsbury was "quick with her needle, and . . . one of those persons to whom nothing comes amiss." Even better, she was "fond of the children, and they are fond of her, so that when I am out, I feel as if all would go on well." Nor was Peabody exceptional. In 1844, a bout of the whooping cough made middle-aged Arethusa Howe more dependent than ever on good help. "If Sally Mills had not been homeless at that time I could hardly have done my work," she wrote. Recommending Mills to her sister, she reported that "she washes dishes & clothes & floors very well if you can put up with her oddities." Whatever misfortune left Sally Mills "homeless" worked to the benefit of Arethusa Howe.[16]

Any "oddities" servants displayed were overshadowed by their capac-

[15]Harriet Adams Aiken to Eliza Adams, 7 January 1828, Adams Family Papers, MS 420, Box 3, Folder 39, DCL. Elizabeth Phelps Huntington to Elizabeth Porter Phelps, 17 Febru-ary 1802, 20 June 1801, PPHFP, Box 13, Folder 2. For other accounts of the significance of help for newlyweds, see Hannah Fulton Reed to Lyman Reed, 20 June 1853, Reed Family Papers, HSCC; Amelia White Peabody to Mary Jane White, 22 June 1823, Everett-Peabody Family Papers, MHS.

[16]Arethusa Howe to Fanny Negus Fuller, 17 April 1844, Fuller Family Papers, PVMA. Amelia White Peabody to Mary Jane White, 22 January 1835, October 1834, Everett-Peabody Family Papers, MHS.

ity for work. When a Rutland, Vermont, couple set up house in the 1820s, they found "full subjects for mirth" in the "whim-whaws & superstitions" of their "housekeeper," Miss Betsey Sheppard. But they also acknowledged that it was Sheppard's capable labor that allowed them to "get along very well." Even hired women whose efforts failed to meet their mistresses' standards counted as valuable additions to a provincial household. For example, Elizabeth Bradley Dorr complained that her servant, Mary, had become "old and so _fat_ that she can hardly get about and I find I have all the running to do and much of the cooking." Still, she would not dismiss Mary but waited until Mary chose to retire before hiring a replacement.[17] By the 1830s, the scarcity of domestic help prompted Amelia Peabody and other Springfield women to take in young girls from the city's orphan asylum, bringing up the girls in exchange for housework. If an eleven-year-old girl failed to match a Hannah Kingsbury, she still eased the press of housework. Even in 1831, when Peabody planned to "chang[e] her young girl," she recognized that the girl was "strong and capable." Unfortunately, she was "better calculated for kitchen work than children," and it was child care that Peabody desired, for, as she later confessed, "there is no work so wearing to me as the tug of children."[18]

Provincial women prized hired help when they had it, but the full value of that help was most conspicuous in its absence. After several years spent in Northampton with little or no help, Lizzie Cochran observed that "it is very hard to give up every thing else for the mere cares of eating—drinking and keeping clean—but it is all for the best." It was not simply that women lost what leisure they had, although they did. When housework mounted, or when female kin were incapacitated, women faced more work than they could manage. For example, in the winter of 1846, Abigail Alden Freeman found herself facing the full range of household tasks without husband or help. Under the circumstances, "milking, bringing water, making fires, &c. &c., must be performed by us if done at all. You may imagine how pleasant these things are in the bitter cold." Left in the same position as Freeman, Fanny Fuller complained, "I am very sensible of my inability to discharge every duty that seems to be put on me to perform alone all I ask is patience." Mary Ann Webster Sanborn was not content with patience; she demanded help. She and her father shared the time of

[17]Elizabeth Bradley Dorr to Susan Bradley, 30 July 1846, SL. Amelia White Peabody to Mary Jane White, 22 June 1823, Everett-Peabody Family Papers, MHS.

[18]Amelia White Peabody to Mary Jane White, 16 January 36, 26 August 1831; see also Amelia White Peabody to Mary Jane White, 20 September 1835, 5 December 1835, Everett-Peabody Family Papers, MHS.

Mrs. Poole, who sewed for both households. In 1850, Sanborn grew impatient and insisted that her father send Poole back to her house. "Don't think I am lazy for I really do try to be industrious," she wrote. The problem was that she had more work than she could perform. She pointed out that after "the oversight I have to take of every thing by day," her evenings were "devoted to hearing Catharine read and helping Caty when her figures dont add up—receiving calls—going to meeting—letter writing & newspaper reading." It is no wonder that she had "not much time for efficient sewing."[19]

Mary Palmer Tyler had always worked hard. As the mistress of a household that included numerous children, boarders, and visitors and that never attained economic stability, much less great wealth, she was rarely idle. Through the 1810s, the family's finances enabled her to hire women to assist with the sewing, cleaning, and laundering. Like many provincial women, she could count on access to regular, if not frequent, help. Around 1820, hard times made it impossible for Tyler to hire even day help, forcing her to rely solely on the assistance of her daughter Mary. The two women managed to keep up, but just barely. Worse, Tyler noted that the housework took a toll on the girl, who was "not so well as I wish or as she used to be." More than health was at stake. "I tremble for fear she should give out," she wrote. "We should then have to hire someone unavoidably. I regret we cannot do it long enough to let her rest—but know not how we can." Indeed, women regularly reported that the absence of help led to illness. Elizabeth Parson's mother suffered from chronic side pain in 1847. She wrote that Dr. Prescott confirmed her diagnosis that the pain was a "neuralgic difficulty . . . almost invariably brought on by over exertion." But "with a family of nine boarders & five of her own," her mother could hardly "avoid working beyond her strength." When Mrs. Lyman, wife of a prosperous Northampton judge, found herself without help for three weeks, her friends reported that she looked "completely exhausted," having "worked herself sick washing, ironing, and everything!"[20]

To say that provincial women valued the services of the women they

[19]Mary Ann Webster Sanborn to Achsah Webster, 27 December [ca. 1850], Sanborn Family Papers, NHHS. Fanny Fuller to Aaron Fuller 31 May [n.d.], Fuller Family Papers, PVMA. Abigail Alden Freeman to Eliza Adams Young, 26 February 1846, Adams Family Papers, MS 420, Box 5, Folder 10, DCL. Lizzie Cochran to Agnes Cochran Higginson, 16 December 1838, Fuller Family Papers, PVMA.

[20]Marianne Cochran to Agnes Cochran Higginson, 28 October 1838, Fuller Family Papers, PVMA. Elizabeth Parsons to Elizabeth Tenney, 29 March 1847, Parsons Family Papers, SL. Mary Palmer Tyler to Amelia Palmer Curtis, 10 October 1824, Royall Tyler Collection, Gift of Helen Tyler Brown, VHS; Royall Tyler Daybook, 14 August 1817, 1–12 September 1818, Royall Tyler Collection, Gift of Helen Tyler Brown, VHS.

hired is not to say that they were always sensitive to the servants them-selves. The relations between mistress and maid were hardly immune to conflicts that arose from differences in class, ethnicity, and age—conflicts that were only exacerbated as women shouldered demanding work in close quarters. The most condescending comments about provincial help came from those who were furthest removed from it. Women and men who possessed considerable wealth, an urban back-ground, or both, could be especially nasty. And disparaging comments about servants sharpened noticeably at the end of the antebellum period, when even provincial help became proletarianized.

William Czar Bradley, who served on the New Hampshire Supreme Court in the 1840s, displayed all of the expected prejudices in a poem about the trials of securing good help. After the abrupt departure of the stalwart Becky, the family was visited by a succession of domestics who were overpaid, lazy, dishonest, promiscuous, and Irish or African American as well. Although the Bradley family had high hopes for two Irish servants, they quickly wished to dispatch the wretches to the "Lake of Killarney / For we found they were made up of sponging and blarney." "Dr. Jackson's fam'd cook and John Randolph's mulatto" only "made matters worse for to beat all creation / They took in their heads to try 'malgamation." Next came Mrs. Whiting, "a worker indeed but she'd lie like Sapphire," who quickly moved to Walpole to "get near her admirers." Mercifully, Becky and her "well-stuffed bureau" returned, rescuing the beleaguered Bradleys: "Thus six months have passed and now they are over/And if Becky holds out we may yet be in clover."[21]

Such attitudes were not simply the stuff of light verse. Consider the protracted battle between Agnes Cochran Higginson and Bridget, her Irish servant. In 1854, Higginson reluctantly moved with seven of her ten children to Deerfield, Massachusetts, which she disdained as a rural backwater. Leaving her husband behind in Boston tending to business, she commenced life as a provincial housekeeper—a role for which she had little enthusiasm and less aptitude. At first, she was happy to have the help of Bridget, for although the Irish woman was a "character," she was "very good-hearted to the children and the *dogs*." But the honeymoon was soon over. By the end of 1855, the Higginsons owed Bridget some $200 in back wages. They couldn't pay, and Brid-get refused to quit until she received her money. Predictably, tempers mounted. "I am tormented out of my life with Bridget whose impu-

---

[21]William Czar Bradley to Emily Bradley Dorr, 4 March 1846, Sarah Merry Bradley Gam-ble Papers, SL.

dence is beyond all bounds," Higginson complained to her husband. "This P.M. she positively refused to manage [Higginson's son] Arthur as I wished." Later that evening, Higginson overheard Bridget trying to quiet the fussy child by "threatening to open the window and throw him out if he did not be still in a loud cross voice." The incident was all the more frustrating because Higginson was unable care for her son herself, "he has such an aversion to coming to me." She urged her husband to sell a life insurance policy to "make me independent of [Bridget]—for I see no peace for any of us while she stays." Two days later, Bridget quit, although it isn't clear whether she ever obtained her money. Describing the final scene for her husband, Higginson cast herself as the gracious lady and Bridget as the repentant if ignorant servant: "She begged me to forgive her . . . which I did, of course." After all, Bridget probably never *really* intended to toss Arthur out the window. With cloying condescension, Higginson supposed "it was only an Irish way, & the poor child cried so & [Bridget] was sick & needed sleep, it was not strange she should do all she could to quiet him, according to her lights." Not once did Higginson acknowledge that Bridget's anger might owe more to back wages than to different philosophies of child-rearing.[22]

Agnes Cochran Higginson was unusually harsh and self-serving by any standard. But even when provincial women displayed far greater regard for their help, they were hardly immune to the prejudices of an Agnes Higginson or a William Czar Bradley. Jokes about servants' "oddities," "whim-whaws," and "superstitions" reinforced the distance between mistress and help—a distance measured by refinement as well as wealth. Caroline Clapp Briggs described the servants of her Northampton girlhood as creatures of almost exotic rusticity, with their "hard, sharp Yankee faces" and "curious old-fashioned names, Sabina and Orpah, Naomi and Thankful." But more than genteel breeding separated Briggs from her mother's help. She recalled Thankful W., "a perfect specimen of a Yankee" whose work indoors and out gave her "hands as hard as her face." Surely Briggs's own body never revealed such a life of labor.[23] And it is difficult to imagine that Amelia Peabody, whose household help was drawn largely from Springfield's orphan asylum, was free from the middle-class maternalism that colored so many of antebellum women's encounters with the "deserving poor." Indeed, the primary virtue of orphan girls, aside from their

[22]Agnes Cochran Higginson to Stephen Higginson II, 1 January 1856, 30 December 1855, 28 December 1855, 20 April 1854, Fuller Family Papers, PVMA.

[23]Caroline C. Briggs, *Reminiscences and Letters of Caroline C[lapp] Briggs*, ed. George Merriam (Boston: Houghton Mifflin, 1897), 33, 31.

availability, was that they had been brought up with "regularity & strictness" and arrived "admirably instructed in sewing, knitting, reading, writing & spelling." Certainly, there were no guarantees, for bad girls were everywhere. But asylum girls posed "not half so much [risk] as . . . girls from poor families."[24]

Not surprisingly, distance and disdain increased when the servant in question was African American. In the same letter that Amelia Peabody sang the praises of Hannah Kingsbury, she observed almost as an afterthought, "as to help, I have a pretty good coloured woman." Elizabeth Phelps Huntington, who had no difficulty acknowledging her dependence on the labor of her African-American servants Clara and Chloe, found the servants themselves harder to accept. She could not resist condescension in describing Clara as a woman with "something such a temper as Lydia Atwood's, tho' more obliging." Nor was Huntington pleased that both Clara and Chloe entered the Huntington household with a child. She described Clara's two-year-old as "<u>tolerably troublesome</u>" and only grudgingly accepted Chloe's three-year-old daughter. Hoping to keep the child out from underfoot and preferably out of sight, Huntington planned to banish the little girl to the "lower kitchen."[25]

While provincial women stopped short of treating their help as their equals, they did acknowledge their debt to hired labor. And complaints about the scarcity of servants outnumbered complaints about their insolence and incompetence. This regard, coupled with the relative absence of conflict, increasingly set rural service apart from its urban counterpart. Nineteenth-century observers generally explained the distinctiveness of rural help by pointing to the fierce pride of New England's farm families, crediting it with creating a kind of social equality. Caroline Clapp Briggs recounted that the servants her family had employed in Northampton were "sturdy, self-reliant independent Yankee women, who would have scorned to be called servants" and who were "very impatient with anything they considered an infringement on their rights."[26] Historians have similarly looked to rural social relations to explain rural service. They have suggested that traditions of reciprocity between families and neighbors minimized the social dis-

[24]Amelia White Peabody to Mary Jane White, 16 January 1836, Everett-Peabody Family Papers, MHS. For a discussion of the practice of binding out orphan girls as domestic servants that differs somewhat from my own, see Dudden, *Serving Women*, 20–24.

[25]Elizabeth Phelps Huntington to Elizabeth Porter Phelps, 20 June 1801, 17 February 1802, PPHFP, Box 13, Folder 1. Amelia White Peabody to Mary Jane White Peabody, 22 January 1835, Everett-Peabody Family Papers, MHS.

[26]Briggs, *Reminiscences*, 31.

tance between mistress and help, protecting domestic service from the damning decline in status that eventually rendered it the exclusive dominion of immigrants and African Americans. Women who were well acquainted with their servants' kin, who worked alongside their servants, and who had spent a season or two working as hired help in their own youths could be expected to treat domestics with respect.[27] Certainly, there is some truth to this formulation, although after 1820, it was increasingly rare for middling women to perform paid labor in the homes of nonkin. But the relatively high status of provincial help was embedded in women's appreciation of demands of housework itself. Provincial women valued "help" not because they identified with the women they hired but because they understood the value of the labor those women performed—understood it personally, immediately, and physically.

Women, Work, and Cash

If provincial women's primary work was housework, they hardly found their labor confined to the domestic sphere. Through the antebellum period, women remained knowledgeable about and even involved in family business ventures. Certainly provincial New Englanders relied on and elaborated the gender division of labor that had dominated Anglo-American society from the earliest years of settlement and that located women's primary responsibilities in the household and surrounding yards. But as historians have come to recognize, there was enormous flexibility, permeability, and overlap between women's and men's work.[28]

The daily journal kept by Royall Tyler and Mary Palmer Tyler in the

[27]On the distinctive nature of rural service, see Osterud, *Bonds of Community*, 194–98, and Dudden, *Serving Women*, 93–104. On the increasingly rigid hierarchies of class, race, and ethnicity that characterized urban service over the course of the antebellum period, see Dudden, *Serving Women;* Lasser, "Domestic Balance of Power"; Christine Stansell, *City of Women: Sex and Class in New York, 1798–1860* (Urbana: University of Illinois Press, 1987), 155–92; and John F. Kasson, *Rudeness and Civility: Manners in Nineteenth-Century America* (New York: Hill & Wang, 1990).

[28]A large and growing literature examines the significance and contours of eighteenth- and nineteenth-century women's labor in ways that illuminate its relation to men's work and to household strategies. See, among many, Boydston, *Home and Work;* Clark, *Roots of Rural Capitalism;* Osterud, *Bonds of Community;* Karen V. Hansen, *A Very Social Time: Crafting Community in Antebellum New England* (Berkeley: University of California Press, 1994); Ulrich, *Midwife's Tale;* Mary H. Blewett, *Men, Women, and Work: Class, Gender, and Protest in the New England Shoe Industry, 1780–1910* (Urbana: University of Illinois Press, 1988); and Jensen, *Loosening the Bonds.*

late 1810s offers a graphic representation of the daily interplay between women's and men's work. The Vermont couple kept a single daybook to note family events, domestic expenditures; the comings and goings of family members, visitors, and hired help; and the records of Royall Tyler's struggling law practice. Mary Palmer Tyler generally wrote about housework and child care. Royall Tyler's entries centered on his professional concerns. He frequently made note of wash day, perhaps because it involved hired help, which it often did, or perhaps because after a day of laundry, Mary Tyler was too tired to pick up the pen. Entering her descriptions of shirts sewed, children nursed, and help hired in between entries that detailed her husband's attempts to generate new business and secure payment for old, Mary Tyler hardly inhabited a separate sphere—either in practice or imagination. She understood not only the daily workings of her husband's sphere of activity but also the ways in which his responsibilities, his successes and failures impinged upon her own.[29]

This understanding was hardly an abstract, intellectual exercise. When Royall Tyler's declining health put an end to his legal career, Mary Tyler worked ceaselessly to help revive his literary career. She stopped taking in sewing (the family's one source of cash) to transcribe the pieces he was preparing for publication. Along with her children, she drummed up strategies to bring Tyler's name to the attention of the Boston publishing establishment. She also familiarized herself with the copyright laws that would determine how much money Tyler's work might generate. While Royall Tyler was updating the *Algerine Captive*, hoping to capitalize on the "rage especially in England for American litterature," Mary Palmer Tyler was concluding that in order to finance printing, her husband would have to sell his "copy right for 14 years for such sum as he could get," for "the destruction of the poor is their poverty."[30]

A crisis brought on by illness and poverty drove Mary Tyler to add the tasks of secretary and literary promoter to her daily responsibilities. Through the 1840s, however, the labor that many women performed for their families within their houses was routinely augmented by work they performed beyond them. Especially when their families' fortunes depended on farming and small-scale manufacturing, provincial women might find themselves shouldering responsibility for

[29]Royall Tyler Daybook, 1817–21, Document 45:15, Royall Tyler Collection, Gift of Helen Tyler Brown, VHS.
[30]Mary Tyler to Amelia Tyler, 19 January 1825, Mary Tyler to Edward S. Tyler, 15 May 1825, Royall Tyler Collection, Gift of Helen Tyler Brown, VHS.

"men's work." For example, Fanny Fuller, whose husband owned a cranberry farm in Deerfield, Massachusetts, expected to manage the farm in his absence, although it added considerably to her workload and her cares. Under the press of an especially large cranberry harvest in 1832, she wrote to her husband in New York, "I feel sometimes that if ever you wish to see me again you will come soon," for she was "almost worn out with care & fatigue."[31] Fuller's participation in the harvest demanded notice not because she was doing *men's* work but because she was doing *so much* work. It was the quantity, not the gendering of the work that was remarkable.

Persis Hastings Russell assumed an unusually active role in her family's many business ventures during the 1830s. Although the extent of her involvement was unusual, her experiences do provide some sense of the possible range of women's work within family enterprises and the place of that work in local and regional exchange networks. Married in 1815, Persis Hastings and Charles Russell set up housekeeping in Princeton, Massachusetts, a rural community in which both families were well established. Enterprising and ambitious, Charles Russell's commercial interests included a farm, a general store, and a tavern. Like many provincial merchants, Russell played a key role in furthering the development of rural capitalism. Drawing on the commercial connections he developed in his mercantile business, he supplemented income from his store by serving as a broker for outwork: The straw hats, axes, and scythes produced in local households found their way to regional and national markets through Charles Russell's store. Economic success brought political recognition. During his career, Charles Russell served as Princeton's justice of the peace, its postmaster, and, by 1832, its representative in the Massachusetts Senate. Russell's commercial and political ambitions regularly drew him away from home for extended periods of time. And in his absence, Persis assumed responsibility for the family's business.[32]

Evidence of Persis Russell's business activity begins to appear in the 1830s in letters she and her husband exchanged during his absences.[33] While Charles Russell cataloged the availability and the cost of goods

[31]Fanny Negus Fuller to Aaron Fuller, 5 August 1832, Fuller Family Papers, PVMA.

[32]Charles Russell's economic and political progress can be traced in Charles Russell, General Correspondence, Charles Russell Papers, MHS.

[33]It is not clear whether this correspondence signals the beginning of Persis Russell's involvement in the family's business enterprises. It may be that earlier letters detailing her participation have not survived or that she worked alongside her husband, which wouldn't have required written exchanges of information. It may also be that before the 1830s, her responsibilities for the family's three children kept her at home; letters between the Russells begin to appear around the time that their youngest child turned eight and required

in Boston, Persis Russell shared information about the pace of commerce at home. "We have found it much easier this Winter than we did last so far business has been rather dull but not to wonder at for the peoples attention are entirely ocupied by" conflicts within Princeton's Congregational church, she reported in 1831.[34] When Charles Russell shipped goods home, he specified the selling price. For example, in 1834, he forwarded "1 Box Brown Sugar—1 Chest Fancy Soochong Tea—1 Bar Flour—1 Box Raisins & 2 pounds linen thread" to Princeton. "The sugar you may sell 1 ctl or 10 by quantity—fancy tea 50 cts Flour &c. as usual," he instructed. The authority to set prices surely reflected Charles Russell's position as final authority in all business matters. But it also reflected his greater knowledge of regional market prices. And he was careful to apprise his wife of market fluctuations so that she might better justify the prices. He explained that the walnuts shipped in 1835 were "new & fresh & cost about double to what they last did." Moreover, there were no other nuts to be had. Quality and scarcity demanded that these nuts "must be sold as high as 12 cts."[35]

While her husband was on buying trips to Boston, Persis Russell assumed daily responsibility for the store, stocking and pricing goods and carrying on trade. Persis Russell relied on her husband's instructions to set local prices, but they both expected that she would use her knowledge of local markets and prices to make decisions about the sale and distribution of outwork. In the spring of 1835, with "time to write only a few lines," she reported that she had opted to sell their stock of "corse" hats to "White of Holden" for "9/ the dozen." White also wished to buy the "fine ones," offering to pay "5 dollars a dozen for a part . . . and 3.50 for the rest." But Persis Russell declined, for "I thought it was not enough." Quick to solicit her husband's opinion, she added that "if you think it is [enough], he will take them now but I think you can get more."[36]

Persis Russell's involvement in the distribution of local outwork brought her into contact with regional buyers, like "White of Holden." But it also embedded her within the web of debt, credit, and exchange that characterized the local economy. Consider her conflicts with Joel Howe, who assembled at least some of the axes that the Russells sold

---

far less care and supervision. For accounts of the ways in which women's work outside the home was shaped by family life cycle, see Ulrich, *Midwife's Tale*.

[34]Persis Russell to Charles Russell, 9 January 1831, Charles Russell Papers, MHS.

[35]Charles Russell to Persis Russell, 1 January 1835, 31 January 1834, Charles Russell Papers, MHS.

[36]Persis Russell to Charles Russell, 6 March 1835, Russell Family Papers.

in Boston.[37] In 1834, Howe agreed to deliver "100 hatchets." On the appointed day, he arrived with only 46, promising to deliver the balance within the week. As if that wasn't enough, he demanded that Persis Russell extend him his full payment of "33 Dollars," claiming that Charles Russell had offered him an advance. Given "the character of the man," Persis Russell turned him away; she doubted both that Howe was good for the missing hatchets and that her husband would consent to such an arrangement. But Joel Howe was not to be deterred. The next day, he returned, requesting a $20 loan. When Persis Russell refused him, he threatened to borrow the money elsewhere, leaving the Russells responsible for payment against his future wages. "He wanted to go to Maj. Lamb and Borrow 20 Dollars and I should be responsible I told him I would not be responsible for 1 cent he also sent Col. Watson to me and told him I would pay his taxes I told Col Watson I should not pay them," she fumed. Furious at the possibility that her husband might actually have volunteered to help such a man, she wrote, "If you have agreed to pay all Joel Hows Debts please to furnish me with some money," for in order to pay for "finishing and for Scythes," Persis Russell had exhausted her own cash supply and borrowed all of her mother-in-laws's money.

The experiences of Persis Russell suggest the flexibility in provincial New Englanders' gender division of labor, the permeability between housework and household affairs. Serving as the kind of deputy husband identified by Laurel Thatcher Ulrich in colonial New England, Persis Russell kept store, managed a thriving outwork business, dispensed wages, and might even have been held liable for another man's debts and taxes. In her husband's absence, she carried on business in his stead. But she did not simply represent *his* interests. Instead, she helped shape the family enterprise, as did her mother-in-law, who pumped cash into the business on at least one occasion.[38]

Women possessed of Persis Russell's energy, acumen, and opportunities were always rare. But they almost disappear after around 1840. In part, their disappearance resulted from the ways in which the development of rural capitalism undermined older social and economic structures, eventually divorcing commerce and manufacture from older patterns of neighborhood exchange. Land shortages, combined with the growing scale and complexity of commerce and manufacture, ensured that increasing numbers of men would never become propri-

[37]The following discussion is drawn from Persis Russell to Charles Russell, 12 January 1832, Charles Russell Papers, MHS.

[38]Laurel Thatcher Ulrich, *Good Wives: Image and Reality in the Lives of Women in Northern New England 1650–1750* (New York: Oxford University Press, 1983), 35–50.

etors. And although a majority of provincial business establishments remained family owned and operated through the 1850s, the context of business changed in subtle and significant ways, as Christopher Clark has shown. Following the depression of the 1830s, new concentrations of credit along with the growing concentrations of capital and labor restructured the provincial economy. By the 1850s, although the majority of businesses in the Connecticut River Valley remained family owned and largely family operated, those businesses no longer dominated the local economic landscape. Instead, wealth and power increasingly concentrated in the hands of entrepreneurs who had established close ties to nonlocal credit and markets.[39] Each of these factors worked to remove middle-class women from their husbands' shops and stores. Deputy husbands stood in for men who were small proprietors, not men who were professionals or incorporated partners, much less employees.[40]

But the transformation of provincial business was matched by a hardening of the bourgeois domestic ideology that relegated men and women to separate spheres—a hardening that took place along generational lines. Whatever tender feelings Charles Russell harbored for his wife, he also respected her business savvy. And if Persis Russell's letters inscribe her as an "affectionate wife," they reveal her as a respected partner. Their children, however, elaborated a different understanding of family life. Theodore Russell enjoyed memories of his family that surely owed more to the literary conventions of bourgeois domesticity than anything he had ever witnessed in Princeton. Alone in his Harvard College "chamber," with "the hum of business long ceased," he fantasized about "home and scenes of pleasurable childhood." Most striking was his imagined rendition of his family, those "dear objects of affection." In 1835, the same year that Persis Russell was dickering over the price of hats with "White of Holden," Theodore Russell conjured up images of the "little family circle . . . quietly seated around the domestic fireside." Astoundingly, he went on to contrast the "warm and devoted friendship" of this charmed circle with the "cold and heartless applause" that rewarded the "mad

[39]This process is described in greater detail in Clark, *Roots of Rural Capitalism*, 228–72; Randolph A. Roth, *The Democratic Dilemma: Religion, Reform, and the Social Order in the Connecticut River Valley of Vermont, 1750–1850* (New York: Cambridge University Press, 1987), 118–30, 265–79; and Jonathan Prude, *The Coming of the Industrial Order: Town and Factory Life in Rural Massachusetts* (New York: Cambridge University Press, 1983), 188–91, 198–202.

[40]The continued role of women in struggling and marginal business enterprises underscores this point; see, for example, Christopher Clark's discussion of Mary Bullard Graham's "self-exploitation" in *Roots of Rural Capitalism*, 240.

ambition of the outside world." Persis Russell might well have been a "warm and devoted" mother, but she was also a deeply ambitious woman whose daily activity owed far more to the cold calculations of the bottom line than to any womanly sensibilities. Nor was Theodore alone in accepting the gender conventions that relegated women to the "domestic fireside." The Russells' daughter, Sarah, regularly spent time at the family store with her mother. The girl took little interest in the basics of commerce, although she was mightily intrigued by the intricacies of fashion. More to the point, working at the store was at odds with her sense of genteel refinement. "I have been rather lazy [at the store] today," she confessed to her father, "but I suppose it wont do for such poor girls to be lazy." Despite her family's substantial income and her mother's example, by the time she turned thirteen, Sarah had internalized the notion that only want drove women into the market and only poverty justified keeping them there.[41]

By the end of the 1830s, provincial New Englanders narrowed the range of employments that a woman might pursue and still lay claim to a measure of gentility. If women continued to help out in stores and shops and on farms, this labor played a less critical role in middle-class family strategies than it once had. It also assumed a far smaller place in women's self-representations. Indeed, this narrowing, as much the result of economic as ideological change, was central to the emergence of the middle class. It exaggerated the distinction between home and work, obscured the full range of women's productivity, and and sharpened class distinctions. Yet even within the middle-class imagination, this recasting of women's market labor never entirely removed women from the market, although it decisively changed the context of their market participation.

Provincial New Englanders expected that middle-class women would contribute to their men's attempts to secure a competency, partly through prudent and thrifty housekeeping and partly through the many "hidden" services that wives or daughters routinely performed by producing goods for trade and credit.[42] But especially when family finances seemed uncertain, middle-class women were enjoined

[41]Sarah Russell to Charles Russell, 8 October 1835, and Theodore Russell to Sarah Russell, 25 April 1835, Charles Russell Papers, MHS. Charles Grier Sellers (*The Market Revolution: Jacksonian America, 1815–1846* [New York: Oxford University Press, 1991], 242) also points to the generational dimensions of family transformation, although his analysis of that transformation differs from my own.

[42]Leonore Davidoff and Catherine Hall (*Family Fortunes: Men and Women of the English Middle Class, 1750–1850* [Chicago: University of Chicago Press, 1987], 279–89) describe women's "hidden" investments in family enterprises. See also Ryan, *Cradle of the Middle Class*, 200–202; and Boydston, *Home and Work*, 77–88.

not only to succor their kin but also to help supply them with cash. The nineteenth-century fictional heroines whose pluck and industry save their families' farms were not simply the stuff of middle-class myth. The most genteel lady could augment her family's income and remain a lady as long as she labored at tasks that were understood as extensions of women's sphere or, more to the point, those that seemed to replicate the unpaid labor that middling and middle-class women performed within their homes. Accordingly, impoverished ladies took in boarders and sewing, produced fancy work for sale, and sent their daughters out to teach. If the papers of provincial families reveal the treacherous snare that debt and credit created in a market society, these same papers testify to women's efforts to free their kin from that snare.

Louisa Bradlee, for example, aimed to relieve her parents of a crippling debt while they were still alive. In addition to painting window hangings, she took in boarders; in one year, she earned $400 above expenses by assuming sole responsibility of 12 boarders, including 8 children.[43] Thirty years earlier, Anne Laura Clarke left her Northampton home with her younger sister Elizabeth in tow. The two headed south, where Anne taught in a series of female academies and seminaries and served as a governess. Her decision to leave Northampton was undoubtedly inspired by multiple motivations—her commitment to provide an education for her sister, her desire to further her own education, and, not least, her ambition to forge a career as a speaker, writer, and woman of letters in America's emerging culture industry. But Anne Laura Clarke's early career choices were more immediately shaped by her family's pressing debts, for she felt that she could not return home until the debts had been paid.

Between 1818 and 1822, Clarke's letters to her father are dominated by family finances. She raised pointed questions about her father's current financial status and offered advice on which creditors must be paid first and which could wait. "After the payment of $750—pray—what still remains on the mortgage—I should like to know," she asked.

> And also what the amount of the taxes is and how you have managed to pay them—how you procure money—and whether you are in want of it—and if when all the debts are paid whether there will be any income—and whether Elizabeth and I could, in that case, get along tolerably well if we were at home.[44]

[43]Louisa Bradlee to Samuel Colcord Bartlett, 4 May 1846, 30 March 1844, Bartlett Family Papers, NHHS.

[44]Anne Laura Clarke to Joseph Clarke, 18 October 1818; see also Anne Laura Clarke to Joseph Clarke, 17 January 1819; both in Anne Laura Clarke Bound Letters, 1817–24, NHS.

Above all, she described her ceaseless efforts to earn and save and her anticipation of the day when she might step free of such a burden. In 1820, after three years in the South and in Philadelphia, she entertained the hope that one more year's labor would finally clear the debt. "Then how rejoiced I shall be," she wrote. But it took two years of "deny[ing] myself so many comforts and submit[ting] to so many privations" before the debts were finally paid.[45]

If women like Anne Clarke and Louisa Bradlee successfully maneuvered within the labor markets created by and for middle-class women's industry, many more found themselves all but shut out. The ambitions and needs of particular families as well as the general expansion of the market created a pressing need for cash. By the 1850s, the growing reluctance of town merchants to accept trade or long-term credit meant that even local exchange had become dominated by cash. Surveying the array of bills she had accumulated in the 1850s, Agnes Cochran Higginson declared Deerfield, Massachusetts, "a place where you can only live for *cash*."[46] This demand for cash pulled growing numbers of women into the market in search of wages only to lodge them within a remarkably narrow and increasingly overcrowded range of occupations. As early as the 1820s, provincial centers such as Brattleboro, Vermont, and Northampton, Massachusetts, contained far more women who aspired to earn money teaching or sewing than the local populations could possibly support. Mary Palmer Tyler saw marked continuities between the prospects for lawyers and genteel seamstresses. In Brattleboro, the "law business even for the well and young amongst its profession is very dull," she wrote in 1823. Women fared no better: "There is nothing to be done here by which we females could earn a penny there are more workmen than work already in the market—and Schools in abundance." Around the same time, Anne Clarke's younger sister Elizabeth reported that the competition for students in Northampton had reached almost comic proportions. In addition to her young nephews, Elizabeth had secured "five schollars." But she had also lost two: "Helen and Ann Clapp have gone to Miss Howe and Miss Mills by way of variety." Worse, one "Miss Davis from Boston has or is to commence a finishing school and I guess <u>mine will</u> be before a great while."[47]

[45]Anne Laura Clarke to Joseph Clarke, 15 November 1820, 8 July 1821, Anne Laura Clarke Bound Letters, 1817–24, NHS.

[46]Agnes Cochran Higginson to Stephen Higginson II, 18 December 1855, Fuller Family Papers, PVMA. On cash in the Connecticut River Valley, see Clark, *Roots of Rural Capitalism*, 221–27.

[47]Elizabeth Clarke to Anne Laura Clarke [n.d.], Anne Laura Clarke Papers, NHS. Mary Palmer Tyler to Amelia Curtis, 12 January 1823, Royall Tyler Collection, Gift of Helen Tyler

This kind of competition did little to improve women's earning capacity. It also contributed substantially to the persistent difficulties women faced in securing money. For all its value within households and as a form of exchange between them, women's labor was radically undervalued in the world of cash transactions, as Jeanne Boydston has demonstrated.[48] Given the growing significance of cash within even local exchange networks, women's limited access to money bore significant consequences for their efforts to contribute to their families' competence, much less to support themselves. On one hand, the money women earned along with the money that their unpaid labor saved could and often did make the difference between maintaining middle-class status and sliding over the edge into diminished circumstances. On the other hand, when families found themselves especially short on cash, women's most Herculean efforts could not guarantee financial stability.

Yet provincial New Englanders maintained their expectation, however unrealistic, that women could somehow continue to pick up the slack during hard times. Overlooking the transformation of the rural economy, they insisted that a woman could continue to shape her household's relation to the market. With effort, the middle-class lady could serve the same function as the yeoman's productive mistress. When Francis Higginson, a Vermont "country Physician," ran up enormous debts in the 1850s, his mother and brothers came to his assistance. Eventually, they found him a clerkship in Worcester, Massachusetts, that carried an annual salary of $600. No one doubted that most of Francis's woes stemmed from his own poor judgment. And at least one family member complained that Francis lacked the "bustling qualities" demanded by the antebellum marketplace; such a man should count himself lucky to land as a middling clerk. But if the clerkship enabled Francis to support his family in a "strictly economical manner," it would not begin to cover his debts. Surely, it fell to his wife and daughters to make up the difference. The "ladies can give lessons perhaps," one brother supposed, "& at any rate they can do plain nice sewing—making shirts at $1.25 & such work." One might well question the value of "plain nice sewing" for a man whose butcher bill alone exceeded $200. But the Higginson family never doubted that their women would be able to transcend the gendered

Brown, VHS. For a similar narrowing of occupations in provincial England, see Davidoff and Hall, *Family Fortunes*, 312–13.

[48]Boydston, *Home and Work*, 116–19, 153–59. See also Davidoff and Hall, *Family Fortunes*, 304–15.

constraints of the marketplace to help Francis Higginson regain a modest competence.[49]

Mary Palmer Tyler could have told them otherwise. From the 1820s through the 1850s, her life was driven by the struggle to procure cash. Although she and her daughters took in sewing and boarders and operated a successful and highly regarded school, they could not have survived without regular assistance from the Tyler sons, who sent cash and guaranteed the household's credit with local merchants. Accordingly, fluctuations in her sons' finances wreaked havoc with her own. When illness threatened the health of her son William in 1825, it also threatened Mary Tyler's economic security. After all, William had given a local storekeeper "his word to pay anything . . . now I fear this sickness will swallow up all his wages and added to time lost before he will be able to attend to business, will prevent his paying." The family was "as prudent as possible using no sugar except" to indulge Royall Tyler, who was dying of cancer. Still, with a bill of "nearly thirty dollars," she had reason to fear for her continued credit. Some thirty years later, her lot had not improved much. When her son Thomas neglected to send a monthly check for twenty-five dollars, she found herself entirely without money, despite boarding numerous schoolboys. After three days, she wrote for help, explaining that "it is no small thing to have so many hungry boys to feed when the funds get exhausted. Every eatable is so high, now, that it requires the strictest economy to provide enough of the simplest food, with the income I have."[50]

Women who could not turn to male kin fared far worse. The structure of the provincial economy had always made life especially precarious for unmarried and widowed women and orphaned girls. Persis Russell speculated in 1834 that Mrs. Mirick's "verry melancholy situation" owed less to loneliness and grief, as her neighbors supposed, than to the fear of poverty that accompanied widowhood. "I think it is her property which makes her so: she said she had an idea her property was all a going and she should come to want," Russell explained. And only five years earlier, the Princeton widow Lucinda Dillingham committed suicide, explaining in a note that "Lucinda cannot live and see her children come to want—Farewell dear Children & friends."[51]

Over the course of the antebellum period, however women's desper-

[49]Waldo Higginson to Stephen Higginson II, 4 January 1854 and n.d. [ca. December 1854]. See also Louisa Storrow Higginson to Stephen Higginson II, 13 November 1853, 23 December 1853, and 29 December 1853; all in Fuller Family Papers, PVMA.

[50]Mary Palmer Tyler to Thomas Pickman Tyler, 3 June 1859, and Mary Palmer Tyler to Edward R. Tyler, 15 May 1825, Royall Tyler Collection, Gift of Helen Tyler Brown, VHS.

[51]Charles Russell to Joshua Dillingham, 25 May 1832, and Persis Russell to Charles Russell, 23 January 1831, Charles Russell Papers, MHS. Daniel Scott Smith, "Female House-

ation was increasingly measured in flat dollar figures. Louisa Bradlee, who had taken in boarders and painted window hangings to earn money, learned the full significance of cash and of a male head of household after the deaths of her father and her brother. At first, it seemed as though her brother's legacy of $3,500 was sufficient to leave Bradlee and her mother in "very comfortable circumstances." Yet despite her inheritance, she found that the struggle to survive in a cash economy left her "ever anxious, ever watching, and laborious." For one thing, much of the inheritance was swallowed up by the family's debts, especially the mortgage on the "the homestead" and the loan an aunt had advanced for her brother's education. As a safeguard against the future, she invested $1,000 in bonds paying 7 percent interest. Then she confronted the costs associated with caring for her ailing mother, improving the house and farm, buying stock, and hiring help. With great effort, she managed to reduce the family's debts to $250, which she expected to pay off within a year. But when her last creditors demanded immediate payment to finance their migration to the West, she found herself without resources. No one would advance the single woman a short-term loan. "I am <u>completely</u> discouraged," she wrote. After she had "thought and worried till I can think no longer who to look to," she finally turned to the husband of a sister who had died more than ten years earlier. Without cash, and without male kin to help secure it, she found herself "very much alone—for all practical purposes <u>entirely</u> alone in the world."[52]

This is not to suggest that the combination of bad luck and economic transformation that sent women like Mary Tyler and Louisa Bradlee scrambling for cash left provincial men untouched. On the contrary, the growing numbers of men who found themselves trapped among the ranks of wage earners faced similar dilemmas. Nor is it to suggest that the development of rural capitalism consigned all women to poverty or that it increased women's dependence on their men. Within the household economy, the most energetic, productive yeoman's wife found that her fortunes depended on those of her male kin in general and her husband in particular. Some women managed very well despite the absence of a male head of household; Charles Russell's mother, who helped finance the Russells' ax-brokering business,

holding in Late Eighteenth-Century America and the Problem of Poverty," *Journal of Social History* 28, no. 1 (Fall 1994): 83–107.

[52]Louisa Bradlee to Samuel Colcord Bartlett, 20 Febuary 1857, Bartlett Family Papers, NHHS.

was not the only provincial widow with cash enough to help her kin. The development of rural capitalism reinforced women's economic dependence even as it led to subtle changes in the nature of that dependence.

The Household Economy and the Cult of Domesticity

The same changes that recast women's domestic dependence gave them new ways of imagining their work. The growing distinction between paid and unpaid work, which was itself increasingly conflated with the sexual division of labor, led to a new awareness of women's work. Women and men alike elaborated a new vocabulary for describing what women did and for asserting its value. This reconceptualization of the relation between women's and men's work—and, by extension, between home and market, private and public—was central to the creation of the middle class. From the 1830s, provincial women increasingly drew upon and contributed to a transatlantic canon of domesticity to describe their work, to distinguish it from their men's, and, by implication, to distinguish it from the labor of their poorer neighbors. Yet many of these same women were slow to abandon the vocabulary that had described women's labor within the household economy. Both vocabularies incorporated women's work into the lexicon of family structure and gender identity. But although the language of the household economy situated the value of women's work in its productivity and its utility, the domestic canon located the value of women's work in its femininity, its removal from the economic calculations that governed the relations between households and markets. Until the close of the antebellum period, provincial women drew upon two potentially contradictory languages.

For example, tensions between the domestic ideal and the values of the household economy even pervaded women's attitudes toward sewing, perhaps the most domestic of domestic tasks. Women had always sewed. But as textile manufacture moved out of the household and standards of dress became more elaborate, urban and rural women tended to spend more time sewing and mending; hours liberated from the spinning wheel and the loom were gobbled up by the sewing box. Indeed, by the middle of the nineteenth century, the image of the middle-class lady, ensconced in a parlor with her needlework, female friends, and relatives assumed an almost mythic quality, capturing the imagination of nineteenth-century novelists and twentieth-century women's historians. It was in just such a setting, historians have suggested, that an autonomous women's culture took shape.[53]

Certainly, provincial women understood their needlework as a distinctly female activity.[54] From childhood, girls sewed. Describing the "good girl" for young readers, Northampton writer J. H. Butler stressed that she "likes to sit by her mother, and sew, or knit." Although the "good girl" was careful not "meddle" in the kitchen and diary, she knew all about sewing:

> She does not take long stitches, nor pucker her work; but does it very neatly, just as her mother tells her to do. And she always keeps her work very clean; for if her hands are dirty, she washes them before she begins her work; and when she has finished it, she folds it up, and puts it very carefully in her workbag.[55]

After mastering the small stitch and the straight seam, the "good girl" could expect to spend much of her life plying a needle, usually in the company of other women. Mothers, daughters, and sisters spent hours sewing, mending, and knitting in one another's company. Although women most often sewed alongside their kin, they frequently benefited from neighborhood "help" hired in for a day or two. Sewing might also take on a social dimension, part of the prosaic mutuality that structured provincial women's friendships. In 1822, for example, Mary Tyler of Brattleboro, Vermont, took time out from her own fam-

[53]On domestic manufacture of clothing, see Strasser, *Never Done*, 130–35. Carroll Smith-Rosenberg ("Female World of Love and Ritual," 62, 65) suggests that nineteenth-century women's culture owed much to an "apprenticeship" system in which girls learned a variety of tasks, including sewing, from other women. For literary productions that deploy the image of the middle-class woman at her needlework, see, for example, Harriet Beecher Stowe's *Uncle Tom's Cabin* (New York: New American Library, 1966), and Louisa May Alcott's *Little Women* (New York: Viking Penguin, 1989). Antebellum reformers inverted this image to describe the virtuous working-class woman as a starving seamstress. Christine Stansell (*City of Women: Sex and Class in New York*, 110) describes the middle-class construction of the "solitary, pallid and timid" seamstress. For an especially nuanced account of the different meanings women could bring to sewing, see Elizabeth Fox-Genovese's discussion of mistresses and slaves in *Within the Plantation Household: Black and White Women of the Old South* (Chapel Hill: University of North Carolina Press, 1988), 120–28, 179–85.

[54]Social and rural historians have challenged prevailing assumptions about the sexual division of labor in rural communities, finding women in stores, workshops, and fields and, less frequently, men assisting within the household. With few exceptions, however, sewing seems to have been women's work. For a discussion of one provincial man who defied the sexual division of labor by sewing and quilting, see Karen V. Hansen, "Challenging Separate Spheres in Antebellum New Hampshire: The Case of Brigham Nims," *Historical New Hampshire* 43 (1988): 120–35.

[55]J. H. Butler, *The Good Girl* (Northampton, Mass.: John Metcalf, 1842), n.p.

ily's sewing to make silk hoods for her friend Madam Denison and Denison's daughter Sophia. At a dinner the next month, Denison "roasted her last Turkey (which she reared herself)" while Tyler "quilted comforters for Sophia, or rather helped quilt one." And, after the 1820s, provincial women regularly assembled as members of benevolent societies, wielding their needles for God and the poor.[56]

If the practice of sewing gave shape to provincial women's sense of themselves as women, the garments they stitched and mended underscored their identities as the wives, mothers, and sisters of provincial men. Mary Tyler, who honored her friend with a silk hood, set great store by the sewing she did for her sons. The journal she kept from the late 1810s through the 1820s reveals her as a woman who sewed almost continuously. In addition to sewing for Madam Denison and her daughter, she sewed for her husband, nine of her ten children, and herself. After 1823, when her husband's illness and her eldest son's business failure left the family destitute, she and her two daughters took in sewing from their neighbors and friends. Describing endless rounds of needlework, Tyler took care to mention sewing for particular sons, noting that she was mending Edward's shirts for his return to New Haven and that despite illness, she had "made out to finish Ch[arles]'s great coat" and that daughter Amelia was "kniting stockings for Pickman." As a matter of course, women sewed not only for the men they lived with but also for sons and brothers whose schooling or work had drawn them away from home. Sisters Mehab Ann and Emily Bradley took a special pride in their contributions to their brother's wardrobe. Mehab assured him that on his next visit home he would find "a little more gentleman's linen done." Busy spinning wool in 1820, Emily hoped that her labors would eventually provide her brother with "a very handsome suit of clothes." For Mehab Ann and Emily Bradley, a growing sense of craft merged with the affection they bore a cherished older brother.[57]

Even aging mothers who had stitched countless shirts and darned endless piles of socks found that needlework could evoke the love they bore their absent sons, reinforcing the ties that bound child to mother and, perhaps, to household. Forty-two years old and in failing health, Fanny Negus Fuller of Deerfield, Massachusetts, continued to sew for her sons Elijah and George, who were seeking careers beyond the fam-

[56]20 March 1822, 16 February 1822, Mary Palmer Tyler Diary, 1821–43, Document 49:1, Royall Tyler Collection, Gift of Helen Tyler Brown, VHS.

[57]Emily Bradley to Jonathan Dorr Bradley, 27 March 1820, and Mehab Ann Bradley to Jonathan Dorr Bradley, 19 April 1819, Bradley Family Papers, SL; 28 December 1821, 12 January 1822, and 12 October 1822, Mary Palmer Tyler Diary, 1821–43, Document 49:1, Royall Tyler Collection, Gift of Helen Tyler Brown, VHS.

ily farm. In 1841, she promised that she and her stepdaughter Elizabeth would tend to Elijah's shirts as quickly as possible. "I cannot work much, and we have no help," she warned, "but I think I shall be able to sew some part of the day." She added that "I shed many tears because cannot do more and suffer much more on my familys acount than my own approaching disolution." Near death three years later, she wrote to George, "I am too feeble to work any more for any of you but I trust you will all get along comfortable when you have no Mother to do your sewing." In Fuller's mind, plain sewing gave concrete form to her duties as a mother, the love she bore her sons, and, finally, her own mortality.[58]

Like Fanny Negus Fuller, Elizabeth Phelps Huntington worked for her sons long after they had left home. She attacked the worn socks of her son Frederic Dan Huntington, a married minister living in Boston, with a missionary's zeal. "Don't think me crazy about socks," she wrote, "if I send you a pair well mended—and ask you to send back . . . all you have and can spare, that need mending or will do to have new feet knit upon them." She teasingly reminded him that "there is honourable mention made in an ancient Record, of those who had 'washed the saints feet'—What if I should aspire to be ranked among them?"[59]

Provincial women like Mary Tyler, Emily and Mehab Ann Bradley, Fanny Negus Fuller, and Elizabeth Phelps Huntington imbued their needlework with special significance. Indeed, sewing rivaled nursing and child care in its power to evoke women's love for their kin, male and female. They imagined their work in language drawn from the domestic canon, language that transformed housework into a labor of love. Juxtaposed against the self-interested scramble of the marketplace, housework emerged as a divinely sanctioned calling, as Huntington's gentle joke suggests.[60]

Although provincial women described their domestic labors in the language of middle-class sentiment and feminine service, sewing carried other meanings as well. Certainly, sewing was a labor of love. But it was also a valuable contribution to the household economy. While this contribution stopped short of elevating women to ranks of those who "washed the saints feet," it did entitle them to a certain return. Fanny Negus Fuller may have shed tears because her ill health

[58]Fanny Negus Fuller to George Fuller, 22 September 1844, 18 April 1841, Fuller-Higginson Papers, PVMA.

[59]Elizabeth Phelps Huntington to Frederic Dan Huntington, n.d. [ca. 1842], PPHFP, Box 12, Folder 9.

[60]On the construction of housework as selfless service, see Boydston, *Home and Work*, 142–63; Brown, *Domestic Individualism*, 63–96; Cott, *Bonds of Womanhood*, 64–74.

deprived her sons of fresh shirts, but she did not hesitate to appropriate their earnings when she saw fit.

In 1841, Fuller agreed with her daughter Elizabeth that the Fullers' parlor was in need of improvement. The two women braided palm-leaf hats to buy wallpaper and to "cover the sofa new," but the fifteen dollars necessary for a carpet exceeded what they could hope to earn by braiding. Negus Fuller approached her husband for the carpet money, but he refused her, saying "he cannot let so much money go as he owes Uncle Sid D. six hundred & sixty dollars, which must be paid." She then turned to her son Elijah, reasoning that he could "send us the sum out of his wages, as he can get along with less than he had last year." Fanny Negus Fuller never requested a contribution; instead, after explaining her need, she simply reminded her son that she "wish[ed] him to send the money soon.''[61] The next week she called on two other sons to "defray" the expenses of a much-needed vacation to "Washington City" for their sister Elizabeth. She could not turn to her husband, who was struggling to pay for the musical education of yet another Fuller son, Joseph, in the hopes that "he can have a profession by which he can live hereafter." But if Joseph's demands were more pressing, Elizabeth's claim to a share of the family's resources was equally valid. Fuller reminded her sons that their own progress had been aided by their sister's efforts. "You know verry well how hard she has worked and confined herself at home almost exclusively at home for the last 3 years," she wrote. Indeed, Elizabeth had been "so truly faithfull to me and you all" that Fuller was willing to "forgo most any inconvenience that she could have a respit from care and toil." Fuller expected her sons to respond in kind. When Fanny Negus Fuller wanted assistance from her men, she did not request it in the sentimental language of middle-class motherhood, although she was not above deploying a small measure of guilt. Instead, she reminded them of the work that she and her daughter had performed, and continued to perform, on their behalf. Fuller laid claim to her sons' earnings not in the language of domesticity but in the language of the household economy.[62] Sewing may have figured as an especially selfless form of service, emanating from women's love for their kin, but it also counted as labor that carried economic value and entitled women to some share of the household's resources.

These same tensions—between household economy and middle-class domesticity, between sentiment and labor—extended beyond

[61]Fanny Negus Fuller to George Fuller, 18 April [1841], Fuller-Higginson Papers, PVMA.
[62]Fanny Negus Fuller to George Fuller, 25 April 1841, Fuller-Higginson Papers, PVMA.

work to shape women's relations with their female kin. Mothers, daughters, sisters, and cousins formed deep bonds that resonated with their shared destinies as women. They looked to one another to provide an ideal of womanhood that owed as much to women's experiences as members of particular households and families as to any transcendent female identity. Certainly, the patterns of material reciprocity that shaped relations between female kin within the household economy of the eighteenth and early nineteenth centuries continued through the antebellum era. But that mutuality took on new meanings and was put to new purposes by members of an emerging middle class.

Because female kin both reflected and reinforced provincial women's sense of self, kin played a pivotal role in shaping provincial women's identities. After her marriage in 1800 necessitated a move to Litchfield, Connecticut, Elizabeth Phelps Huntington struggled to construct an identity separate from her connections to her family, especially her mother, Elizabeth Porter Phelps. She anxiously awaited a visit from her mother, writing, "I cannot feel at home untill you have been here—I want your opinion of everything and every body." After the treasured visit, Huntington returned to the room that had served as her mother's chamber and "took a long view of the road you had left," giving way to tears. "It was long before I was decent to be seen," she admitted. In the first years of her marriage, Huntington was so distraught over their separation that her mother began to worry about the effect her homesickness would have on her marriage. But Huntington urged her mother not to "fear that my attachment to my parents, will at all lessen the regard of my husband." On the contrary, Dan Huntington thought that his wife's feelings spoke well for her character; he hoped that she would "always love as much as you now do those dear parents, who have been so good to you all your life." She assured her mother that "I have room in my heart for both parents, and husband, and shall always cherish a proper affection for both."[63]

Forty years later, Caroline Clapp Briggs was relieved to find a husband equally tolerant of her attachment to her only sister. Shortly after marrying Mr. Merrick, an old family friend, Briggs's sister suffered an emotional breakdown. Following her doctor's advice, the new Mrs. Merrick left her husband to live with her sister and brother-in-law, a situation no doubt made easier by the timely death of Mr. Merrick. For thirty years, until her sister's death in 1879, Caroline Clapp Briggs basked in the company of her beloved sister and husband. "We lived

[63]Elizabeth Phelps Huntington to Elizabeth Porter Phelps, 17 February 1802, 14 February 1801, and 11 January 1801, PPHFP, Box 13, Folder 2.

absolutely one life together," she wrote. "It was a sort of triple marriage, and an arrangement perfect in all things. . . . I think there was never a happier home." Drawing on the conventions of a female literary culture, she described her sister's death, and her sister's love, in language that combined the sensual and the sacred:

> In those last few days she gave full and free expression to all her love for me. Then I realized that even as I loved I had been loved, and neither time nor death nor any other thing can ever separate me from my own. She gave herself to me then, fully, freely, and without reserve, and the prayer of my life was answered.[64]

Faced with the loss of a sister with whom she had spent her life, Briggs appropriated her sister's essence for herself.

Sarah Parsons was haunted by the fact that she had failed to "give full and free expression" to her feelings before her sister Hannah died in 1848. During Hannah's last illness, Parsons underestimated the seriousness of the young woman's condition, complaining that she was less ill than lazy. Several weeks later, when Hannah Parsons died, Sarah Parsons finally realized how deeply her sister had touched her life. "Sorrow & gloom is thrown over every thing which we used to enjoy in common—I was not aware how closely my thoughts feelings & & interests were connected—I placed a great deal of reliance upon her judgement & discernment," she wrote. Plagued by "doubts and regrets," Parsons worried that her feelings were of "no avail the past is forever fled & its events sealed for Eternity." Six months later, unable to master her grief or her guilt, she confessed, "my Faith has been shaken." Questioning herself and her God, Sarah Parsons turned to *another* sister, Elizabeth Parsons Hidden, for solace. She found that Hidden's reassuring letters "tore away some of the cold callous feelings that have been washing around me." Promising to "read & endeavor to profit" from her sister's words, she wrote, "Let me have another [letter] when you have time to write." The comforts of one sister slowly compensated for the loss of the other, restoring Parsons's sense of self.[65]

In a moment of crisis, Elizabeth Parsons Hidden sustained her sister with words. But provincial women were just as likely to sustain one another with tangible forms of comfort. The emotional tenor of their

---

[64]Briggs, *Reminiscences*, 45, 42–43, 98–100.

[65]Sarah Parsons to Elizabeth Parsons Hidden, 8 January 1849, 28 June 1848, and Elizabeth Parsons Hidden to Emily Parsons Tenney, 29 March 1847, Parsons Papers, SL.

relationships was embedded in a complex web of material reciprocity. Even middle-class women were bound to one another through a system of everyday give-and-take. At least until the late 1850s, their exchanges were governed by the same principles that had governed the household economy from the eighteenth century through the 1830s.

Social historians who contend that the rural North was characterized by a distinctive household economy have long pointed to the differences between local exchange and long-distance trade to support their arguments. Michael Merrill and James Henretta early discovered a pattern of reciprocity between households that belied the image of the New England farmer as a yeoman capitalist; their studies demonstrated that farmers were more interested in maintaining a "competence" or "independence" than in becoming market-oriented producers. Christopher Clark has extended this argument, suggesting that rural men and women adhered to an "ethic" of local exchange quite distinct from the principles governing long-distance trade. In contrast to long-distance trade, local exchange often entailed face-to-face transactions between neighbors and kin, noncash payment, extended indebtedness, and "recognition of particular households' needs and abilities." Although he is careful not to romanticize this reciprocity, which regularly collapsed into small-minded wrangling, Clark nevertheless demonstrates that local exchange created "networks of obligation," embodying the "distinctive moral demands rural people made on each other when they exchanged goods, labor, and other services." Like most scholars interested in local exchange, Clark primarily examined the ways in which men traded goods and labor. Tracing the activities and strategies of provincial men, he concluded that this older pattern of exchange had begun to collapse by the late 1830s.[66]

Yet long after it had disappeared from transactions between farmers and craftsmen, the ethic of local exchange continued to govern the prosaic trades and mundane obligations that punctuated women's lives. Women lent their mothers, daughters, sisters, and cousins dress patterns, cloth, foodstuffs, and, when it was both necessary and possible, cash. Provincial families offered their kin the labor of their women and children for days, weeks, or months. Exchanges between female kin were frequently so small and so common that they escaped mention even in women's writings. At times, women's reciprocity was conspicuous only in its absence. In 1834, Polly Flint Tarble of Vermont listed

[66]Clark, *Roots of Rural Capitalism*, 33, 31; Henretta, "Families and Farms"; Merrill, "Cash Is Good to Eat." Compare Osterud, *Bonds of Community*, 187–201, for a systematic examination of women's exchange.

relatives who had visited, helped, and departed only to conclude, "Now I am left alone, nobody to depend on."[67]

Amelia White Peabody, wife of a Springfield, Massachusetts, Unitarian minister, was more forthcoming. The dozens of letters she wrote to her father, sisters, and cousins between her marriage in 1825 and her death in 1843 provide a rare account of the ways that women's reciprocity structured the ties between female kin and between households. Peabody, her sisters, and her cousins regularly bestowed small gifts on one another, keeping an eye out for items another woman might have difficulty obtaining. Not surprisingly, these exchanges often centered on the women's needlework. In 1825, Peabody was most grateful for some pins sent by her cousin Eliza White in Salem, Massachusetts, for "tho so common an article, such nice ones are not to be got here." Several years later, she sent patterns for dress trim to her sister Mary Jane White who was living in rustic Lancaster, New Hampshire. Indeed, fashions, trimmings, and fabrics form a minor theme in the sisters' correspondence. They frequently provided each other with information about styles, and Peabody, at least, regularly purchased cloth for her sister. Although the pins and patterns appear to have been gifts, Peabody expected to be reimbursed for more expensive items, such as fabric. But Peabody and White approached the financial aspects of their exchange with the flexible standards of the household economy. Knowing that she owed her sister money, White in 1831 arranged for her brother to send on thirty-six dollars, leaving Amelia with a credit of more than fifteen dollars. Both women assumed that White would eventually request purchases against the credit; in the meantime, the balance was Peabody's to use as she saw fit. This was fortunate, for, as she explained, money was "a commodity scarce with us at this time."[68]

Exchanges of pins and patterns might seem to be trifling matters, owing more to the frivolous pastimes of fashionable ladies than to the serious strategies of provincial households. But the reciprocity that marked these small exchanges was part of the wider practice of mutual obligation that linked not just Peabody and White but the households of their kin. Through the 1830s, for example, Peabody put up a series of nieces and nephews, whose parents were eager for them to obtain good educations without incurring full boarding expenses. From Peabody's perspective, the extra children certainly created extra work

[67]Polly Flint Tarble to Mary Anne Tarble Haile, 16 November 1834, Haile Family Papers, MS-130 VHS.

[68]Amelia White Peabody to Mary Jane White, 17 June 1831, 8 July 1827, and Amelia White Peabody to Eliza White, 25 September 1825, Everett-Peabody Family Papers, MHS.

and possibly extra expense, but in providing for her young kin, she and her husband conformed to older customs of family obligation, making a significant contribution to the budgets and family strategies of her brothers and sisters.[69]

Amelia White Peabody did not simply participate in a system of exchange between households. She attempted to shape it, ensuring that an ethic of mutual obligation continued to govern relations between her kin. At the end of the 1820s, Peabody's father, Moses White, was close to settling a protracted land dispute. Peabody was delighted at his good fortune, for the claim stood to rescue him from financial embarrassment and restore him to "independence." But she was concerned that her father's windfall might prompt her cousins Mary and Harriett to pursue an old claim of their own against Moses White. Certainly, Peabody was irked about the women's claim, which they had inherited from their father and which had been the source of a long-standing feud within the family; a loyal daughter, Peabody took her father's part. Still, she urged her father to settle with the women. As she pointed out, a willingness to negotiate might enable her father to reach a less expensive compromise. More to the point, the sisters' miserable poverty demanded that White come to their assistance. She assured him that Mary and Harriett were "the most forsaken beings in the whole of my knowledge." Mary did "all the work of the family," in addition to caring for Harriett, whose fits were "more distressing even than they formerly were" and whose "mind [was] greatly weakened." As she pointed out, "If it were in any other shape, you would be desirous under existing circumstances of doing something for those poor forlorn girls." Despite his daughter's pleas, White refused to settle; after his death in 1833, Amelia White Peabody acknowledged her cousins' claim to a share of her father's estate.[70]

Women who wrote less frequently and less garrulously were more apt to comment only on the assistance they gave one another in times of unusual need. For example, provincial women routinely recorded that they assisted their kin during and after childbirth. The unmarried Cochran sisters of Northampton, Massachusetts, expected that one of them would tend their married sister in New York for the birth of her

[69]Amelia White Peabody to Mary Jane White, 26 August 1831, 31 July 1831, Everett-Peabody Family Papers, MHS. This seems to have been common practice. See, for example, Arethusa Howe to Fanny Negus Fuller, 10 April 1837, 19 November 1839, Fuller-Higginson Papers, PVMA.

[70]Amelia White Peabody to Moses White, 2 April 1828, 14 June 1829, and Amelia White Peabody to Mary Jane White Williams, 8 February 1834, Everett-Peabody Family Papers, MHS.

second child in 1836. Elizabeth Phelps Huntington counted on her mother's presence during the birth of her first child in 1802; more than twenty-five years later, she traveled from South Hadley to Oswego, New York, to assist her daughter, Elizabeth Fisher, after the birth of her fourth child. The value of this support was not lost on the Huntington men. When Elizabeth Phelps Huntington returned to Massachusetts, her husband could "hardly divine" what their daughter would do without her help. "What will she do with four babys"? he wondered. "I used to think you had your hands full with three." Illness, like childbirth, could summon a woman to the household of her kin. In 1849, a woman named Sarah and her children stopped to visit her sister's family in Amherst, Massachusetts, "expecting to stay for a week or two." But when her sister succumbed to illness, Sarah "staid and done the work most all summer." Only eight weeks later, when her sister was well enough to "be about the house a little," did Sarah consider returning home.[71]

This pattern of mutuality and exchange structured women's daily routines, but it also shaped their feelings of love and obligation. The fusion of love, labor, and exchange was especially poignant at death. Women remembered one another as companions and confidantes, but the most devoted kin also remembered one another as fellow laborers. After the death of her daughter, Mary Dwight Huntington, in 1839, Elizabeth Phelps Huntington mourned the loss of a child, a friend, and a helpmeet. "Bethia and I go on in our labour alone," she wrote. "Our pleasant companion, and kind assistant is remov'd." Esther Goodell, a young Amherst, woman, shared Huntington's perspective. Just before she died in 1840, she summoned her kin so that she might dispose of her money and possessions. She left her watch to her fiancé. She bequeathed the bulk of her small savings to her father, returning her income to the household coffers. But she also set aside twenty-five dollars for her mother and ten dollars for her brother, saying that "her Brother was helping her and she wanted to help him to an education." The rest of her belongings she divided up among her sisters and sisters-in-law. To her sister Lucinda, who was also looking to marry, Goodell offered the trousseau she had been unable to use—"her gold beads and wedding dress and Crokery." She requested that "the rest of her

[71]Harriett Goodell to Angelo Goodell, 31 July 1849, Goodell Family Papers, JL; Martha Cochran to Agnes Cochran Higginson, 16 August 1836, Fuller-Higginson Papers, PVMA; Elizabeth Phelps Huntington to Elizabeth Porter Phelps, 17 February 1802, PPHFP, Box 13, Folder 1; Dan Huntington to Elizabeth Phelps Huntington, 26 May 1828, PPHFP, Box 15, Folder 6; see also Mary Jane White to Charlotte White, 4 July 1830, Everett-Peabody Family Papers, MHS.

Clothes . . . be divided between her sisters, and remember her brothers wives and give them some thing that was hers." Esther Goodell remembered her kin, and asked that they remember her, not through the flowery conventions of domesticity but through the reciprocity of the household economy.[72]

Gender and Family Strategies

Salvaging the ethic of local exchange from the remains of the household economy, provincial women also adapted that ethic to serve the aspirations of an emerging middle class. To be sure, middle-class women acquired the "advantages" that set them apart from struggling farmers and the laboring poor largely through their men's purchasing power. But provincial women worked hard to turn themselves, and their kin, into ladies. Mothers, in particular, were inclined to shoulder extra chores to provide their daughters with a proper "finishing." For example, girls attended school not simply because their fathers could afford the expense but because their mothers were willing to forfeit their help for months at a time. When Bethia Huntington was a student at Troy Seminary, her father assured her that "we get along quite cleverly" without her help. He joked that "Ma groans some, after washing &c.," but insisted that "parents are willing to groan if they can go to rest at night thinking that their children . . . are doing well in their stations." Deeply committed to educating her four daughters, Elizabeth Phelps Huntington undoubtedly was "willing to groan," although the work probably weighed on her more heavily than her husband realized. Fanny Negus Fuller found her life was "very hard" after she sent her eldest daughter to Boston to read French early in 1837. "I am tugging along alone for the sake of her advantages," she wrote. Fuller nevertheless resolved that her daughter "must continue for six months if we can afford to board her there so long."[73]

The same sisters who assisted one another in childbirth and nursed one another through illness offered their services to help with increasingly elaborate "affairs." Several years after sending her daughter to read French, Fanny Negus Fuller agreed to host an ambitious wedding for her sister, Caroline Negus. With "so much to do in arranging and

[72]Susanna Goodell to Ira Chafee Goodell, 24 March 1840, Goodell Papers, JL; Elizabeth Phelps Huntington to Edward Huntington, 7 December 1839, PPHFP, Box 12, Folder 4.

[73]Fanny Negus Fuller to George Fuller, 11 December 1837, Fuller-Higginson Family Papers, PVMA; Dan Huntington to Bethia Huntington, 8 October 1882, PPHFP, Box 15, Folder 4.

putting the house in order" and "no boy to help," Fuller worried that Elizabeth "will get worn out before the wedding," adding that "I also feel the same." She was finally forced to enlist the services of her reluctant husband; as she explained to her son, she had no choice but to "call on your father untill he is out of patience."[74]

To approximate a middle-class standard of living, provincial families especially counted on the periodic assistance of single female kin. When estimating their budgets for a coming season, provincial women used the labor of daughters, sisters, nieces, and cousins to reduce expenditures on hired nurses, domestics, and seamstresses. In return, girls and women received "payments" such as board, a new dress, schooling, or, less frequently, cash.[75] More important, their own families were assured that they in turn would benefit from the supply of female labor during their own time of need. These exchanges of women's labor took the form of visits, merging labor, leisure, and sociability. For example, after the death of Royall Tyler, Mary W. Tyler was sent to stay with Boston cousins, for she had been a "blessed good girl" during her "Father's long illness and deserve[d] a good rest." But her mother reminded Mary that her "rest" depended on her usefulness to her aunt. "You can and I doubt not you will do a great deal of sewing and if I hear you do I shall feel very easy, otherwise not," her mother wrote. More than twenty years later, Aurelia Smith found herself "enjoying peaceful mountain air & working" while visiting her relatives; she reported to her family that she had made twenty-three sunbonnets for her cousins and a dress for herself.[76]

Under the best of circumstances, these exchanges of labor functioned as "working vacations," offering provincial women a change of scenery, a chance to expand their circle of friends and acquaintances, and the opportunity to renew treasured family relationships.[77] Al-

[74]Fanny Negus Fuller to George Fuller, n.d. [ca. 1841], Fuller-Higginson Family Papers, PVMA. The elaboration of provincial sociability is discussed in Chapter 6.

[75]For accounts of payments, see, for example, Mary Palmer Tyler to Mary W. Tyler, 12 April 1827, Royall Tyler Collection, Gift of Helen Tyler Brown, VHS; Aurelia Smith to Family, 19 December 1845, Aurelia Smith to Parents and Brothers, 21 July 1850, Hooker Collection, SL; Milla Haile to Mary Ann Tarble Haile, 2 November 1858, Haile Papers, VHS.

[76]Aurelia Smith to Parents and Brothers, 21 July 1850, Hooker Collection, SL. Mary Palmer Tyler to Mary W. Tyler, 12 April 1827, Royall Tyler Collection, VHS.

[77]Under the worst of circumstances, such visits could saddle women with unduly heavy burdens. In 1827, Eliza Adams's friend Lucia planned to leave Hanover, New Hampshire, where she had been boarding with "Mrs. W." and return to her family. "I think it will be much better for her, for they have no help, so the whole care of Mrs. W who is always sick, & of her large family, devolves on Lucia," Adams wrote. Eliza Minot Adams to Harriet Adams Aiken, 19 January 1827, Adams Family Papers, MS 420, Box 5, Folder 2, DCL.

though many women stressed the female bonds these visits occasioned, their working vacations should not be seen as the expression of an emerging, autonomous women's culture. This is not to discount the genuine pleasure and significance that women derived from their visits. But women's visits among their kin point both to ways in which middle-class provincial households continued to depend on the labor of their women and the extent to which they maintained control over the labor of their women.[78]

Married women's visits were certainly determined by the needs of their children, but they were also determined by their husbands' needs and wishes. When Amelia White Peabody and Mary Jane White Williams wanted each other's company, they found their husbands uncooperative. Peabody was only half-joking when she wrote her sister that "as to my husband's gallantry, I have never boasted of it . . . & it is not very high praise to yours to say he is not better . . . though your owning horses & vehicles makes the sin more preponderate on your side."[79]

Single women found their visiting, and their labor, similarly managed by their mothers, fathers, older brothers, and married sisters. These women were dispatched to their kin with little regard for their own plans or preferences. Young women, in particular, lacked control over the timing or duration of their visits. Eliza Adams "despair[ed] of ever seeing" her recently married sister, Harriet, who had repeatedly requested the girl's company and her help. "Pa though he has no great desire to keep me at home, still cares so little about my going that he will make no sort of exertion," she complained in 1827. Several years later, a young woman named Hannah found herself "once more" postponing "long anticipated plans for pleasure" to care for a married sister who was experiencing "liver complaint, indigestion, tic doloreaux, & the whole list of dolours" that followed childbirth. "One would imagine that we spinsters could have few sympathies to offer in these afflictive troubles," she wrote. "But my dear Sisters have almost succeeded in their object to make me feel that I am at all times indispensible to their comfort and again they have prevailed, and according to promise I must be on my way."[80]

---

[78]For an insightful discussion of visiting as a form of social and labor exchange, see Hansen, *A Very Social Time*, 79–113.

[79]Amelia White Peabody to Mary Jane White, 16 January 1836, Everett-Peabody Family Papers, MHS.

[80]Hannah to Elizabeth Sprague, 20 July 1831, Sprague-Dinsmore Papers, HSCC. Eliza Minot Adams to Harriet Adams Aiken, 17 September 1828, Adams Family Papers, MS 420, Box 5, Folder 2, DCL.

It isn't surprising that the family claim not only took precedence over young women's "plans for pleasure" but also prevailed over their plans to earn money. Hannah Fulton, who lived with her sister in the early 1850s, was quite willing to spend a few weeks tending to Mrs. Gillis's boarders while that woman visited her relatives. The Gillises boarded only three people, and besides, she "felt under some obligation to Mr. & Mrs. G therefore make an effort to accommodate them." But Fulton's sister was less enthusiastic about the arrangement, for "sister thought she could hardly spare me." To accommodate both her sister and the Gillises, Fulton "rose very early & did her [sister's] washing before" she left for the Gillis household. Many women delayed or canceled plans to keep school to assist in the households of their kin. When Sarah Parsons's sister managed to secure her a much-desired teaching position, Sarah responded that she could accept the position only if another, ailing sister "continues to improve so as to be comfortable again." "You may think this a very indefinite answer," she conceded, "but at present all is uncertain." And other women closed schools on their families' request. Mary Giddings Coult, for example, "dismissed [her] school to go & take care of Cousin Lydia C."[81]

Middle-class families were able to swap the labor of their women in part because women had so few alternatives beyond the household. In the late eighteenth century, provincial fathers had begun to lose control over their sons' labor because they could no longer provide for their futures. In the precarious economy of the 1830s and 1840s, these same families were no more able to guarantee their daughters' futures than their sons'. Weighed against the dismal life that awaited any provincial woman cut loose from kin and household, however, the uncertain care offered by her family must have looked comforting indeed.[82]

This is not to suggest that the exchange of young women's labor rested on coercion alone. Influenced by an ideology that elevated the

[81]Mary Giddings Coult is quoted in Hansen, *A Very Social Time*, 95. Sarah Parsons to Elizabeth Parsons Hidden, n.d. [spring 1848], Parsons Family Papers, SL. Hannah Fulton to Lyman Fulton, 8 December 1851, Fulton-Lyman Papers, 1991–007, NHHS. Women frequently consulted with their families before accepting teaching positions to determine whether teaching would interfere with the family's plans. See, for example, Dan Huntington to Bethia Throop Huntington, 11 July 1851, PPHFP, Box 15, Folder 4; Hannah Fulton to Lyman Fulton, 22 March 1852, Fulton-Lyman Papers, 1991–007, NHHS.

[82]Karen Hansen, *A Very Social Time*, 95–98, argues that among the "working women" she studied, families granted single women a great deal of latitude in these exchanges, respecting women's need to weigh their need for self-support against the family claim. But middle-class women who continued to depend on and who expected to benefit from their families' support were not granted this latitude. On the changing strategies of middle-class families to provide for their offspring, see Ryan, *Cradle of the Middle Class*.

needs of kin over the rights of individuals, provincial women accepted their responsibilities to their households and the households of their families even as they accepted the unequal distribution of power within those households. Individual women surely resented the demands placed on their time, or the lack of consideration they were sometimes shown, but they accepted their families' authority to make those demands.

By the end of the antebellum period, many provincial women found it increasingly difficult to accommodate the tensions between the values and practices that had prevailed in the household economy and those that characterized the emerging market society. Women in the upper reaches of the provincial middle class described their labor, when they described it at all, as a manifestation of gentility and femininity. Slowly, they stopped turning to female kin for assistance, relying instead on store purchases and on the hired help of domestic servants, however unreliable. Family visits came to consist of a strenuous round of parties, dances, teas, and "afternoons at home." Agnes Higginson frequently traveled from Deerfield, Massachusetts, to Brattleboro, Vermont, to visit her grandmother, aunts, and cousins and to attend plays, tableaux, and parties. But her contribution to their households was found in her charm and pleasant disposition rather than in her sewing box.[83]

Women at the lower margins of the middle class also experienced the contradiction between market and household, although in very different ways. For these women, the need to contribute both income and labor to their families created tremendous burdens. By the end of the antebellum period, some began to weigh the family claim against their own needs, to think about their contributions to their kin in the language of the market rather than in the language of the household. In the late 1840s, Julia Dutton, a single woman working in a Clintonville, Massachusetts textile mill, was called to help nurse her ailing brother-in-law in nearby Grafton. By the time Julia arrived, Leander Withersby had recovered enough to take his wife visiting, leaving an empty house to welcome his sister-in-law. Julia was understandably furious that her sister would invoke the family claim so carelessly. She carefully calculated the expense of her mishap, writing her mother that the fare to Grafton, combined with her lost wages, had set her back two dollars.

[83]See Agnes Higginson [Fuller] Diary, 1855–1856, PVMA. For an account of a similar transformation in the visual representation of provincial women's work, see my " 'The Consummation of Rural Prosperity and Happiness': New England Agricultural Fairs and the Construction of Class and Gender, 1810–1860," American Quarterly 49 (1997): 574–602.

Several years later, Julia was again called to the Withersby home. This time, her sister Jane was ill, and Julia nursed her for several months until she died. After her sister's death, Julia felt justified in presenting her brother-in-law with a bill for $ 6.75.[84]

Neither Agnes Higginson nor Julia Dutton made sense of her life by the lights of the household economy, which had fused family obligations, women's work, and female identity into a seamless whole for women like Elizabeth Phelps Huntington. Both Higginson and Dutton had assimilated the categories of a market society—categories that drew sharp distinctions between paid labor and labor for families, between production and reproduction, between public and private. But for much of the antebellum period, provincial women had successfully negotiated the tensions between middle-class domesticity and household economy; in the minds and lives of many women, the two coexisted in an uneasy peace. Only gradually, almost unwittingly, did women reshape their identities as mothers, sisters, and daughters to accord with a bourgeois ideal. Part of a much broader process of economic, social, and cultural change, this transformation in women's roles and identities was so uneventful precisely because it left unchallenged their primary obligations to—and dependence on—their households and families.

[84]Julia Dutton to Lucretia Wilson Dutton, 29 August 1847, 5 September 1848, 5 November 1848, 17 December 1848, and R. Leander Withersby to Lucretia Wilson Dutton, 17 December 1848, Lucretia Wilson Dutton Papers, UVM.

3

"Never was a separation
so painful"

In an 1856 memoir recalling her days at Mount Holyoke Seminary and dedicated to an "old friend," a Northampton, Massachusetts, woman described the school as a world set apart.[1] In her telling, girls looked out at the surrounding landscape from the school's attic windows. They reached across the fences enclosing the school only to grab peaches from the branch of a neighbor's tree. The school was an island, completely separated from the community beyond it. But the school was not only a separate physical space. It was also a distinct social space in which girls and young women could create their own worlds. The school building figured as little more than a backdrop for female bonding. The woman took her friend on a journey from the school's cellar, "the resort of many childish hours of childish innocence and glee," where girls constructed make-believe households out of cubby houses, to the school attic, the "hallowed resort" that the students appropriated for themselves, arranging the " 'green benches' in a sort of semi-circle, for our own accommodation." Education depended on the distinctly feminine companionship of "faithful teachers" and, especially, "loving schoolmates."

Yet these pleasures and lessons proved transitory, more the stuff of nostalgic memory than the basis of adult identity. The writer saw little connection between her school years and her adult life. Although she had lived to regret the childish "impatience and want of perseverance"

[1]A. C. A., "School Reminiscences," *Hampshire Gazette*, 22 January 1856.

that had once hampered her progress on "difficult problems," she entertained no hopes of making up for lost time. Intellectual striving disappeared in the face of adult responsibility. Friendship suffered the same fate as learning. The companions who "tripped so lightly and laughingly into our large 'school-room' were now scattered far and wide." Like those golden days, those good friends were "all over—we can never enjoy them again." "We prize not our privileges while we possess them," she wrote. "We value not our blessings until deprived of them."[2] If Mount Holyoke was an island in the New England countryside, her student days were an island of intellectual engagement and female friendship receding across an ocean of womanly responsibility.

In her "School Reminiscences," the Northampton woman fused the culture of the women's academy with the culture of female friendship, celebrating their power even as she mourned their passing. To be sure, the language and structure of her account owe much to prevailing literary conventions. But they owe much more to New England women's experiences of the contradictory processes of social and cultural change that accompanied the development of rural capitalism. As part of a "Village Enlightenment," the expansion of female academies, seminaries, and select schools in antebellum New England testified not only to the spread of ideas but also to the growth of the middle class and the expansion of bourgeois culture.[3]

Academies offered provincial young women many things—chief among them the opportunity to enter into new imaginative worlds and new kinds of relations with one another. And as the Northampton woman's "School Reminiscences" suggest, these opportunities were inextricably connected. If only for a few months, academies loosened the hierarchical obligations of kinship and community that dictated so many aspects of provincial women's lives, freeing them to develop voluntary bonds with one another. At the same time, these schools inculcated the refined sensibility and the literary technique demanded by

[2]Ibid.

[3]On the growth of female seminaries and academies in the nineteenth century, see Nancy F. Cott, *The Bonds of Womanhood: "Woman's Sphere" in New England, 1780–1835* (New Haven, Conn.: Yale University Press, 1977), 101–25, and Thomas Woody, *A History of Women's Education in the United States*, vol. 1 (New York: Science Press, 1929), 363–79. For a detailed account of the development of one early female academy, see Lynne Templeton Brickley, "Sarah Pierce's Litchfield Academy" (Ed.D. diss., Harvard University, 1985). On the emergence of academies in the antebellum South, see Christie Anne Farnham, *The Education of the Southern Belle: Higher Education and Student Socialization in the Antebellum South* (New York: New York University Press, 1994). On the "village enlightenment," see David Jaffee, "The Village Enlightenment in New England, 1760–1820," *William and Mary Quarterly*, 3d ser., 47 (1990): 327–46.

the emerging culture of friendship. The feelings of friendship might first manifest themselves in the heart, but they assumed their fullest shape through the pen in letters, diaries, poems, and friendship books. Indeed, a mastery of the studied effusions demanded by sentimental friendship was strikingly similar to the mastery of arts and letters that stood at the center of a genteel education. The cultivation of a capacity for friendship merged with the cultivation of intellect, sensibility, and religious faith. These pursuits occupied the attention of male and female students alike, but whereas young men found themselves free— and even compelled—to continue their process of self-cultivation beyond the academy walls, young women discovered that the identities they had so carefully crafted at school were ill-suited for the realities of provincial households. It is no accident that study and friendship suffered the same fate when young women returned to the embrace of their families.

Education and Friendship

Examining the lives of nineteenth-century women, scholars have been struck by both the emotional intimacy and the duration of their subjects' friendships. The diaries and letters of urban, middle-class women, in particular, testify to loving and lifelong relationships. Perhaps even more striking than the devotion women offered their closest friends is the attention they lavished on friendship itself.[4] Embracing bonds of choice rather than blood, women consciously cultivated their capacity of friendship at the same time that they nurtured particular relationships. More than simply making friends, urban middle-class women created an entire culture of friendship. The attention accorded female friendship was part of a more general privileging of peer relations that accompanied the emergence of a liberal capitalist

[4]The social structure and emotional dimensions of nineteenth-century female friendships are described in William R. Taylor and Christopher Lasch, "Two 'Kindred Spirits': Sorority and Family in New England, 1839–1846," *New England Quarterly* 36 (1963): 23–41; Carroll Smith-Rosenberg, "The Female World of Love and Ritual: Relations between Women in Nineteenth-Century America," and "Hearing Women's Words: A Feminist Reconstruction of History," in her *Disorderly Conduct: Visions of Gender in Victorian America* (New York: Oxford University Press, 1985), 53–76, 11–52; Cott, *Bonds of Womanhood*, 160–96; Christine Stansell, "Revisiting the Angel in the House: Revisions of Victorian Womanhood," *New England Quarterly* 60 (1987): 466–83; and Carol Lasser, " 'Let Us Be Sisters Forever': The Sororal Model of Nineteenth-Century Female Friendship," *Signs* 14 (1988): 158–81. Lasser is especially sensitive to women's changing understanding of friendship; my thinking about nineteenth-century female friendships owes much to her fine essay.

society between the eighteenth and nineteenth centuries. Democratization, geographic and social mobility, and the Second Great Awakening all worked to erode systems of deference and hierarchy in the young republic.[5]

Although this decline of deference signaled a new emphasis on egalitarian relationships for both men and women, the special qualities of women's friendships derived from a growing sense of the differences between men and women, for the economic and political revolutions that leveled old hierarchies simultaneously recast social categories. Within bourgeois ideology, the decisive division between male and female supplanted the innumerable distinctions that had run up and down an older social scale. Emphasizing the divergence between men's and women's gender roles, domesticity sharpened women's gender identity. Both the style and the substance of female friendships owed much to this heightened sense of gender identity and to the cultural autonomy that some women derived from that identity.[6] Nineteenth-century female friendships thus derived from a particular configuration of political, social, and economic change. One strand in a broader pattern of change, the culture of female friendship merged with the culture of capitalism.

Christian and sentimental discourses were central to the idealized vision of female friendship that flourished between the middle of the eighteenth century and the end of the nineteenth. In both the First and Second Great Awakenings, Protestant theologians, ministers, and writers of various denominations created and expanded a vocabulary of

[5]See, among many, Richard D. Brown, "Modernization and the Modern Personality in Early America, 1600–1865," *Journal of Interdisciplinary History* 2 (1972): 201–28; Wilson Carey McWilliams, *The Idea of Fraternity in America* (Berkeley: University of California Press, 1973); Cott, *Bonds of Womanhood;* Mary P. Ryan, *Cradle of the Middle Class: The Family in Oneida County, New York, 1790–1865* (New York: Cambridge University Press, 1981); Jay Fliegelman, *Prodigals and Pilgrims: The American Revolution against Patriarchal Authority, 1750–1800* (New York: Cambridge University Press, 1982); Alfred D. Young, "George Robert Twelves Hewes (1742–1840): A Boston Shoemaker and the Memory of the American Revolution," *William and Mary Quarterly*, 3d ser., 28 (1981): 561–623; Lee Virginia Chambers-Schiller, *Liberty, a Better Husband: Single Women in America: The Generations of 1780–1840* (New Haven, Conn.: Yale University Press, 1984); Nancy R. Folbre, "The Wealth of Patriarchs: Deerfield, Massachusetts, 1760–1840," *Journal of Interdisciplinary History* 16 (1985): 199–220; Susan Juster, *Disorderly Women: Sexual Politics and Evangelicalism in Revolutionary New England* (Ithaca, N.Y.: Cornell University Press, 1994); Jan Lewis, "The Republican Wife: Virtue and Seduction in the Early Republic," *William and Mary Quarterly* 44 (1987): 659–721; and Richard Rabinowitz, *The Spiritual Self in Everyday Life* (Boston: Northeastern University Press, 1989).

[6]On the connections between domesticity and friendship, see Taylor and Lasch, "'Two Kindred Spirits'"; Smith-Rosenberg, "The Female World of Love and Ritual"; Cott, *Bonds of Womanhood;* and Lasser, "'Let Us Be Sisters Forever.'"

religious affections that associated Christian faith and practice with the affectional as opposed to the cognitive faculties. By encouraging men and women alike to heed their hearts and to cultivate intimate relations with those who shared their sensibilities, ministers offered up a model of Christian community that spoke to entire congregations. But ministers also recognized and endorsed the special friendships that resulted when religious women opened their hearts to one another. As Rev. Daniel Dana asked in 1804, "Who but a woman can know the heart of a woman?"[7]

The sermonic image of one devout Christian woman piously revealing her soul to another was mirrored by the secular image of two young ladies whose attachment was exceeded only by their refinement. In bourgeois didactic and imaginative literature, an elaborate process of self-fashioning fused the cultivation of an interior identity, the sympathy demanded by friendship, and the practices of refinement into the seamless bonds of friendship. The capacity for friendship, especially female friendship, was all but indistinguishable from the capacity for refinement, for the same writers who insisted that true friendship was artless also detailed the arts through which it could be realized: charming conversation, carefully selected tokens of appreciation, and especially engaging and expressive letters. Delineating the permissible, the desirable, and the expected, these sacred and secular discourses, as much as personal affinity or gender role, set the boundaries and the tone for young women's friendships.[8]

Provincial girls and young women looked to the images of intimate and loving relationships sanctioned in sermons, didactic literature, and fiction and poetry to structure their imaginative worlds and peer relations. Not surprisingly, they often cast their appreciation of friendship in a distinctly literary form. Vermonter Susan Mina Crossman carefully copied "lines to the memory of Mrs Belinda Wells" into her commonplace book in the late 1820s, memorializing Wells alongside verses praising God and Harriet Martineau's observations on fiction. The poet praised the young matron's "mild discourse," "bright intelligence," and deep piety. But she also remembered her as

<hr>

[7] Quoted in Cott, *Bonds of Womanhood*, 168. Although Rabinowitz (*The Spiritual Self in Everyday Life*, 184–85, 186, 207–11, 218) notes that intense, Christian friendships were more prevalent among women than men, he fails to address the implications of this observation for understanding nineteenth-century gender roles.

[8] On the connections between Protestantism and refinement, see Richard Bushman, *The Refinement of America: Persons, Houses, Cities* (New York: Vintage Random House, 1993), 313–52.

The dear companion, I can ne'er forget,
Who tho' so lately found, I grieve to lose,
And fondest feeling of sincere regret,
With tributary tears, these eyes suffuse.[9]

Dead at twenty-four, Mrs. Wells's gift for friendship was included among her many virtues.

It is not clear that Crossman wrote the lines memorializing Belinda Wells. It is not even certain that she knew her. Susan Crossman neither signed the poem nor attributed it to another writer; widely reproduced in the early national and antebellum press, poems like the one honoring Wells may well have caught her eye solely for their literary merits and the feelings they evoked. Reflecting Crossman's grief over the death of a beloved friend or her participation in a community of letters, the poem suggests both the respect accorded female friendships generally and women's emotional investment in particular friendships.

The stylized, sentimental language that honored Belinda Wells was not limited to overtly literary endeavors. Many young women brought this discourse to bear on their own experiences, using it to describe and reinforce special relationships. At sixteen, Sophronia Grout of Hawley, Massachusetts, was especially close to a girl named Miranda. Learning that Miranda's father had plans to "remove to a distant part of the land," Grout wrote, "O must I be parted from my dear Miranda her heart is united to mine with the strongest ties." Ten months later, after giving "dear Miranda" the "parting hand & bid[ding] her adieu," Grout wondered, "How shall I dry my tears, how can they cease to flow?" "Never expecting another interview with her," Grout could only look forward to meeting "at the bar of God . . . where tears cannot enter."[10]

When emotions ran high, even taciturn girls called on the language of friendship. For example, Mary Hoyt Wilson of Deerfield, Massachusetts, wrote regularly in the diary she received in 1826 for her seventeenth birthday. Faithfully recounting the rhythms of work and leisure, the hours spent at home and in the village, she eschewed the painful introspection that marked the diaries of so many Protestant women. Describing her days in language bereft of expressive detail, Wilson likely approached writing with more duty than pleasure. Rereading a

[9]"The following lines to the memory of Mrs. Belinda Wells who died at Boston Mass aged 24," writing book of Susan Mina Crossman [Bradley], Bradley Family Papers, SL.

[10]Diary of Sophronia Grout, April 1817, 15 June 1816, Pocumtuck Valley Memorial Association Library, PVMA. Christine Stansell has also called attention to the discursive dimension of female friendships. See "Revisiting the Angel in the House," 473–74.

month's entries, she herself admitted that for the most part, her narrative was "little diversified with memorable or interesting events." But faced with the unexpected death of Amelia Lyman, a friend "valued most dear," even Wilson turned to the language of friendship, capturing her feelings in its formulaic imagery and elaborate constructions. She consoled herself that the beloved Lyman had joined her God, but added, "Could tears revive the dead, then should I be happy for mine could do it." A year later, she continued to struggle with the meaning of her friend's death; surely, it was "no common event that one so young, so beautiful and innocent should be called hence." Wilson eased her feelings of abandonment by appropriating something of her friend's essence, claiming her inheritance in the dead girl's virtues. If Amelia's "frame" lay "slow mouldering in the dust," her spirit survived in Hoyt's heart. Fusing piety and sentiment, Wilson prayed that "the mantle of purity with which [Lyman] was enrobed while here on earth, might fall upon and continue with me so long as I remain a wanderer here below."[11]

If literary culture set the standards for the expressive style of female friendship, academies broadened girls' exposure to that culture. Equally important, academies and seminaries provided girls with an institutional setting in which to develop friendships. Young women made friends at Sunday school and day school, and through their neighbors and kin. But the academies that proliferated in nineteenth-century New England proved especially important in reinforcing the kind of sentiments shared by Mary Hoyt, Sophronia Grout, and Susan Crossman.

Over the first half of the nineteenth century, provincial centers offered young women a choice of increasingly advanced and costly schools. In 1814, Catharine Fiske established one of the first female academies in the United States in Keene, New Hampshire, where she offered instruction in reading, writing, English grammar, composition, arithmetic, history, geography, and "the use of maps and globes."[12] The residents of Keene were hardly alone in their desire to stake out an interest in women's education. Between 1817 and 1821 in Northamp-

[11]Diary of Mary Hoyt Wilson, 17 August 1827, 15 September 1826, and 16 September 1826, PVMA. Wilson continued to mourn Lyman for several years after her death, memorializing her in her diary with prayers and poetry.

[12]*Catalogue of the Young Ladies Seminary, in Keene, NH*, 1823, 1829, 1830, 1832; Gardner C. Hill, M. D., "A Famous Institution: Miss Catherine Fiske's Boarding School of the Early Days," unpublished typescript, HSCC; Sara Josepha Hale, *Woman's Record; or, Sketches of all Distinguished Women, from the Creation to A.D. 1854* (New York: Harper Brothers, 1855, reprinted by New York Source Book Press, 1970), 866–68.

ton, Miss Bancroft, sister to historian George Bancroft, instructed young ladies from that town and the neighboring communities in the basic arts of reading, writing, arithmetic, and sewing. By the mid-1820s, the younger sisters of these scholars could choose from far more sophisticated courses of study. Miss C. M. Snow offered her students a background in history, rhetoric, natural philosophy, painting, and needlework; at a competing school, Miss Fiske transformed spelling into "orthography" and included ancient and modern geography and "elements of criticism" among the course selections. These schools were superseded in 1835 by Margarette Dwight's Gothic Seminary, which raised the standards against which curriculum and cost were measured. Offering a program similar to that of Miss Fiske, Dwight pledged to endow each student with "the power of abstraction, quickness and clearness of conception" along with "habits . . . essential to the practical purposes of life" for one hundred dollars per term, board included. Dwight and her sponsors succeeded in their bid to attract the finest members of New England society. Her students counted among their fathers gentleman farmers, prominent physicians, ministers, the president of Dartmouth College, and a Massachusetts senator.[13]

Drawing attention to Northampton as a regional educational center, Dwight's academy also created new divisions within the town. The tuition proved prohibitive for many local families who admired her methods and goals. Even middling parents who had managed her fees when she was offering less formal instruction under her mother's roof found themselves unable to afford the grander program offered at the Gothic Seminary. After sixteen months under Miss Dwight's excellent supervision, Apphia Judd was forced to withdraw from school. As her father regretfully acknowledged, "Today closes a quarter, & closes the school to Apphia. . . . Miss Dwight is an excellent teacher, but her price is too high for me."[14]

[13] *Third Annual Catalogue of the Teachers and Scholars in the Gothic Seminary, Northampton, Massachusetts, September 1838*, NHS; Ingeborg Hotze, "The Gothic Seminary, the Meaning and Influence of a Female Seminary for the Community and for the Liberation of the Students," unpublished manuscript, FL; Virginia White James, "Development of the Education of Girls in Northampton, Massachusetts, 1654–1850," unpublished manuscript, FL. On elite support for private women's education in Northampton, see Kathryn Kish Sklar, "The Schooling of Girls and Changing Community Values in Massachusetts Towns, 1750–1820," *History of Education Quarterly* 33 (1993): 511–42.

[14] Even with the reduced rate for students who boarded at home, Sylvester Judd was unable to afford the Gothic Seminary for very long; after paying thirty-three dollars for six quarters, he withdrew his daughter in 1834. Apphia Judd left Dwight's school before the seminary officially opened. Dwight instructed girls in her mother's home for at least five years before John Tappan donated the King Street property to give the school a permanent home. Sylvester Judd, "Notebook," vol. 1, 22 April 1834, FL.

Girls like Apphia Judd, whose fathers could not afford tuition at the Gothic Seminary, might take advantage of the countless smaller, less prestigious, and less expensive schools that dotted the New England hinterland. At the beginning of the 1838 winter term, for example, the Greenfield *Gazette and Mercury* carried advertisements for seven local academies and select schools, each promising the advantages of an elite education at a fraction of the cost. The Franklin Academy in Shelburne Falls Massachusetts, managed by J. Mason Macomber with the assistance of "Misses Sarah A. Lee and Marcy W. Bigelow," offered instruction in English, "Higher Math," and foreign languages as well as opportunities to pursue mezzotinto and Chinese painting, all for around half the cost of the Gothic Seminary. Students enrolling at Massachusetts's New Salem Academy benefited from a female department directed by Maria Howe, a former Mount Holyoke pupil, and from an affordable quarterly tuition for "Higher English" and foreign languages; additional instruction in drawing, needlework, and waxwork was available for only a few dollars more. Board was arranged with private families for $1.50 to $1.75 per week, but, the advertisement promised, frugal parents could make their own arrangements for "much less expense."[15] Less expensive still was the Marlow Academy, located in the "quiet, but thriving village of Marlow," New Hampshire. With 1847 tuition for study in the "Higher English Branches" totaling only $3.50 per term (with languages, music, and ornamental arts extra) and board available for around $1.00 per week, school officers could well boast that their academy "offered superior inducements to all of those who wished to fit themselves in the preparatory studies for college, for teaching, or for discharging honorably the common duties of life." Like countless other schools, the New Salem and Marlow academies catered to the contradictory impulses of accomplishment and economy.[16]

Academies such as the Gothic Seminary and Emma Willard's Troy Seminary in New York State catered to the daughters of the wealthy, training them for marriage to merchants, lawyers, large landowners, and prominent ministers, just as Mary Lyon's Mount Holyoke Seminary fitted the daughters of middling farmers and country profession-

[15]On 4 December 1838, the Greenfield *Gazette and Mercury* carried advertisements for the Franklin Academy, the Shelburne Falls Select School, the New Salem Academy, the Conway Select School, the Deerfield Academy, the Fellenberg Academy, and the Buckland Select School.

[16]*Catalogue of the Officers and Students of the Marlow Academy, Marlow, New Hampshire, 1847* (Keene, N. H.: J. W. Prentiss & Co., 1847).

als for a season of teaching and a life of Christian service.[17] Yet other schools, with less distinct missions and less rigorous standards, attracted scores of antebellum women, if only for a few months.[18] Consider the Negus and Fuller families. Not wealthy by any means, Joel Negus, who worked as a sign painter, surveyor, and schoolmaster in Petersham, Massachusetts, sent his daughter Rosana away to school in 1815. After his death in 1816, his widow found herself in financial trouble. Still, she somehow managed to send their next daughter, Fanny, for a year's education at a school of questionable academic merit in Putney, Vermont. Piecing together an adequate school wardrobe by rotating the clothes out of the closets of her other daughters, Mrs. Negus nevertheless managed to scrape up the money for the girl's tuition and board. Her mother's example was not wasted on Fanny Negus. Some fifteen years later, she and her husband, Aaron Fuller, struggled to save the $56.90 necessary to provide her stepdaughter Elizabeth with two quarters at Catharine Fiske's prestigious Young Ladies Academy, where she studied botany, chemistry, "Arethmetick and Watts on the mind." Fifteen years after Elizabeth was dispatched to New Hampshire, Aaron Fuller demonstrated his own commitment to female education. After his wife's death, Fuller sacrificed both tuition money and housekeeping services to provide their daughter Hattie with a season of musical instruction in Boston.[19]

For families such as the Neguses and Fullers, female education was obviously not a luxury that announced their place among New England's upper strata. But neither was it a necessity, part of a rational

[17]This distinction between the aspirations of the different groups of students was drawn by Nina Baym, "Women and the Republic: Emma Willard's Rhetoric of History," *American Quarterly* 43 (1991): 1–23. Compare Anne Firor Scott, "The Ever Widening Circle: The Diffusion of Feminist Values from the Troy Female Seminary, 1822–1872," *History of Education Quarterly* 18 (1978): 3–25.

[18]Attendance at the majority of female academies appears haphazard by contemporary standards. Lynne Brickley ("Sarah Pierce's Litchfield Female Academy, 1792–1833," 94–102) found that the majority of students at Sarah Pierce's Litchfield Academy departed after only one or two semesters but that they often enrolled in another academy for a term or two; moreover, the attendance patterns of female and male students were roughly comparable.

[19]Hattie Fuller to George Fuller, 2 April 1848, Fanny Negus Fuller to Aaron Fuller, 15 June, n.d. [after 1832], receipts of George Fuller, Arethusa Negus to Fanny Negus, 19 May 1816, Rosana Negus to Fanny Negus, 18 June 1815. Disparaging comments about the Putney school were made by Fanny's former schoolmate Helen, who compared their education with the much better one she was getting in New York, probably at Emma Willard's seminary. Helen's assessment is supported by Fanny Negus's spelling, which ranged from idiosyncratic to deplorable. See Helen to Fanny Negus, n.d., all in the Fuller-Higginson Papers, PVMA.

plan to prepare their daughters for careers in teaching.[20] After her turn in Putney, Fannie Negus obtained work not as a schoolteacher but as "help." It is difficult to imagine that Elizabeth Fuller's brief stay at Catharine Fiske's would have qualified her for a really good teaching position; had the Fullers imagined Hattie as a self-supporting teacher, they would have sent her to normal school rather than to piano lessons. Instead, their rather haphazard approach suggests that they sought some approximation of a genteel education at middling prices.

However uneven, the training offered by these antebellum academies superseded that which was available in village common schools. If the majority of these academies failed to provide a systematic education in the arts and sciences, they did afford young women with at least a rudimentary exposure to the higher branches of learning and with the dainty accomplishments that were regularly disparaged by moralists and regularly sought by women. Equally important, these academies also inculcated in their students the gender consciousness that stood at the heart of the middle-class cult of domesticity. As Nancy Cott, Anne Firor Scott, and others have observed, women's academies sought to increase gender awareness, if not feminism, and to encourage feelings of sisterly solidarity.[21]

Parents shared this perspective. They expected their daughters to benefit from the presence of other young ladies as well as from formal instruction. In 1822, Dan Huntington was delighted when his daughter Bethia Throop Huntington reported that she was taking advantage of the social and the intellectual opportunities at Emma Willard's Troy Seminary. Exposure to the society of other young ladies was part of her father's objective in sending her to school. After arranging for her to share a room with the daughter of an old family friend, her father pointed out that at Emma Willard's, Bethia was "surrounded by the best society in the young ladies, collected from the best families in our country." Ten years later, the next Huntington daughter was dispatched to Troy. When Mary Dwight Huntington wrote home for advice about manners, her mother urged her to observe "some of the young ladies who are accustomed to good company." By following the

[20]This interpretation was forwarded by David F. Allmendinger, Jr., "Mount Holyoke Students Encounter the Need for Life-Planning, 1837–1850," *History of Education Quarterly* 18 (1978): 27–45.

[21]See Cott, *Bonds of Womanhood*, 114–25, 123–35, 176–78; Scott, "The Ever Widening Circle: The Diffusion of Feminist Values from the Troy Female Seminary, 1822–1872"; Allmendinger, "Mount Holyoke Students Encounter the Need for Life-Planning"; and Baym, "Women and the Republic: Emma Willard's Rhetoric of History."

example set by her peers, she wrote, "you can easily adopt such manners as will enable you to move among your companions or others without embarrassment."[22]

Girls could learn more than manners from their classmates. Especially at schools with evangelical leanings or in moments of revival, girls pushed one another toward conversion.[23] Adeline Young earnestly hoped that both her "heavenly Parent" and the brother who was subsidizing her education would find her "an altered person" when she returned home. In a correspondence that centered more on spiritual than intellectual progress, Adeline detailed faith and practice for her brother's approval. After a month under the watch of teachers and classmates, she could claim a "<u>trembling</u> hope."[24] Ten years later, when Edward Hitchcock learned that "some individuals" at Mount Holyoke Seminary were "seriously enquiring what they must do to be saved," he pushed his daughter Mary to follow their lead. Both he and her mother felt "extremely anxious to have you also seize upon so favorable an opportunity," he wrote. Whether they sent their daughters to academies to acquire a final polish, to prepare for a lifelong Christian mission, or both, parents hoped that exposure to other, like-minded, young ladies would have an improving effect.[25]

Providing a social space in which young women were encouraged to emulate one another, academies also offered girls the chance to build new relationships. Mehab Ann Bradley, who enrolled at the Troy Seminary the same year as Bethia Huntington, shared Huntington's pleasure in her schoolmates. After only one week away from home, she had befriended her roommates, a Miss Foster from Watertown and a Miss Francis Skinner, whose father was the governor of Vermont. She also sought out a Miss Whiting, who had been recommended to her by a mutual friend. Too excited to wait for the standard letter of introduction, Bradley brashly presented herself to Miss Whiting. Writing to her brother later, she explained that the letter "would have been uneces-

[22]Elizabeth Phelps Huntington to Mary Dwight Huntington, 1 June 1832, PPHFP, Box 5, Folder 12; Dan Huntington to Bethia Throop Huntington, 22 October 1822, PPHFP, Box 15, Folder 4.

[23]See Joan Hedrick, *Harriet Beecher Stowe: A Life* (New York: Oxford University Press, 1994), 39–42, and Brickley, "Sarah Pierce's Litchfield Female Academy," 319–37. Brickley emphasizes the role of teachers and ministers in encouraging conversion, but her evidence also points to the pressure that students exerted on one another.

[24]Adeline Young to Ira Young, 13 August 1831, Adams Family Papers, MS 420, Box 5, Folder 55, DCL.

[25]Edward Hitchcock to Mary Hitchcock, 26 December 1841, Box 4 Folder 45, Edward and Orra White Hitchcock Papers, ACASC.

sary" for the generous Miss Whiting; she added that she was "very much pleased" with her new friend.[26]

Many young women wove their new friendships into social circles that recalled the networks of kin and neighbors they had left at home. Girls may have developed intense feelings for particular friends, but they were also inclined to build more diffuse networks with women of similar backgrounds, sensibilities, and religious beliefs. For example, Eliza Perkins of Amherst became particularly close to Weltha Brown while the two were students at Lydia Huntley's Hartford Connecticut academy during the 1810s. During their school years and after, the two shared a friendship dominated by religious convictions and educational principles. But these two close friends also shared connections with Brown's sister Clarissa, Abby Dillingham, Mary Hooker of Springfield, and probably other students as well. Indeed, when Eliza left school in 1817, she relied on Weltha Brown to remind her other friends of their promises to write. The network comprised of Perkins, Brown, Hooker, and their other friends was but one small part of a much larger group. As Nancy Cott observed, the entire student body at Huntley's school joined together to envision themselves as a loosely knit "sisterhood."[27]

Although the structure of these networks paralleled that of the girls' mothers', the geographic reach was far more extensive. Drawing students from throughout New England, even small academies enabled girls to make connections with similar young women whose homes were far apart. Even when a scholar remained close to home, she enjoyed the chance to broaden her social horizons. While a student at South Hadley's Hopkins Academy in the early 1820s, Rachel Strong of Northampton developed friendships with a number of other girls. Like Strong herself, the majority of her companions were drawn from the surrounding Hampshire County towns: Eliza Franklin and Mary Ann Williams from Amherst, Clarissa C. Smith from Hadley, and Sally Emmon from Chester. But the academy also offered Strong the opportunity to become friendly with several girls from neighboring counties and the Massachusetts coast, and one, Mary Ann Little, from St. Albans, Vermont.[28]

[26]Mehab Ann Bradley to Jonathan Dorr Bradley, 1 July 1822, Bradley Family Papers, SL.

[27]Eliza Perkins to Weltha Brown, 26 June 1817 and 17 July 1819, Hooker Collection, SL; Cott, *Bonds of Womanhood*, 177.

[28]1821 Friendship Book of Rachel Strong, 1833–35, and Friendship Book of Sarah P. Adams, both in FL.

The Culture of Friendship

If it is relatively easy to trace the outlines of young women's networks, penetrating these boundaries to assess the interior dimensions of these women's friendships is far more difficult. Friendship books, which contained girls' tributes to their dearest friends as well as meditations on friendship itself, offer one window into these networks. A common part of both male and female student culture in antebellum New England, friendship books were regularly circulated among close friends for an inscription and signature. In script that ranged from the plain to the baroque, girls carefully transcribed epigrams, poems, and extracts from improving essays, each chosen to describe and celebrate the virtues of the album's owner: piety, sincerity, loyalty, innocence, and beauty were especially prized. Writers sought to capture not only the essence of their friends but something of their friendships as well. Girls understood that the collected inscriptions simultaneously fixed and preserved precious connections. As one New Hampshire poet wrote,

> . . . on this page, so purely white,
> I'll trill a simple, heartfelt lay,
> With other friends my name I'll write,
> And bind in Friendship's sweet boquet.[29]

Or, as another young woman wrote in the frontspiece to her own friendship book, the following pages were

> Not for folly's idle strain;
> Not for love's fictitious pain;
> Not for heaps of senseless praise,
> That fools on beauty's altar raise—

Instead, her friends were called to write in "friendship's voice sincere," to capture "feeling's genuine tear," "gentle, feeling, soulfelt mirth," and "virtues lessons—praise deserved." She concluded, "For many truths this book's reserved."[30]

---

[29]Adaliza Cutter Phelps, "For My Cousin's Album," *The Life of Christ and Other Poems by Mrs. Adaliza Cutter Phelps with an Introductory Notice by Her Husband* (Boston: John P. Jewett & Co. 1852), 175. Phelps wrote no fewer than three poems on the theme of friendship albums for the volume.

[30]Untitled poem by H. W. C., 11 September 1833, Friendship Book of Sarah P. Adams, FL.

A Memento of Affection

May fortunes smiles attend thee ever
Around thy bed sweet roses strew
The bud of innocence forever
Within thy heart still bloom anew
May you through all your life possess
Sweet peace of mind and happiness
May troubles never haunt your breast
Be thou my friend forever blest

Mary M. Hutchinson

Mary Hutchinson's 1833 friendship book illustrates the fusion of literary culture, gentility, and female friendship. New Hampshire Historical Society #F4651.

Yet the truths of friendship were not eternal. Changes in these books reflect shifts in the culture of friendship as well in provincial society. Small chapbooks covered with colored or printed paper, albums dating from the first quarter of the nineteenth century generally contained messages that urged their readers to heed their religious obligations. For example, in 1821, Betsey Wright and a friend named Caroline each reminded Rachel Strong that "this world is all a fleeting show. . . . There's nothing <u>true</u>, <u>but</u> Heav'n." Reflecting the self-abnegation that characterized the faith of so many nineteenth-century women, Maria Gilbert offered Strong this verse:

> The finest flower that ever blow'd
> Open'd on Calvary's tree
> When Jesus' blood in rivers flow'd
> For love of worthless me.[31]

Although Christian sentiments never disappeared from friendship books, they did soften considerably. Fifteen years after Rachel Strong was reminded that "Jesus' blood in rivers flow'd," Sarah Adams was warned to "guard well thy thoughts, thy thoughts are heard in heaven." But this rather ominous thought was countered by the message of another friend, who hoped that "if there's a spot on earth all fresh & fair," where "pleasure reigns, unbounded & serene . . . May that same place be thine."[32]

By the 1850s, friendship books, like so many other aspects of provincial sociability, had become more elaborate and more secular. Flimsy chapbooks had been replaced by volumes bound in elegantly tooled leather. Inscriptions about religious duty had given way to verses celebrating the power of memory, the nature of beauty, and the myriad requirements for friendship. As Fannie Hunt wrote for her friend Lizzie Smith, friendship was a "union" that demanded "reciprocated duties," beginning with sincerity. But sincerity was not enough. In a girl worthy of true friendship, "every virtue of the soul / Must constitute the charming whole."[33]

Despite these changes, two themes persisted. Throughout the antebellum period, young women's inscriptions testified at once to the preciousness of friendship and to its fragility. One girl confidently swore to the permanence of her affection for Sarah Adams, asking, "Can I forget or cease to love thee?" She answered, "Yes! when the sun forgets to rise, / Or, when the fadeless stars above thee / Forget to shine or leave the skies."[34] More frequently, girls pointed to the many dangers that might erode or end a friendship despite the deep affection one girls bore the other.

Sudden death posed the most obvious threat. Provincial women frequently lost friends and kin unexpectedly. Resigning themselves to

---

[31]Friendship Book of Rachel Strong, 1821, FL.

[32]Untitled poem by E. J. P., epigram signed Elizabeth A. L., in Friendship Book of Sarah P. Adams, FL.

[33]Untitled poem by Fannie Hunt, 5 March 1857, Friendship Book of Lizzie S. Smith, FL.

[34]Untitled poem from "Laura," Friendship Book of Sarah P. Adams, 1833–35, FL.

God's will, they consoled themselves with the image of a loved one called to heaven. Still, the death of a young friend could seem especially bitter. As one young woman wrote,

> When Heaven would kindly set us free,
> And earth's enchantment end,
> It takes the most effectual means,
> And robs us of <u>a friend</u>.[35]

Contemplating their own mortality, some girls hoped to survive in the albums of their friends. Reminding Elizabeth Strong that "I have known thee very well / In hours of joy as well as sorrow," a girl named Electa asked,

> If righteous Heaven eternal King
> Should call me to the grave before thee
> Elizabeth! preserve this little thing
> In token of the love I [gave] thee.[36]

There is no reason to suspect that Elizabeth Strong was called to honor Electa's request. But other young women did use their friendship books to mark the passing of beloved friends. Two years after Fannie Hunt rehearsed the requirements of friendship for her friend Lizzie Smith, Smith recorded Hunt's death in the margin next to her poem.

Less dramatic disruptions could also rend the bonds of friendship. In particular, girls and young women mourned the inevitable separations that accompanied the end of a student's school days. If these departures often prompted friends to relive their shared histories, they also summoned visions of an uncertain and lonely future. Sally Emmons, who described herself as Rachel Strong's "chum," wrote in 1821 that although "dear is that spot, I saw thee first/ The school where oft we met," she would "ne'r forget" the place where she "took the last farewell." Although they lived less than thirty miles apart, Emmons and Strong did not fantasize about frequent visits between Chester and Northampton. As they left the Hopkins Academy, they could only pledge their friendship and hope for the best:

> Though fortune destined we should part,
> We'll hope to meet again;

[35]Untitled verse from "Ellen," ibid.
[36]Untitled poem by "Electa," Friendship Album of Elizabeth Strong, ca. 1822, FL.

> In friendship let us now unite,
> And innocence retain.[37]

Rather than planning friendships that would span their lives, young women prepared themselves to lose contact with their closest companions. Almost forty years after Sally Emmons and Rachel Strong shared their "last farewell," Helen Wooster said good-bye to her friend Lizzie Smith. Although she wished her friend a "bright and joyous" life, "unclouded by care or sorrow," Wooster did not imagine herself playing any role in her friend's future. Instead, she underscored the finality of their separation. She wrote, "Soon, very soon, we shall be called upon to leave this place where we have spent so many happy hours. We may never meet this side of Heaven."[38]

Intensely aware of their participation in a community of letters, provincial young women looked to prevailing literary conventions to shape their depictions of loss and separation. Both in the poems they chose to quote and in their original verse, they infused an older Protestant tradition that reminded Christians of the immanence of death with the nostalgia of domestic imaginative and didactic literature. But if these poems conformed to prevailing literary conventions, they also portended young women's adult experiences. Provincial women were unable to maintain their student friendships beyond the academy walls. Ending their educations, young women prepared themselves to end their friendships. In 1822, Sophronia Grout lamented that she had "parted, perhaps forever, with my dear school companions." Then, remembering her Christian convictions, she corrected herself: "I may never more behold those countenances until I meet them before the Living God." Grout was not alone in her feelings. Shared piety had created especially close ties among her classmates. As she observed, "Never was a seperation so painful I think to any of us as the close of this school." Similar feelings clouded the ceremonies that marked the end of Mary Hoyt Wilson's term at the Deerfield Academy. In the last week of school, she attended a round of parties and teas honoring the students. She proudly noted that the public "Examination of Academy Schollars" attracted a "numerous audience," filling the meeting hall. But even these grand occasions did not compensate for "bid[ding] adieu to Miss Barton and other of my schoolmates." Following the death of her beloved friend Amelia Lyman by only a few months, the loss of these friends must have been especially distressing. After

[37]Friendship Book of Rachel Strong, 1821, FL.
[38]Inscription for Helen A. Wooster, Friendship Book of Lizzie Smith, 1857–861, FL.

watching her new friends depart, she confessed, "I fear I shall never see them again." Hoyt's fears were entirely justified. Far from receiving the longed-for visits, in the months that followed, Hoyt received only two letters from former schoolmates.[39]

Even provincial women who were seriously committed to preserving their friendships encountered almost insurmountable obstacles. Eliza Perkins and Weltha Brown, for example, made some attempt to maintain the network of "sisters" formed at their Hartford school. For several years, they passed along news of their classmates and encouraged their "sisters" to remain in touch with one another. But these efforts were dwarfed by their struggle to sustain their own friendship, which offered each woman a satisfying mixture of personal affection and Christian fellowship. When Perkins left school in 1816, the two pledged to continue their "ideal converse" through the mail. Hoping to retain a sense of emotional immediacy, Brown asked Perkins to "write [her] feelings with freedom." Such a request was easily granted, for Perkins expected that the "endearing mark of confidence" would be mutual. Over the next few years, the friends shared their struggles to attain true grace and their experiences as women suspended between school and marriage. Later, they traded their thoughts on the duties of Christian husbands and wives and news about their menfolk. Throughout, they noted revivals, sermons, and conversions, eager for evidence of God's presence in the Connecticut River Valley.[40]

Containing pious speculations on the nature of faith and affectionate accounts of daily life, the letters from Eliza Perkins to Weltha Brown also contain hints that their friendship was slipping away. From the time they separated, any delay in their correspondence alarmed Perkins. After one silence, Perkins wrote, "So long time had elapsed . . . since I had heard from you . . . that I was almost afraid I should never hear from you again." When the "long-wished-for letter" arrived, it inspired "ten thousand thanks . . . for Oh how did it rejoice my heart." Unfortunately, such delays were common. An erratic postal service and unreliable couriers guaranteed that some letters arrived late and others

[39]If any of Hoyt's friends returned to the academy the next term, there is no indication that they tried to renew their contact with Hoyt. Her diary contains no mention of visits from returning scholars. Diary of Mary Hoyt Wilson, 25 October 1826, and 24 October 1826, PVMA. Hoyt noted receiving letters from schoolmates in Halifax and New Haven on 10 December 1826, Diary of Sophronia Grout, May 1822, PVMA.

[40]Eliza Perkins to Weltha Brown, 17 July 1819, Hooker Collection, SL. Brown's request is quoted in Perkins's reply. The Hooker Collection contains only half of the correspondence between Eliza Perkins [Gunnell] and Weltha Brown. For the reference to "ideal converse," see Eliza Perkins to Weltha Brown, n.d. [ca. 1819], Hooker Collection, SL.

not at all. More to the point, despite a sincere desire to continue their "ideal converse," both women found the burdens of letter-writing difficult to manage. While teaching school in Greenfield, Perkins "gladly" postponed tedious preparations for an assignment in logic to write to her "absent & very dear" friend. More often, writing demanded that she postpone sleep.[41]

For a schoolteacher, finding the leisure to write was no easy task; for a wife, it was well-nigh impossible. After her marriage in 1820, Eliza Perkins Gunnell discovered that her new responsibilities left very little time for writing. Worse, by the time she managed to scrape together an hour, the thought of writing looked less like "ideal converse" than a dreaded chore. She advised Brown, "When you are married I beg of you not to neglect letter writing till it becomes a task even to a dear friend. This is the fact with regard to myself." As she had learned, the perfect confidence demanded by long-distance friendships depended as much on a woman's leisure as on her sincerity. The following year, the birth of a son added considerably to her happiness, but it also increased her workload, for even a healthy infant and a small household demanded considerable attention. Caring for her husband and son, Perkins Gunnell had less free time than ever. The only sure way to command leisure was to purchase it, an option she could ill afford. Explaining an unusually long silence, she defended herself by telling Brown that "when you are a wife, and a mother of a crying babe, and feel it necessary to curtail your expenses, as it respects help, your own feelings will supply a sufficient excuse."[42]

Eliza Perkins Gunnell and Weltha Brown created an epistolary friendship that aspired to more than a continuing acquaintance. They sought to preserve the emotional intimacy and immediacy that had marked the "ideal converse" of their school days. But after five years, a correspondence begun in faith and affection lapsed into anxiety and guilt. The problem was not so much that the written word could not accommodate the experiences of everyday life; the two captured both the spiritual and the prosaic with perfect "freedom of feeling." Rather, the rhythms of provincial housekeeping could not accommodate the rarified friendship the women had cultivated at school. The relation-

[41]Eliza Perkins to Weltha Brown, 17 July 1819, n.d. [ca. 1819], Hooker Collection, SL. This difficulty was by no means limited to Perkins and Brown; comments on the difficulties of writing letters and writing in diaries are ubiquitous in the papers of antebellum provincial women.

[42]Eliza Perkins to Weltha Brown, 10 December 1821 and 9 December 1820, Hooker Collection, SL.

ship prized by Eliza Perkins and Weltha Brown belonged not to the household economy but to the sheltered environment of the ladies' academy. For provincial young women, a sojourn at an academy constituted a time out of time, an interlude that was in many ways at odds with their lives within homes and communities.

Educated Women

Like friendships, the sustained and purposeful intellectual endeavors and sophisticated accomplishments promoted by academies and select schools seemed to have a limited place in provincial households and towns. As students, young women turned their attention to mathematics, science, history, painting, and music with varying degrees of enthusiasm and success. Yet much of the substance of an academy education seemed superfluous compared with the knowledge demanded by even the best provincial circles. John Todd, a Northampton minister and a staunch advocate of women's education, observed in 1854 that "every one who goes to school knows that, for some reason or other, the object is to study. But many seem to know nothing as to *why* they must study."[43]

Todd attempted to resolve the discrepancy between elite education and everyday experience through a dialogue between a flighty, fashionable girl and her "judicious, *sensible*" father. The older man explained that girls needed instruction in the liberal arts to improve their powers of concentration and memory, to provide them with cultivated tastes and discriminating judgment. Girls needed a rigorous education to exorcise the frivolous tendencies fostered by bourgeois society. But pressed to explain in concrete detail how the virtues he described would serve his daughter, he faltered. Good taste offered the most obvious return on his daughter's investment of time and energy. Called to select a library for a village school, to read aloud from Milton, Cowper, or Shakespeare, or to preside over a seminary writing contest, she would stand prepared. But in explaining how the concentration gained from working algebraic equations or the memory honed by "stor[ing] up the dry facts of history" would prove relevant, even Todd's "*sensible*" father was forced back onto vague and empty abstractions. Indeed, Todd argued that girls needed to attend academies precisely because their mothers, "amid the cares and toils neces-

[43]Rev. John Todd, D. D., *The Daughter at School* (Northampton, Mass.: Hopkins, Bridgman & Co., 1854), 20.

sary to provide for a family," were unable to remember the "particulars of their own education."[44]

Like the Reverend Todd, provincial parents and daughters agreed on the value of an education, and they were uncertain as to how the particulars of that education might be turned to the service of kin and community. Sophronia Grout, blessed with literary talent and intellectual ambition, was torn between her desire for an education that transcended the limits of Hawley, Massachusetts, and her need to acquire an education that would fit her to live within those limits. In 1828, after "much prayer" and extended discussions with her parents, she decided to continue her schooling, enrolling in Mary Lyon's Select Female School in Buckland, Massachusetts. Grout considered the months at Buckland "perhaps the most important era of my adult life." But while her "desire to gain knowledge was ardent," the utility of her studies was not apparent. Neither she nor her family could imagine that her "literary acquirements" would ever "produc[e] a good effect on others." She decided, with more resignation than enthusiasm, to withdraw from school, to "improve my leisure by the fireside of my own home & store my mind with what I could glean from good writers and good society."[45]

But the demands of provincial housekeeping left little time for intellectual pursuits, just as they left little time for epistolary friendship. Even John Todd warned his female readers that once home, "You will soon feel that all the knowledge acquired during these years of hard study is useless." Urging women to continue their educations at home, he conceded that it was nearly impossible to do so, for every member of the household could exercise some claim on a young woman's time. He could only suggest that young women rise early, claiming an uninterrupted hour before the rest of the household rose for breakfast. Small wonder that women abandoned their studies. Returning to her parents in Amherst, Eliza Perkins found study "all but impossible." Hattie Fuller was more emphatic, assessing her musical education as "money thrown away." Caring for her widowed father and younger brothers,

[44]Ibid., 42, 45, 36. In the 1830s, Todd played a key role in organizing local support for Margaret Dwight's Gothic Seminary and published several essays promoting female education in the Hampshire *Gazette*. (See, for example, his "Female Education: Address Delivered at the Opening of the Northampton Female Seminary, Nov. 17, 1835," *Hampshire Gazette*, 2 December 1835.) By the time he wrote *The Daughter at School*, Todd had long since left the area, but Northampton's citizens continued to claim him as one of their own. His didactic and religious works remained popular in the region long after he moved on. The dilemma facing educated women—all dressed up and no place to go—was by no means limited to provincial or even antebellum society. See Lynn D. Gordon, *Gender and Higher Education in the Progressive Era* (New Haven, Conn.: Yale University Press, 1990).

[45]Diary of Sophronia Grout, 28 March [ca. 1828], PVMA.

she despaired of ever having the time to practice. "If I have got to wait until the children are grown up, I shall be an old maid—too old to learn music," she complained.[46]

Even the most gifted, committed, and privileged scholars confronted virtually insurmountable obstacles when they attempted to continue their educations at home. Consider Harriet and Eliza Adams. Daughters of a Dartmouth College professor, the two young women grew up in a household that valued and encouraged female education. Each spent a season or so at a New England academy and each availed herself of Hanover's vibrant intellectual community, taking advantage of lectures, addresses, and especially the reading societies organized to help pass the long New Hampshire winters. And each sister was unflagging in her support of the other's intellectual progress; in the letters they exchanged, sisterly devotion was suffused with the love of learning. Yet despite their relatively supportive environment, their access to a community of letters, and the steady encouragement they offered each other, both found that their adult obligations to families and households sorely compromised their attempts to sustain lives of learning.

When Harriet Adams left Hanover in 1827 at the age of twenty-two as the wife of John Aiken, a Concord lawyer, she naively imagined that married life would allow her time to extend her education. Long frustrated by her lack of mental discipline, she also hoped that access to her husband's office would "correct my vague habits of reading thinking & reasoning," for surely a "lawyers office would be the best place in the world to acquire close investigating habits of study." She planned to commence reading Blackstone at once: What better way to realize her new role as a young lawyer's companion and helpmeet? Instead, she found that even the minimal housekeeping demanded of boarders encroached upon her time and energy. Only three months after her marriage, she confessed to Eliza, "I am creeping along in Blackstone at rather a slow pace—I am ashamed of my winters' work I confess for I have not accomplished much & I shall hereafter look back upon it as a lost opportunity of improvement." The future looked worse. "After I am fairly <u>Madam</u> I suppose I must lay by books, tho' I hope not to lose my taste for them," she wrote.[47]

[46]Hattie Fuller to George Fuller, n.d. [ca.1852], Fuller-Higginson Papers, PVMA; Eliza Perkins to Weltha Brown, 26 June 1817, Hooker Collection, SL; Todd, *Daughter at School*, 233–34. On women's pursuit of education, see Mary Kelley, "Reading Women/Women Reading: The Making of Learned Women in Antebellum America," *Journal of American History* 83 (1996): 401–24.

[47]Harriet Adams Aiken to Eliza Adams, 19 March 1827, Adams Family Papers, DCL, MS 420, Box 3, Folder 39.

Sadly, her predictions proved correct. The much-dreaded house-keeping and the birth of a son left her "plodding on" in a "routine of domestic duties almost forgetting there are books in the world." She did manage to read a bit in *Bonaparte's Life* while she nursed her baby, for she could do "nothing else then." Although Harriet adored both husband and child, this was hardly the life she had imagined.[48] "Do come and read to me," she begged Eliza. "Just give an abstract of all your acquisitions." In the letters she wrote to Eliza during her first two years of marriage, Harriet's hunger for her sister's company grew apace of her hunger for books.[49]

Harriet Adams Aiken hoped that her younger sister's life would afford greater opportunities for reading and contemplation. "Improve your time well, & read thoroughly & think deeply," she cautioned. "At Hanover there is such a world of knowledge open before us, that we are constantly excited by a desire for <u>more</u>, while we do not perhaps dwell long enough upon one subject to make ourselves master of it." Eliza must put her single years to good advantage, for who knew what marriage would bring? Pointing to her life as an example, Harriet warned Eliza against "losing half the profit of the present by grasping at the future."[50]

Harriet was preaching to the converted. Both before and after Harriet's marriage, Eliza made steady progress in mathematics, geography, the sciences, literature, theology, and philosophy, although she did eventually abandon "the dead languages."[51] She purchased her progress with sleep. Counting five hours of sleep as her "<u>quantum</u>," she generally studied past midnight, dismissing her family's concern about the consequences for her health. "All the comfort I take is in the night," she explained, "for if deprived of that I should have no time to <u>read</u>, <u>write</u>, or <u>think</u>." Occasionally, she mustered a determination that

[48]Harriet Adams Aiken to Eliza Minot Adams, February 1828 and n.d. [ca. 1828], Adams Family Papers, DCL, MS 420, Box 3, Folder 39.

[49]Harriet Adams Aiken to Eliza Minot Adams, n.d. [ca. 1828], Adams Family Papers, DCL, MS 420, Box 3, Folder 39. In 1829, Harriet Adams Aiken became seriously ill with consumption, which would kill her the following year; after 1829, her letters focus on her illness and fears for her children's future.

[50]Harriet Adams Aiken to Eliza Adams, 19 March 1827, Adams Family Papers, DCL, MS 420, Box 3, Folder 39.

[51]Eliza Minot Adams Young's letters to her siblings contain extensive references to her current reading and plan of study. See, for example, Eliza Adams (Young) to Ebenezar Adams Jr., 14 May 1827, 30 January 1832, and 2 October 1833, Box 1 Folder 8; Eliza Adams to Harriet Adams (Aiken), 23 September 1826 and 17 September 1828, Box 5, Folder 2; all in Adams Family Papers, DCL, MS 420.

would have warmed the heart of John Todd. One winter, she proudly reported that she had been rising "before the first prayer bell, that is to say, before daylight" in order to study.[52] But even these efforts were not sufficient to protect her time. Any disruption of the normal rhythm of household duties disturbed the fragile calculus of sleep and study. Ironically, Harriet herself compromised Eliza's ability to "read thoroughly & think deeply." Harriet may have been a beloved companion and a judicious mentor, but she was also a source of labor whose departure from the Adams household increased the demands on the younger girl's time. With Harriet gone, Eliza "had work in abundance." It was not simply that the pace of work increased—although it did. As the only remaining daughter, Eliza had little choice but to master a battery of new sewing and cooking skills. Harriet's marriage moved Eliza one step closer to assuming the full repertoire of responsibilities that accompanied provincial womanhood.[53]

When Eliza did have time to study, she found herself increasingly dissatisfied. The pleasure of the process was one thing, but what end would it serve? Like Sophronia Grout, she struggled to reconcile her ambitions and her options. "I seek for improvement to be sure, & try to cultivate my mind but what good does it all do? & who will ever be made better or happier by it?" she asked. She had become, by her own account, "an useless sort of commodity . . . whose presence at home is neither pleasant nor disagreeable." Perhaps comparing herself with the energetic, ambitious Dartmouth students who surrounded her, she wished that "young ladies had something to live for, something to do, like men." Without a "marked course," a "definite aim," life seemed "to vapid, too trifling to deserve the name." "I must be something—do something, & not thus slothfully lie like the dull lakes, in stagnant marshes bred," she wrote. She resolved to abandon her advanced education in favor of the "elementary studies, so that I may become qualified to go & keep school among the Indians."[54]

In the end, Eliza Adams never did teach "among the Indians." Harriet's declining health and her eventual death from consumption in 1830 made Eliza's obligations to her family more critical than ever.

[52]Eliza Adams to Harriet Adams Aiken, 19 January 1827 and 23 November 1826, Box 5, Folder 2; Eliza Adams to Ebenezar Adams Jr., 23 December 1827, Box 1, Folder 8; all in Adams Family Papers, DCL, MS 420. Adams's reference to the prayer bell is a literary allusion.

[53]See Eliza Adams to Harriet Adams Aiken, 17 September 1828 and 19 January 1827, Adams Family Papers, DCL, MS 420, Box 5, Folder 2.

[54]Eliza Adams to Harriet Adams Aiken, 17 September 1828, Adams Family Papers, DCL, MS 420, Box 5, Folder 2.

From 1829 until 1832, when her brother-in-law remarried, she assumed primary responsibility for rearing Harriet's two small children. The following year, Eliza Adams married Ira Young, a Dartmouth College mathematics professor. Marriage not only increased Eliza Adams Young's sense of purpose, but also her time for study. Ira Young arrived at the altar with a demonstrated commitment to women's education. As a Dartmouth tutor, Young had saved the tuition to provide his younger sister with a year at Mary Lyon's Ipswich academy.[55] As a new professor and husband, he extended that commitment to Eliza, serving as both tutor and intellectual companion. And as the wife of a rising young professor, Eliza Adams Young gained a permanent, prominent place in Hanover's intellectual and cultural circles.

Nor was she overly burdened with housework. Indeed, it is likely that she was less encumbered after her marriage than before it. The couple took up residence in her parents' home, which was for the first time free from boarders and the extra work they created. More important, Eliza's mother refused to relinquish any control over day-to-day household affairs. If Eliza hoped that "sometime mother will be willing to let me become housekeeper, & take the sceptre into my own hands," she must also have relished the freedom that her new life afforded her. Her only real regret was that Ira's study had been moved out of their home and into the college. "I cannot now interrupt his studies to obtain his assistance in mine half as much as I should like," she wrote.[56] Even the birth of a son the year after her marriage seems not to have diminished her energy or appetite for study, although the birth of twins in 1836 took a predictable toll.

Unlike most antebellum women, Eliza Adams Young managed not only to extend her education beyond the academy but also to integrate it into her adult identity. Yet the very factors that determined her success only point up the extraordinary difficulties encountered by other women. After all, the majority of provincial women did not live in lively cultural centers such as Hanover. They did not marry professors who regarded their wives as star students and intellectual companions. They did not spend the early, most demanding years of wife-and-motherhood with mothers who hoarded the most time-consuming branches of housework. Far more common was the experience of Harriet Adams Aiken, whose aspirations to shape herself as a woman of letters crum-

[55]Adaline Young to Ira Young, 10 June 1831 and 2 July 1831, Adams Family Papers, DCL, MS 420 Box 5, Folder 55.

[56]Eliza Adams Young described her early married life and housekeeping arrangements in a letter to Ebenezar Adams Jr., 2 October 1833, Adams Family Papers, DCL, MS 420, Box 1, Folder 8.

As a girl, Eliza Adams Young, of Hanover, New Hamsphire, rose before dawn to continue her studies. Courtesy of Dartmouth College library.

bled beneath the weight of her roles as wife, mother, and mistress of a household.

Like the schools in which they were cultivated, the intellectual improvement and the intense female friendships of the antebellum middle class distanced girls from the household economy, from the reciprocal obligation that shaped their relations with kin and their places within households and communities. Certainly, the learning that girls obtained at school connected them to a world of letters that stretched well beyond provincial New England. And the bonds they forged offered them a glimpse of another culture, a broader culture, perhaps even a woman's culture. But provincial households and communities offered them no way to sustain those bonds or that culture. Returning to their households and their kin, young women reentered a world of particularism and mutual obligation, of familial interdependence and female dependence.

It is in this context that the distinct contours of provincial women's friendships must be understood. The bourgeois paradigm of female friendship may have articulated both the ambitions of an emerging middle class and women's aspirations within that class, but it was sharply at odds with the realities of provincial life. Both the language and the practice of middle-class friendship drew women's attention toward one another and away from the web of relations that structured households and communities. Setting voluntary association above corporate obligation, the culture of friendship offered women a fantasy of female bonding unchecked by either the demands of husbands and fathers or the claims of the household economy.[57] From this perspective, it is hardly surprising that the vision of friendship celebrated by nineteenth-century didactic writers, "Victorian ladies," and women's historians as the hallmark of middle-class womanhood gained only a tenuous hold in the towns and villages of antebellum New England.[58] The culture of friendship may have encompassed the lives of urban women, providing a sense of continuity within and between generations. But in the countryside, the culture of friendship rarely survived the transition from girlhood to adulthood. Indeed, it was usually coter-

[57]On the connections between sisterhood and liberalism, see Elizabeth Fox-Genovese, *Feminism without Illusions: A Critique of Individualism* (Chapel Hill: University of North Carolina Press, 1991), 11–17.

[58]Scholars have recently challenged the primacy of female friendships (and, more generally, autonomous female networks or communities) for understanding the experiences of nineteenth-century women. Studies of southern, rural, and working-class women have revealed the richness of these women's connections to one another; however, they have also revealed a marked resistance to the ideals embodied in bourgeois female friendships. Taken together, these studies indicate that the paradigm of friendship that has decisively shaped our understanding of American women's history was limited by region and class. They also suggest that this culture of friendship, profoundly implicated in bourgeois ideology, may have been contested by women as well as by men. See especially Nancy Grey Osterud, *Bonds of Community: The Lives of Farm Women in Nineteenth-Century New York* (Ithaca, N.Y.: Cornell University Press, 1991); Elizabeth Fox-Genovese, *Within the Plantation Household: Black and White Women of the Old South* (Chapel Hill: University of North Carolina Press, 1988); and Nancy A. Hewitt, "Feminist Friends: Agrarian Quakers and the Emergence of Women's Rights in America," *Feminist Studies* 12 (1986): 27–49.

minous with the time that girls and young women spent in academies and seminaries.

Provincial women shared powerful and sustaining connections with women outside their families, make no mistake, but adult friendships were governed by very different conventions and expectations than those that shaped more youthful attachments. The bonds that adult women forged with neighbors and even with kin were shaped less by declarations of undying love than by understated reciprocity between households, less by an appreciation of women's shared identity than by a persistent localism. Within that world, they could only agree with the young Deerfield woman who observed in the 1850s that "my welfare is inseparable from home & all there."[59]

[59]See also [Illegible] to Elijah Fuller, n.d. [ca. 1853], Fuller-Higginson Papers, PVMA.

4

"With joy I bear his name and pay the duties which his virtue claims"

Rising from the dinner table one fall evening in 1818, Aaron Fuller considered his prospects. A widower of only a few months, the father of four young children (two of them deaf-mutes), not yet established in farming or business, his chances must have seemed questionable at best. Perhaps intimidated by the future he expected, Fuller turned instead to the future he desired. In the essay "The Life I should like," he fantasized about the kind of society that might provide him with happiness, at least insofar as earthly happiness was possible. He wished to be situated in a "plesant town amid people well educated," people who were "truly Republican and patriotical." In such a town, a good man stood some chance of securing a livelihood; for Fuller's part, he aspired to "Mercantile Business enough to employ two faithful clerks." Still, he shared the prejudices of his day. Although this imagined enterprise would guarantee an income, Fuller was less certain that any commercial venture could contribute much to the greater good of society or even to individual character. Toward those ends, Fuller also wished for "about fifty Acres of Good Land." The primary purpose of this farm would not be to generate income but to generate virtue: It would provide him with "an opportunity to exercise my mind & Body in forwarding agriculture—a branch of business of the greatest importance to the whole human family—it supports life & health." Fuller did not expect either "Mercantile Business" or farming to lead to wealth and privilege. On the contrary, like many provincial New Englanders, Fuller hoped only for a modest competency. To be

93

sure, he wanted a comfortable house, "with every usefull accomoda-
tion," and money enough to avoid debt and credit. But Fuller insisted
that he "should wish to be obliged to use econemy," lest he should
become "slothfull & indolent."[1]

Yet good society, prosperous trade, and tidy farms could not alone
secure contentment. Fuller understood that the happiness of any
household depended in large measure on its mistress. "With all this,"
he wistfully admitted, "I could not be truly happy without a partner."
At a loss to describe the particulars of his imaginary wife, Fuller nevertheless knew "what she is that would make me happy." Well educated and "used to the best of company from childhood," she would
graciously uphold his own place within the community. Although
Fuller did not explicitly require a Christian wife, his ideal partner did
embrace all the virtues commonly associated with Christian womanhood. She would be "tender hearted, and affectionate to all virtuous
people," detesting "all the vices of the world and all who practice
them."[2] And, of course, Fuller expected that she would be an exemplary housekeeper, "neat in her dress, prudent in all her decisions"
and economical in "all things." Perhaps remembering the dinner he
had just eaten, Fuller also hoped that she "would understand the art of
cooking to perfection."

Finally, he wished to "possess her first," trusting their "<u>affections</u> &
<u>Love</u>" bolstered by the "friendship of her parents and family" to ensure
their happiness. Almost certainly unaware of his pun, Fuller's play on
words yet reflects his preferences and ambitions. It is likely that Fuller
did prefer to be the first man to "possess" his new wife, if only to guarantee that she entered his household unburdened by the extra children
and debt that accompanied many widows; a struggling widower with
four children could hardly be expected to take on additional expense.
Given the contributions of a good mistress to any successful household, he probably also preferred that he would "possess" his wife
before he acquired his farm and business. In both instances, Fuller
planned to enlist the emotional support of his wife's family. While he
could not count on it, he must also have welcomed the prospect of
their "help" or financial support.

Two years later, Aaron Fuller married Fanny Negus, a young woman

[1]Aaron Fuller, "The Life I should like," 15 September 1818, Fuller-Higginson Papers,
PVMA.

[2]It is significant that for Fuller, Christian womanhood could be separated from Christianity itself. On the importance of Christianity for wifehood, see Laurel Thatcher Ulrich,
*Good Wives: Image and Reality in the Lives of Women in Northern New England,
1650–1750* (New York: Oxford University Press, 1983).

thirteen years his junior from Petersham, Massachusetts. Over the course of their twenty-five-year marriage, the two built a life that went a long way toward realizing the goals Fuller had recorded in 1818. Soon after marrying, they moved to Deerfield, a prosperous and "plesant" town on the Connecticut River, where Aaron Fuller opened a bakery and an inn and finally established himself as a successful farmer, taking cattle, pigs, cranberries, corn, and cheese to market. If he never achieved great wealth, he did attain a competency that allowed him to live quite comfortably and to make some provision for the futures of the four children from his first marriage and the seven from his marriage to Fanny Negus. It is easy to imagine Aaron Fuller as an old man at the end of the antebellum period, looking back over his life with a great deal of satisfaction. After all, as he himself had observed in 1818, if a pleasant town, a modest competency, and a good wife could not make him happy, then happiness was "not on earth."[3]

But what of Fanny Negus Fuller? Did the life she shared with Aaron Fuller satisfy her aspirations? Did she measure happiness against the same standard as her husband? Unfortunately, if she ever systematically considered these questions, her answer has not survived. Still, the picture that emerges from the letters she wrote to her husband, children, and kin reveals a woman contented, even happy, with her lot.

Fanny Negus Fuller proved an admirable mistress and helpmeet. A lively and, by some accounts, flirtatious girl before her marriage, she quickly grew into the responsibilities that accompanied her new station as wife and mother.[4] From the time she wed Fuller almost until her death in 1845, she sewed, cooked, managed the farm's dairy production, and braided palm-leaf hats in her spare time. When her husband was away on business, she managed the rest of the farm, keeping accounts, supervising hired labor, and, on at least one occasion, presiding over the cranberry harvest unassisted. She was a devoted mother to the seven children she bore Fuller as well as to her four stepchildren. Not content simply to provide shelter and sustenance, a common school education, and a Christian upbringing, Fuller sacrificed and schemed to offer all her children the "advantages" she sensed

[3]Fuller, "The Life I should like."

[4]On accounts of Fanny Negus Fuller's life before her marriage to Aaron Fuller, see Arathusa Negus to Fanny Negus, 19 May 1816; Sumner Thayer to Fanny Negus, 12 April 1818; Nathaniel Cheney to Fanny Negus, 25 August 1819; Nancy Cook to Fanny Negus, 2 July 1820. For the suggestion that Fanny's behavior might not always have met the strictest standards of decorous maidenhood, see Jonas Howe to Fanny Negus, 27 June 1820. All in the papers of Fanny Negus Fuller, Fuller-Higginson Papers, PVMA.

Fanny Negus Fuller and her twin sons, painted by her stepson Augustus Fuller in the 1830s. Pocumtuck Valley Memorial Association, Memorial Hall Museum, by permission of the Deerfield Academy, Deerfield, Massachusetts.

were of growing importance for success in provincial Deerfield and the world beyond.

The Fullers' marriage seems to have united hearts as well as hands. Describing herself as her husband's "affectionate friend and lover," Fanny confided to him in 1832 that when he was absent, her "thoughts naturally advert to <u>you</u>, the <u>beloved</u> partner of my joys & sorrows." Nine years later, as she approached death, she concluded her last letter to Fuller with the prayer that "God would grant you a long <u>peacefull</u> life, both for your sake and the young children I leave with you, and when you shall have lived Gods appointed time I hope to greet you in Heaven as my only my long-tried friend." Aaron Fuller returned his wife's affection. While traveling in New York State on business, he compared his "blundering, grumbling" companions to his "comfortable fireside," graced by Fanny and their children (those "charming, prattling little urchins") and confessed, "tell the truth I am homesick."[5]

Joining hands and hearts, hard work, and abiding affection, the Fullers' shared life approaches the ideal of companionate marriage described by antebellum social and cultural historians. Locating this new ideal in the broad transformation of society and culture that accompanied the development of Western capitalism, these historians properly associate companionate marriage with the triumph of individualism. Their accounts of young men's and women's increasing control over both the choice of a marriage partner and the timing of marriage, the respectability accorded romantic love, and, perhaps most telling, women's calculated consideration of the benefits of marriage balanced against the loss of personal freedom all point to the growing significance and autonomy of the individual within New England society as well as to women's attempts to appropriate this individualist discourse for themselves.[6] In broad outline, the experiences of

---

[5]Fanny Negus Fuller to Aaron Fuller, 15 June 1832; Fanny Negus Fuller to Aaron Fuller, letter begun on 5 January 1845 and completed 11 February 1845; Aaron Fuller to Fanny Negus Fuller, 17 February 1836; see also Fanny Negus Fuller to Aaron Fuller, 5 August 1832. Fuller-Higginson Papers, PVMA.

[6]The historical literature on the transformation of marriage between the late seventeenth and nineteenth centuries is too extensive to be cited here in any detail. For accounts of courtship and marriage in North America from the colonial period through the American Revolution, see Edmund S. Morgan, *The Puritan Family* (New York: Harper & Row, 1966); Ulrich, *Good Wives;* Linda K. Kerber, *Women of the Republic: Intellect and Ideology in Revolutionary America* (Chapel Hill: University of North Carolina Press, 1980); Mary Beth Norton, *Liberty's Daughters: The Revolutionary Experience of American Women, 1750–1800* (Boston: Little, Brown, 1980); and Jan Lewis, "The Republican Wife: Virtue and Seduction in the Early Republic," *William and Mary Quarterly*, 3d ser., 44 (1987): 689–721. On the decline of parental control of marriage in the eighteenth century, see Daniel Scott Smith, "Parental Power and Marriage Patterns: An Analysis of Historical Trends in Hingham, Massachusetts," *Journal of Marriage and the Family* 35 (1973): 406–18; Robert A. Gross, *The Minutemen and Their World* (New York: Hill & Wang, 1976); and Jan Lewis, *The Pursuit of Happiness: Family and Values in Jefferson's Virginia* (New York: Cambridge University Press, 1983). For perspectives on courtship and marriage in the nineteenth century, see Nancy F. Cott, *The Bonds of Womanhood: "Woman's Sphere" in New England, 1780–1835* (New Haven, Conn.: Yale University Press, 1977); Mary P. Ryan, *Cradle of the Middle Class: The Family in Oneida County, New York, 1790–1865* (New York: Cambridge University Press, 1983); Ellen K. Rothman, *Hands and Hearts: A History of Courtship in America* (New York: Basic Books, 1984); Michael Grossberg, *Governing the Hearth: Law and the Family in Nineteenth-Century America* (Chapel Hill: University of North Carolina Press, 1985); Karen Lystra, *Searching the Heart: Women, Men, and Romantic Love in Nineteenth-Century America* (New York: Oxford University Press, 1989); and William Leach, *True Love and Perfect Union: The Feminist Reform of Sex and Society* (New York: Basic Books, 1980).

provincial New Englanders like Aaron and Fanny Negus Fuller tend to match the patterns described by these historians. But a closer look at the Fullers, their kin, and their contemporaries reveals other dimensions that challenged the individualist ethos that stood at the heart of middle-class marriage.

Couples and Communities

Although the majority of provincial women and men never mounted a thoroughgoing critique of bourgeois courtship and marriage, their vision of the good life and the good marriage derived as much from the household economy as from the standards of the middle class. The provincial couple did not stand apart from society either before or after marriage; if anything, marriage served to anchor men and especially women even more firmly within their communities. Marriage served as both a manifestation and a symbol of the social relations that bound the larger community.[7] Before 1840, the central dilemma symbolized by marriage did not juxtapose individuals against society but positioned households and communities against the market. This vision signaled New Englanders' attempts to maintain their social and economic independence in the face of a growing involvement with market society and to ease the tensions between their personal commitments to a household economy and their increasing dependence on the capitalist market.

The connections between personal satisfaction, household prosperity, social standing, and community welfare were clearly drawn in the *Pastor's Offering on Courtship and Marriage*, which appeared in the Northampton *Hampshire Gazette* in 1837. In separate essays aimed at men and women, the anonymous pastor echoed the prevailing wisdom in urging men and women to take the long view when contemplating marriage. Presenting readers with a conjugal rogue's gallery, he listed the unsuitable partners young people were likely to encounter, describing with great relish the miseries that each occasioned. Bad mates signified more than bad choices; they exacerbated the dangers of the market and undermined relations between household and community. The *Pastor's Offering* condemned the excesses of the market even as it con-

---

[7]For discussions of courtship and marriage as metaphors for political and economic relations in the early republic, see Jan Lewis, "The Republican Wife"; Carroll Smith-Rosenberg, "Domesticating 'Virtue': Coquettes and Revolutionaries in Young America," in *Literature and the Body: Essays on Populations and Persons*, ed. Elaine Scarry (Baltimore: Johns Hopkins University Press, 1988), 160–84.

ceded the market's significance. Ultimately, the essays idealized a society in which the needs of the community contained the operations of the market. Prudent marriages were critical to this process. A solid marriage certainly increased one's chances of happiness. But in addition to providing personal satisfaction over the course of a lifetime, a wise match also met the needs of the middling household and advanced the interests of kin and community.[8]

Given women's economic dependence, it is not surprising that the author of the *Pastor's Offering* suggested that young women examine a man's character for clues to his prospects. Predictably, the essay warned women away from men who were not "industrious in some honorable vocation." Idle and foppish men, who grounded their identities in dress and conversation rather than in productive labor, were apt to "fall into vicious company [and] contract the most destructive employments." Yet in advising women to assess a man's prospects, the writer hardly encouraged them to behave like matrimonial entrepreneurs, eyeing the main chance and speculating on the futures of their husbands. Indeed, moneyed men posed the greatest danger both to their families and their communities. Without the need for economy, a man might become a spendthrift, squandering the family's resources on personal luxuries and ill-advised business schemes. Eventually, cautioned the pastor, the spendthrift would resort to "vices and crimes," trying to win back his fortune as easily as he had lost it, for a spendthrift was little better than a gambler, and the woman who wed him gambled foolishly indeed. Worse than the spendthrift was the wealthy miser, whose "lust for `filthy lucre'" triumphed over his "natural affection, brutalizing the last feeling of humanity in his soul." If a woman had hoped to share in his wealth, she was mistaken, for although she might "tread among gold and pearls," she would never have "a dollar to [her] own convenience." But she risked more than her pride. Avarice would ultimately dissolve the bonds between kin, for the miser "would not scruple to convert" his wife, "little ones and [their] furniture into stock" for sale to the highest bidder. Both the spendthrift and the miser governed their relations to kin and community according to the laws of the marketplace with disastrous consequences.

While men's value as husbands depended on their economic behavior, women's value as wives seemed to depend on more personal qualities—qualities that contributed much to domestic peace but seemed to

[8]For advice to women, see "Courtship," from the *Pastor's Offering on Courtship and Marriage*, *Hampshire Gazette*, 24 August 1836; for corresponding advice to men, see "Courtship," *Hampshire Gazette*, 14 September 1836.

have little bearing on the prosperity of the household or on the well-being of the community. The same pastor who urged women to seek out industrious and preferably propertied men while rejecting fops, idlers, spendthrifts, and misers could only advise men to avoid slatterns, tattlers, scolds, and tyrants. This difference in emphasis acknowledges the emerging ideology of separate spheres just as it reflects men's predominance in the marketplace and in the public sphere generally. But, as the *Gazette* editor observed, the choice of a wife must not rest on personal preferences alone; instead, the "prosecution of this business" should be "govern[ed]" by specific "principles." The selection of a wife bore consequences that extended beyond the home. Women who were slovenly, loose-tongued, shrewish, or dictatorial would certainly make domestic life uncomfortable. But a man married to such a woman faced more than personal disappointment.

The slattern and the tyrant each neglected women's proper duties—the one through negligence and the other through outright rejection. After all, a man wanted a wife who could manage his household and his children. But in slighting women's sphere, these women lowered their husband's stock within the community. Failing to "give an air of neatness to the most humble abode," the slattern would also fail to "impress spectators." The "*unnatural* female tyrant," refused to "yield . . . the prerogative of directing" the household's affairs; instead, she thrust herself into the public sphere, where she insisted on "mak[ing] all the bargains, settl[ing] all the accounts . . . [and] pay[ing] all the debts." Marriage to such a woman portended disaster not because she would ruin the household's affairs but because she would ruin her husband's "influence and character" at home and abroad.

Tattlers and scolds also undermined a man's reputation. The scold promised to unleash a "perpetual stream of hot words" at home and abroad. It was only a matter of time before she dared to reprimand her husband publicly, adding "mortification and disgrace" to his other trials. Worse still was the tattling wife, condemned as "one of the greatest evils that can befall a man, a church, or a community." She proclaimed her family's secrets "from the house top," making her neighbors privy to all her husband's "plans and business." Eventually, the neighbors themselves would shun the house of the gossip, hoping to avoid "the wounds of that two-edged sword which sharpens by age, and wounds but to poison, and poisons but to destroy." A gossiping woman undermined the business of her own household and soured relations between households. These loose-tongued women jeopardized the social order not simply because they challenged their husband's authority, although provincial men and women might well wonder at a man who could not curb his wife's tongue. A more serious threat lay in the words themselves. Women's gossip was not simply a display of bad manners, unseemly but insignificant. On the contrary, to listening neighbors it proved all too significant. The information circulated through women's gossip about their husbands, their households, and their neighbors played an important role in local exchange, if not in long-distance trade. In towns where the majority of business was conducted face to face, and where a man's worth depended on his worthiness, women's words counted for a good deal.[9] Associating women with the household, the pastor nevertheless stopped short of confining them to a special women's sphere, for if the slattern and the tyrant reminded provincial readers that women's primary responsibilities fell within the household, the tattler and the scold suggested that women might retain a place within public culture and local exchange. A good wife, by implication, assumed responsibility not only for her husband's private comfort but also for upholding the authority of her husband and furthering the interests of her household while remaining within the bounds of community propriety.

The *Pastor's Offering* echoed and elaborated many of the assumptions implicit in Aaron Fuller's informal essay. In describing the "life [he] should like," Aaron Fuller had not discerned any opposition between his household and the world beyond it. He pictured his community, his mercantile business, and his farm as extensions of his household. There is a marked continuity between the relations Fuller sought with his well-educated and "patriotical" townsmen, his faithful clerks, and his wife. Fuller and the pastor agreed that the good wife did not counter a man's connections to the world; she enhanced them. However privileged, the relationship between husband and wife could not be held separate from the web of relations that bound the larger community. The point of marriage, after all, was not simply to form a family but also to establish a household. From this perspective, the texts suggest, the prospect of a wedding was a matter of considerable significance for the provincial community as a whole.

[9]On the influence of women's gossip in controlling behavior and shaping opinion, see David S. Shields, *Civil Tongues and Polite Letters in British America*, (Chapel Hill: University of North Carolina Press, 1997), 106–9; Kathleen M. Brown, *Good Wives, Nasty Wenches, and Anxious Patriarchs: Gender, Race, and Power in Colonial Virginia* (Chapel Hill: University of North Carolina Press, 1996), 99–100, 306–18; Ulrich, *Good Wives*, 55–57; and Karen V. Hansen, *A Very Social Time: Crafting Community in Antebellum New England* (Berkeley: University of California Press, 1994), 114–36. On the significance of character and reputation for provincial business dealings, see Christopher Clark, *The Roots of Rural Capitalism: Western Massachusetts, 1780–1860* (Ithaca, N.Y.: Cornell University Press, 1990), 214–20.

Few provincial New Englanders ever bothered to elaborate their views on courtship and marriage with the detail of an Aaron Fuller or the system of the *Pastor's Offering*. Still, evidence suggests that through the 1840s, even middle-class women and men were moved by the values central to each essay—values that stood at the heart of the household economy. New Englanders' persisting emphasis on the corporate dimension of marriage is most vividly demonstrated by the extent to which provincial men and women joined in one another's courtships. Marriage was certainly personal, but it was by no means private. Young people, in particular, were remarkably well informed about the most intimate details of local romances. They introduced their friends and kin to likely young men and women, served as eager confidants, offered copious advice, carried letters back and forth, and arranged moonlight rendezvous. This sort of participation was not limited to peers; older men and women often played decisive roles in encouraging and, less frequently, in squelching particular suits.[10]

This preoccupation with the affairs of others might be dismissed as idle gossip and well-intentioned meddling, as the timeless entertainment of small-town folk. But provincial men and women used gossip and sociability to oversee the courtships of their kin and neighbors, allowing the community considerable authority over seemingly private decisions. Their primary concern was not to police the behavior of individual couples, although they certainly could do so when necessary. Rather, they sought to ensure that men and women selected appropriate marriage partners. Parents rarely attempted to dictate their children's choices, as numerous historians have observed. Instead, parents, siblings, kin, and peers cooperated to present young people with a respectable circle of acquaintances and a large measure of advice to preclude the need for any kind of direct interference. Provincial courtship was not calculated to give young men and women free rein but to give them a carefully circumscribed set of options from which they might freely choose.[11]

Far from resenting the interest of their elders and peers as an intru-

[10]For instances in which suits were discouraged see, for example, Mary Palmer Tyler, *Grandmother Tyler's Book: The Recollections of Mary Palmer Tyler (Mrs. Royall Tyler), 1775–1866*, ed. Frederick Tupper and Helen Tyler Brown (New York: G. P. Putnam's Sons, 1925), 259–64. For a similar, fictive account, see the story of "Patient Emily" in Francis H. Underwood, *Quabbin: The Story of a Small Town with Outlooks upon Puritan Life* (Boston: Lee & Shepard, 1893), 49–61.

[11]Ellen Rothman has argued that by the eighteenth century, "young people . . . made their own decisions when serious courtships developed." But she overlooks the considerable influence that kin and friends exercised in narrowing the field to an acceptable range of candidates. See *Hands and Hearts*, 27–30. For a view similar to my own, see Leonore

sion of privacy, young people actively solicited their advice, gauging their own feelings and decisions against the perceptions of others. When Ebenezer Strong Snell, an instructor at Amherst College, and Sabra Cobb Clark considered marriage in 1825, both maintained that they had come to a decision independently. After all, Clark's father had always urged his daughters to "suit themselves and they would suit him—for he perfectly confided in their discretion." And the couple had "discussed the subject with freedom" before Snell thought to mention Clark in his letters to his parents. Still, neither could dismiss the wisdom of their friends. Although they clearly wished to marry, neither Snell nor Clark would announce a formal engagement without his parents' approval. Ebenezer explained to his mother that Sabra was "filled with anxiety, lest you should be displeased—and urges me to let her know the whole truth respecting the feelings of my friends at home." Before professing their love, Sabra and Ebenezer each conferred with friends regarding the other's character. By the time she agreed to marry Snell, Sabra had been assured that her friends "appear[ed] pleased with the expectation" of their wedding. For his part, Ebenezer took pains to acquaint himself with Sabra's sister, for family was always a good index to character. He also consulted with Mrs. Strong, who boarded Sabra while she attended the local academy, and who vouched for the girl's character and virtue. As Ebenezer pointed out, Mrs. Strong's judgment was entirely reliable, for she was routinely consulted by other Amherst couples in these matters.[12]

The next year, while courting Emily Norcross of Monson, Massachusetts, Edward Dickinson offered to begin a private correspondence, proposing to exchange letters "under cover" of his friend Lyman Cole-

---

Davidoff and Catherine Hall, *Family Fortunes: Men and Women of the English Middle Class, 1780–1850* (Chicago: University of Chicago Press, 1987), 219–22.

[12]Ebenezer Strong Snell to Tirzah Strong Snell, 12 July 1825, Snell Family Papers, ACASC Box 2, Folder 4. This evidence is drawn from Snell's correspondence; Sabra Clark's correspondence dates only from the time of her marriage to Snell. Clark may also have solicited her father's or family's consent, as did many young women. See, for example, Marianne Cochran to Agnes Cochran Higginson, 10 February 1839, Fuller-Higginson Papers, PVMA; Tyler, *Grandmother Tyler's Book*, 181; Nancy Coffey Heffernan and Ann Page Stecker, *Sisters of Fortune: Being the True Story of How Three Motherless Sisters Saved Their Home in New England and Raised Their Younger Brother While Their Father Went Fortune Hunting in the California Gold Rush* (Hanover, N.H.: University Press of New England, 1993). Not surprisingly, provincial men were more likely to marry without regard for their families' counsel. But when Ira Chafee Goodell did not contact his family for three years, leaving them to learn only indirectly of his marriage and the birth of his two children, this was both unusual and unacceptable, according to his mother, Susannah Goodale; see Susannah Goodale to Ira Chafee Goodell, 24 March 1836, Goodell Family Papers, JL.

man, who was pursuing Emily's cousin Maria Flynt.[13] Edward promised that "no one but these two, need know any thing of the letters that pass between us." Such a correspondence, secret and slightly daring, might suggest that Edward hoped to avoid the curiosity and interference of Emily's family. In fact, the opposite is probably true. Lyman Coleman was a minister of irreproachable character; he was also about to marry Maria Flynt. His role as a "secret courier" would not have subverted the authority of the Norcross's family. Rather, it would have incorporated both young men more closely into the Norcross-Flynt family circle.[14]

Almost from the beginning of their courtship, Dickinson and Norcross fostered the bonds between their kin. Although their marriage would primarily join Emily Norcross to Edward Dickinson, it would also unite the Norcross and Dickinson families. In the letters they exchanged between 1826 and 1828, their own relationship assumed pride of place. But this relationship was embedded in an increasingly complex network of ties between the two families. When he promised Emily that "the links of this *Holy Alliance* / Extend through creation's vast range," Edward referred to the persistence of their affection despite the distance between Amherst and Monson. But the sentiment applies equally well to the growing number of "links" between the Dickinsons, Norcrosses and their friends.[15]

Throughout their courtship, both Emily and Edward expected the Norcrosses to entertain Edward's family when they passed through Monson, and Edward made a point of crossing the path of Emily's father, brothers, and cousins in the course of his travels throughout the county.[16] Edward underscored the importance of these family connections in a letter to Emily's father. If they married, he vowed to do everything in his power to secure her happiness. But he also promised "to promote & increase, so far as honorable exertion is any assurance of it, [the happiness] of all her friends and connexions." This pledge was not

[13]My discussion of the courtship of Edward Dickinson and Emily Norcross is drawn from Vivian R. Pollack, ed., *A Poet's Parents: The Courtship Letters of Emily Norcross and Edward Dickinson* (Chapel Hill: University of North Carolina Press, 1988).

[14]Edward Dickinson to Emily Norcross, 18 June 1826, in *Poet's Parents*, 21–24. Immediately after proposing a private correspondence, Dickinson inquired after the health of Norcross's family and asked to be remembered to them. For her part, Norcross ignored Dickinson's suggestion for a secret correspondence.

[15]Edward Dickinson to Emily Norcross, 10 April 1826, in *Poet's Parents*, 7.

[16]On Emily Norcross and Samuel Dickinson, see in *Poet's Parents* Edward Dickinson to Emily Norcross, 10 April 1826, and Emily Norcross to Edward Dickinson, 10 May 1826, 7–10, 12–13; on the Dickinson family's Monson visits, see Emily Norcross to Edward Dickinson, 14 July 1827, 122–23; on tensions between Norcross and Dickinson, see xix–xx, 172–174.

simply for Joel Norcross's benefit. The following year, he wrote to Emily that he looked forward to the day when, as husband and wife, they might "add to the happiness of [their] friends" and advance "the melioration of the condition of all about" them.[17]

Far from imagining a private romance, Edward Dickinson and Emily Norcross expected to court under the watchful eyes of family and friends. Like Sabra Clark and Ebenezer Snell, they understood that the opinions of others not only reflected, but could help determine, the outcome of their courtship. Even the contents of their letters would be shared. Edward admitted that he "should be very glad" to know how Emily's friends "regarded [their] intercourse," for their estimation measured his success as a suitor.[18] Indeed, when Edward offered Emily a formal proposal, he also offered her a list of references. Several prominent attorneys, numerous college and law school associates, and "almost any clergyman in the neighboring towns" could attest to his "real character." He encouraged her to take heed of the impressions and advice of others, for as he explained, "you owe it to your own happiness, & the regard you have for your friends to be fully satisfied respecting the character & standing of the person from whom the proposal comes."[19]

It is doubtful that Emily Norcross or any member of her family ever investigated Edward's references. They did not have to; by the time Edward proposed, his credentials were well established. One of Edward's closest friends, Lyman Coleman, had been accepted into the family circle. He was already acquainted with Emily's uncle, Erasmus

[17]Edward Dickinson to Joel Norcross, 5 September 1826, 42–43, and Edward Dickinson to Emily Dickinson, 9 August 1827, 130, in *Poet's Parents*.

[18]Edward Dickinson to Emily Norcross, 4 June 1826, in *Poet's Parents*, 17–21. Two months later he asked whether Emily's brother William had commented on the prospect of their marriage: "Has he said any thing to your father in relation to our intercourse, & do you know whether he approves, or disapproves of our meetings?—I feel some solicitude to ascertain his feelings, and to know in what light he views my attentions to you. I certainly regard his feelings very much, and should wish to have his countenance in our proceedings." Edward Dickinson to Emily Norcross, 23 August 1826, in *Poet's Parents*, 39. Provincial families routinely circulated letters, and courtship letters seem to have been no exception. See, for example, Marianne Cochran to Agnes Cochran Higginson, 10 February 1839, Fuller-Higginson Papers, PVMA; Mary Palmer Tyler to Thomas Pickman Tyler, 9 December 1838, 29 March 1841, Royall Tyler Collection, Gift of Helen Tyler Brown, VHS; Marilyn S. Blackwell, "Growing up Male in the 1830s: Thomas Pickman Tyler (1815–1892) and the Tyler Family of Brattleboro," *Vermont History* 58 (1990): 17.

[19]Edward Dickinson to Emily Norcross, 4 June 1826, in *Poet's Parents*, 17–21. The following year, Dickinson reiterated, "I wish nothing to be concealed in relation to my circumstances, or my character. . . . My objective has always been to induce you to refer to such sources for information, as would enable you to form an opinion according to the truth." Edward Dickinson to Emily Norcross, 21 February 1827, in *Poet's Parents*, 91.

Norcross, who probably introduced the two during one of Edward's visits to Monson. Promising and prominent, handsome enough, bright enough, Edward Dickinson must have seemed like an entirely satisfactory suitor for the daughter of Monson's largest landowner. Had he been less acceptable, it is unlikely that their courtship would have advanced at all. In such a context, Emily Norcross could well assert that they "ought to form [their] own opinions" and their "own judgments" of each other.[20]

Yet despite Edward Dickinson's sterling credentials, Emily Norcross was not inclined to dispense with parental approval. She admitted to a "warm and increasing attachment" to Edward, and assured him that she "would wish to comply" with his proposal. Nevertheless, until she received the "advise and consent" of her father, she could not accept. She explained, "As I regard his fealings very much should I meet his approbation I will then assure you of my confidence and affection."[21] When her father recommended a lengthy engagement, giving Edward an opportunity to establish himself, Emily Norcross agreed to abide by his wishes. In fact, she complied with an enthusiasm that startled, and at times offended, her fiancé. For two years she used family emergencies, household duties, and parental reservations to postpone her wedding. Like her father, Emily Norcross favored an extended engagement. Yet rather than voicing her own hesitations and desires, she chose to stand behind her family's needs and her father's authority. She prompted Edward, "You would ever wish me to receive [my father's] counsel would you not." By invoking the wishes of her family in general, and the wisdom of her father in particular, Emily Norcross laid claim to a legitimacy that her own desires could never have commanded.[22] Like other provincial New Englanders, Edward Dickinson and Emily Norcross sought and received the advice of family and friends when they contemplated marriage. But the advice they received figured very differently in their lives. For Edward Dickinson, it bol-

[20]Edward Dickinson to Emily Norcross, 4 June 1826, in *Poet's Parents*, 18. Dickinson quoted Norcross: "you remarked, when I saw you last, that we 'ought to form our own opinions, or our own judgments' [about each other]." On the Dickinson and Norcross families, see *Poet's Parents*, xxx–xxxi; Mary Elizabeth Kromer Bernhard, "Portrait of a Family: Emily Dickinson's Norcross Connection," *New England Quarterly* 60 (1979): 363–81; and Richard B. Sewall, *The Life of Emily Dickinson*, vol. 1 (New York: Farrar, Straus & Giroux, 1974), 33, 76.

[21]Emily Norcross to Edward Dickinson, 8 August 1826, in *Poet's Parents*, 37.

[22]Emily Norcross to Edward Dickinson, 30 October 1826, in *Poet's Parents*, 56. On Emily Norcross's reluctance to settle on a wedding date, see *Poet's Parents*, 173, 193, 198, 199, 203. I do not doubt that Norcross invoked the family claim more often than necessity dictated, especially to postpone her wedding, but I give her account of family responsibilities more credence than Pollack allows.

stered his confidence and confirmed his good instincts. For Emily Norcross, that advice represented her best, if not only, chance to articulate her wishes and to advance her interests.

The Meaning of Marriage

If Emily Norcross's elaborate strategies and excuses were extraordinary, her reluctance to marry was not. Having made the decision to wed, many antebellum women happily deferred the ceremony itself, for if marriage bestowed the privileges of full adulthood, it also conferred new and often intimidating responsibilities. Marriage allowed urban and rural women to claim identities as wives, as mistresses of households, and, perhaps most important, as mothers. It offered provincial women nothing less than the opportunity to fulfill their destinies within their particular communities. Still, few women could pass lightly over the responsibility of managing a household, the prospect of sexual intimacy, the dangers of childbirth, or the sacred duties of motherhood. Finally, women understood that the conjugal bonds that joined husband to wife and hand to heart also subjected the fate of a woman to the goodwill, wisdom, industry, and even the luck of her husband. Rivaled only by conversion, the choice of a spouse was the most significant decision a woman would make over the course of a lifetime. It is little wonder that so many middle-class women, urban and provincial alike, hesitated on their way to marriage.

Embodying both hope and risk, promise and threat, the prospect of marriage could arouse misgivings that ranged from vague uneasiness to acute anxiety. When their concerns centered on relatively limited issues, women could communicate their reservations directly and succinctly. One Massachusetts woman, intimidated by the prospect of managing a household by herself, voiced her fears so effectively that she alarmed her fiancé. Worried that her doubts would lead her to break off their engagement, Asel Clark assured Clarissa Warner that her housekeeping skills exceeded his expectations. Indeed, he found her "attainments in Domestic Economy equal and in theory superior to most of the young ladies at the present day." For his part, he could only hope that Warner's "<u>imaginable</u> incompetency in domestic affairs" would never cause her "one unhappy thought." Apparently reassured, Clarissa Warner wed Asel Clark in 1835.[23]

[23]Asel Clark to Clarissa Warner, 7 June 1834, Clark-Warner Papers, SSC. Clarissa Warner may have expressed her fears in person; if they were expressed in her correspondence, the letter has not survived.

But provincial women were more frequently troubled by dilemmas that resisted easy resolution. In these cases, women only partially explored and articulated the source of their fears. Following a 1827 visit to a neighbor whose confinement left her "quite miserable," Emily Norcross confronted the dangers of childbirth. Although she admitted to Dickinson that in such matters she "had rather be a spectator" than a participant, Norcross also knew that married women could not afford to indulge such fears. As she pointed out, her friend was "reconciled to her situation or ought to be." If she herself could not say the same, she understood that in order to wed, she must make her peace with the risks that accompanied marriage, including the hazards of pregnancy and childbirth. Only six months later, her beloved cousin Maria Flynt Coleman fell ill following the birth of her first child. This time, Norcross managed to check her concerns for the safety of her cousin and herself. With admirable equanimity, she observed only that "we must learn from this that there is no happiness but what is mingled with sorrow."[24]

The pattern of doubt and hesitation that marked the courtships of both Clarissa Warner and Emily Norcross was first described by Nancy Cott, who suggested that northern domestic ideology generated conflicts and pressures that resulted in widespread "marriage trauma," revealed most frequently in women's emotional withdrawal from a "too burdened marriage choice." By demanding that women find happiness in marriages that subordinated their interests and desires to their husband's needs and ambitions, the logic of domesticity compelled antebellum women to make a "voluntary choice amounting to self-abnegation." It was this dilemma that prompted women's "marriage trauma."[25] Cott's argument owed much to the observations of Alexis de Tocqueville, who had been struck by the "freedom and pleasure" American women enjoyed within the households of their fathers juxtaposed against the "strict obligations" and "cloister[ed]" confinement they faced in the homes of their husbands. In the United States, de Tocqueville concluded, "a woman loses her independence forever in the bonds of matrimony."[26] Although de Tocqueville was a shrewd observer of American society, his assessment of republican domestic arrangements was informed by a comparison with the habits of the European aristocracy, who raised their daughters in near isolation and

[24]Emily Norcross to Edward Dickinson, 15 November 1827, 150; 27 June 1827, in *Poet's Parents*, 115.

[25]Cott, *Bonds of Womanhood*, 80, 78–83, and passim.

[26]Alexis de Tocqueville, *Democracy in America*, ed. J. P. Mayer, trans. George Lawrence (New York: Doubleday & Co., 1969), 592.

married them off to consolidate alliances and fortunes. Compared with the daughters of continental nobility, American women did enjoy notable latitude before marriage and rather severe restraints after. But it does not necessarily follow that, within the contexts of their own lives and communities, a majority of antebellum women experienced marriage as the sacrifice of personal independence. The tension between freedom and restriction has nevertheless become a commonplace in social historians' descriptions of antebellum courtship and marriage. Despite disagreements over periodization and more serious differences over which aspects of marriage proved most disquieting, a generation of women's historians have drawn on Cott's contention that it was the conflict between women's desire to preserve their independence and their desire to fulfill their roles as wives and mothers that gave rise to antebellum marriage trauma.

Yet there is little evidence to suggest that provincial women equated marriage with "self-abnegation." To be sure, many did experience anxieties similar those described by Cott, yet their misgivings did not stem from a reluctance to trade independence for confinement. Typically, they derived from the prospect of trading the relative security of their parents' households for the emotional risks and the economic uncertainties that accompanied married life. However disruptive, this transition rarely threatened provincial women with a loss of self. After all, relations among kin, friends, and neighbors were more often structured by a system of reciprocal obligations within specific social networks than by notions of the universal rights accorded the individual. The households and communities that bound their lives offered single women, in particular, little autonomy. If anything, married women enjoyed more independence than their single sisters. Accordingly, women found marriage alarming to the extent that it transformed their place within the dense web of relations that connected them to family and friends and determined their identities as members of particular communities.

Rather than fearing self-renunciation, provincial women were more likely to worry that they were abandoning kin and households that depended on them. Before her marriage, Caroline Clapp Briggs and her sister shared the management of their Northampton home, taking in lodgers to support themselves and their widowed mother. With three boarders and "only one servant," Briggs recalled, "we were a very busy family." When marriage to one of her boarders demanded that Briggs move to Walpole, New Hampshire, she found that "it was hard to leave my sister with the care and responsibility of the family on her shoulders." Recognizing the pleasure she took in her new station, Briggs admitted that she felt "very selfish." Still, no one could deny that her new husband had the first claim on her affections and her services. In marrying, she had transferred her allegiance from one household to another. Despite her genuine commitment to her sister and mother, she "belonged to somebody else now, and the stronger love must prevail."[27]

It was precisely this tension that prompted provincial women's most serious misgivings. As Briggs's reminiscence suggests, the trauma of marriage lay not so much in the prospect of "belonging" to another but in the prospect of negotiating the tensions and conflicts that arose when a woman sensed she "belonged" to several others at once. Provincial women did not see themselves as torn between the promise of self-determination and the obligation of the family claim. They were torn, rather, between the claims of competing families and households.

These tensions could become especially acute if a young woman came from a home that was emotionally and economically stable or if the marriage necessitated taking up residence in a new town. So it was with Emily Norcross. In accepting Dickinson's proposal, Norcross accepted all the uncertainties occasioned by beginning a new life in an unfamiliar community while sacrificing the proven security of her place in her father's home and in Monson society. Less than two weeks before her wedding, she wrote to Dickinson, "I have many friends call upon me as they say to make their farewell visit. How do you suppose this sounds in my ear"?[28]

The distress provoked by the prospect of leaving family and friends was compounded by Norcross's attempts to meet the conflicting demands of her family and her fiancé. An unusually energetic correspondent, Dickinson complained regularly that Norcross failed to match his letters either in number or in detail, suspecting that her meager letters were part of a scheme to "practic[e] upon [his] patience." But Dickinson failed to see that whatever else letter-writing signified, it also represented an investment of time and energy, of hours diverted from her commitments to the other members of her household.[29] Writ-

[27]Caroline Clapp Briggs, *Reminiscences and Letters of Caroline C[lapp] Briggs*, ed. George Merriam (Boston: Houghton Mifflin, 1897), 89, 93.

[28]Emily Norcross to Edward Dickinson, 24 April 1828 and 5 February 1828, in *Poet's Parents*, 206. Vivian Pollack insightfully discusses Norcross's fear of separating from her family (xix–xx).

[29]Edward Dickinson to Emily Norcross, 20 October 1827 and 31 January 1828, in *Poet's Parents*, 144, 180. Dickinson's complaints grew more pointed over the course of their courtship, and he was not the last to suspect Norcross's sincerity. Citing the paucity and the lack of detail in Emily Norcross's letters to Edward Dickinson, Vivian Pollack (*Poet's Parents*, xxix, xix, xx) has suggested that Norcross's extreme distress during courtship led

ing demanded that Norcross "lay aside all duties for the sake of gratifying [herself] as well as [her] friend," a luxury she could not always
afford.[30]

This friction plagued Norcross from the beginning of her courtship.
She cut short her second letter to Dickinson because, having "resorted
to my chamber without any one persons knowing how I am occupied," she feared she would "soon be enquired for."[31] During the winter of 1826–1827, her mother's illness further restricted the attention
she could devote to Dickinson. It was only after "some inconvenience" that she could leave her mother's chamber for the "pleasure
of conversing" with her fiancé. Glancing over one such "conversation," she apologized: "This letter appears quite to short but I have
been obliged to write in haste." Several months later she wrote, "I
wish I had time to disclose my fealings to you but I fear my Mother
will ask for me."[32]

Her mother's illness also prevented her from visiting Edward for the
dedication of the Amherst College Chapel in February 1827. She regret-
ted that it was "not in [her] power" to attend the ceremony but believed
that Dickinson would "doubtless presume" that her "cares had been
numerous" and her "solicitude great." Hoping to appease him, Norcross hinted that the constancy that distinguished her as a daughter
would one day distinguish her as a wife. Surely Dickinson would think
her "ungrateful to leave [her] friends when needed so much at home."
Under the circumstances, Edward had little choice but to admit that
she had done "exactly right," for they "owe[d] the first duty to [their]
family and friends."[33] And to her credit, Norcross did make good on
her promise to attend the college's commencement ceremonies that
summer.

Over the next year, Edward Dickinson's invitations became more
demanding. By the winter of 1828, his patience had expired altogether.

---

her to advance the "unlikely claim" that her domestic responsibilities were "so time consuming as to prevent her from writing." Following a strategy of passive resistance, Norcross
"tried to create the impression that her time was not her own but that, given the right circumstances, her time would be Edward's." But it does not follow that because Norcross's
excuses were convenient, they were also feigned. Numerous provincial women, married
and single, complained that household responsibilities kept them from writing to friends
and family.

[30]Emily Norcross to Edward Dickinson, 15 November 1827, in *Poet's Parents*, 150.

[31]Emily Norcross to Edward Dickinson, 10 May 1826, in *Poet's Parents*, 12–13.

[32]Emily Norcross to Edward Dickinson, 15 December 1826, in *Poet's Parents*, 61–62.

[33]Edward Dickinson to Emily Norcross, 7 March 1827, and Emily Norcross to Edward
Dickinson, 25 February 1827, in *Poet's Parents*, 97, 96.

After being "refused times with out number . . . without good reason," he was unwilling to accept anything less than Norcross's "<u>actual sickness</u>" as a reason for "not complying" with his requests. In vaguely threatening tones, he insisted, "I shall not be satisfied with `no,' for an answer . . . let the going be what it may."[34] Loath to leave the security of her family and torn between her duties in Monson and in Amherst, Norcross continued to decline her fiancé's invitations. But the pressure to appease both family and future husband proved exhausting. In this contest of loyalties, Dickinson would simply have to wait his turn. As she explained,

> There are, and have been, reason[s], to prevent me from acting in compliance with your wishes. Perhaps you will say they are all trifling, I am sensible that my feelings are unlike many others at least those within the bounds of my observation, but it is not necessary for me to explain to you why, except that when I am differerently situated I shall enjoy myself much better.[35]

In the meantime, Dickinson could accept her assurances that as her husband, he would assume the first place in her heart and in her attentions. As their wedding approached, Norcross's language increasingly emphasized the authority Dickinson would enjoy when they were married. If he respected the wishes of the Norcrosses, Emily included, before their wedding, afterwards she would never trouble him with "any other objection," for in general she found his "sentiments correct" and "would hope not to deviate from them" when she became "subject to [his] authority."[36]

Throughout her courtship, Emily Norcross waged a battle on two fronts, struggling to meet the often conflicting expectations of her family and her fiancé at the same time she struggled to reconcile herself to the implications of marriage for her own life. But while she was undoubtedly distressed by her impending passage from daughter to wife, Norcross never fully articulated her fears and desires, choosing instead to submerge them beneath her family's more practical concerns. In the midst of wedding preparations, she wrote, "My mind is often completely confused when I allow myself to dwell upon the sub-

---

[34]Edward Dickinson to Emily Norcross, 8 February 1828, in *Poet's Parents*, 185.

[35]Emily Norcross to Edward Dickinson, 9 February 1828, in *Poet's Parents*, 186. For other examples of this kind of internal conflict, see Briggs, *Reminiscences*, and the letters from Elizabeth Phelps Huntington to her mother, Elizabeth Porter Phelps, PPHFP, Box 13. Folder 1–3.

[36]Emily Norcross to Edward Dickinson, 5 February 1828, in *Poet's Parents*, 182.

ject [of her impending marriage], but I usually lay it aside with the reflection that it will result in . . . happiness."[37] Her willingness to "lay aside" her own ambivalence cannot be dismissed as another example of the legendary Norcross-Dickinson emotional eccentricity. Nor can it be explained as a response to the self-abnegation of marriage. Instead, her response is best understood in the context of a culture that generally demonstrated a limited regard for individualism and gave especially short shrift to the aspirations and desires of individual women.

Provincial women whose households were unhappy or unstable understandably experienced relatively little of the anxiety that troubled Emily Norcross Dickinson and Caroline Clapp Briggs. Despite their devotion to particular family members, such women risked little in leaving their families. They experienced little conflict between the households that had commanded their youth and the men who offered them their futures. In the wake of her mother's death and her father's financial reverses, Amelia White spent a number of years moving between her father's house in Lancaster, New Hampshire, and the houses of kin in Salem, Rutland, and Springfield, Massachusetts. Like other young women in similar circumstances, she provided her extended family with sewing, cooking, child care, and good company in return for room and board. As her father observed, although she benefited from the interested guidance of "kind friends who were equally if not more anxious about [her] than what I could be," Amelia White was "pretty much her own mistress."[38] But being one's "own mistress" in someone else's household was no easy task. Even among the most generous families, such arrangements were calculated to promote an uneasy mixture of obligation, dependence, and insecurity. When Unitarian minister William Peabody proposed marriage in 1823, White was almost as eager to claim the security of his home and the approval of his rather prominent family as she was to accept his love. She noted with pride that the Peabodys "class[ed] her with their own children," not "considering themselves quite complete without her, having so long regarded her in the light of a daughter & sister."[39]

Far from feeling the pangs of a divided heart, Amelia White identified

---

[37]Emily Norcross to Edward Dickinson, 22 March 1828, in *Poet's Parents*, 198.

[38]Moses White to William Bourn Oliver Peabody, 6 August 1823, Everett-Peabody Family Papers, MHS.

[39]Amelia White [Peabody] to Moses White, 5 July 1824 and 29 August 1824, Everett-Peabody Family Papers, MHS. On the trials single women experienced while boarding with kin, see Lee Virginia Chambers-Schiller *Liberty, a Better Husband: Single Women in America: The Generations of 1780–1840* (New Haven, Conn.: Yale University Press, 1984), 72–77.

almost wholly with the Peabody family from the time of her engagement. Both Amelia White and William Peabody preferred to marry in Salem, where Amelia had lived with her uncle's family for several years. But Moses White urged his daughter and prospective son-in-law to take their vows in Lancaster, complaining that his age and health argued against a journey to Salem. More to the point, White feared that he would be out of place in cosmopolitan Salem, for his embarrassment had left him "entirely out of fashion."[40] Amelia White took pains to reassure her father that if he was "out of fashion," the republic was "more degenerate" than she realized. But she refused to change her plans and canceled two other promised visits to Lancaster to accommodate Peabody and his family. The first trip, before her marriage, was postponed because "Mr P" was "unwilling" to let her travel alone, although she had certainly made the journey in the past. The second trip, intended as a wedding trip, was rejected in favor of a visit to her in-laws in Exeter; as she explained, Peabody's parents had "fixed their hearts on seeing us after we are married & we promised them that they should not be disappointed."[41]

This should not suggest that Amelia White abandoned her obligations to her own family to curry favor with another. On the contrary, she maintained deep ties to her immediate family, especially her younger sisters, and to the kin whose households and lives she had shared. In the years before and especially after her father's death in 1833, she acted as the head of her family, settling accounts, parceling out loans, overseeing inheritances, and mediating family quarrels. If anything, the social role she assumed as the wife of a respected Unitarian minister increased her sense of familial responsibility. At the very least, the life she shared with William Peabody provided her with emotional and financial resources to meet those obligations. Nevertheless, her marriage offered a welcome relief from the risk and frustration that awaited any provincial woman who found herself "pretty much her own mistress." Shortly after her wedding, she wrote to two of the cousins she had helped to rear, "It will be long before I can be quite reconciled to being away from you, for beside loving you very dearly, the feeling that I was useful to you by my influence makes me often lament our separation." But she added with undisguised pleasure, "I am becoming quite used to my new name."[42]

[40]Moses White to Amelia White [Peabody], 10 June 1824, and see also Amelia White [Peabody] to Moses White, 4 May 1824, Everett-Peabody Family Papers, MHS.
[41]Amelia White [Peabody] to Moses White, 29 August 1824 and 5 July 1824, Everett-Peabody Family Papers, MHS.
[42]Amelia White Peabody to the Misses E. A. and M. W. White, 13 September 1824, Everett-Peabody Family Papers, MHS.

The Specter of Spinsterhood

Provincial New Englanders *expected* that adulthood would bring marriage and that marriage would bring men and women alike their best chance of contentment. Recently married, Charles Russell wrote to a single friend, "that there was no real happiness in celibacy I was conscious of before I married." Time spent in the company of his wife only confirmed this hunch: "I am now fully of the opinion . . . that marriage is necessary to complete happiness," he wrote. Like Charles Russell, the majority of provincial women never questioned either the desirability or the necessity of marriage. Luthera Negus spoke for many when she pronounced a Petersham couple "an excellent match," for "as the times are now, I am glad to see any of the girls <u>marry</u> . . . if they can get good husbands, think themselves old enough, and qualified to make good wives."[43]

Still, arguments enjoining men to marry were far less frequent and far less pointed than comments about spinsters. Published essays that stressed the importance of marriage for men generally emphasized its value in abstract terms, arguing that marriage enabled men to establish households, shore up the republic, or fulfill divine plans. When provincials did notice bachelors, they did so by joking about their virility and sexual potency.[44] A woman poised for spinsterhood was a far more urgent concern for family and friends. When Luthera Negus was still keeping school in 1824 with nary a prospect in sight, her older sister Fanny Negus Fuller began to worry about the "poor girl," admitting "I dont see but she may always keep." In general, provincial women did not self-consciously choose to remain single. Instead, they were troubled by the prospect of spinsterhood making at best an uneasy peace with their futures.[45]

[43]Luthera Negus to Fanny Negus Fuller, 15 April 1823, and see also Hattie Fuller to Elijah Fuller, 30 April 1854, Fuller-Higginson Papers, PVMA. Charles Russell to Joshua Dillingham, 27 July 1815, Charles Russell Papers, MHS. See also Heffernan and Stecker, *Sisters of Fortune*, passim, for an extended discussion of one family's concern about unmarried women.

[44]See, for example, a joke in the 26 January 1841 Greenfield *Gazette and Mercury* in which a schoolmaster asks a little girl to list and explain genders. The girl responds that the teacher is masculine, she is feminine, and "I reckon Mr. Jackson is *neuter*, as he's an Old Bachelor!" See also *Christian Calendar and New England Farmer's Almanac*, 47; S. A., "The Pussyite," *Hampshire Gazette*, 17 May 1842.

[45]Fanny Negus Fuller to Nathan Negus, 18 April 1824, Fuller-Higginson Papers, PVMA. Of the provincial women who openly questioned marriage, the overwhelming majority did so as adolescents. See, for example, Annie Storrow Higginson to Elizabeth and Louisa Higginson, 22 February 1851, Fuller-Higginson Family Papers, PVMA; and the Diary of Sarah Jane Olcutt, UVM. In her study of antebellum southern women, Elizabeth Fox-

If provincial women were unperturbed by the thought of forfeiting their independence at the altar, it was largely because they had so little independence to lose. Historians have long observed that the organization of the antebellum economy committed the overwhelming majority of northern women to a state of material dependence; with notable exceptions, the single and widowed women of New England's cities and countryside relied on the assistance of male kin and their households for their support. For provincial women, this economic dependence was matched by a pronounced social and cultural dependence.[46]

The marginality of unmarried women was underscored in the region's didactic literature. Between 1838 and 1842, Sophia Hewes, editor of a Vermont women's magazine, carefully delineated the special roles played by mothers, stepmothers, aunts, daughters, and eldest daughters in shoring up the republic and furthering the cause of Christ. But Hewes's vision of unmarried women included only the young, who might benefit from her advice as they fitted themselves for marriage and, especially, for motherhood. In four years, she made no mention of those women who would never marry. The *Complete New England Almanac*, on the other hand, acknowledged the possibility that women might never marry by reprinting an English table showing the ages at which 876 women married. Demonstrating that a woman's chances of marriage declined precipitously after she reached her mid-twenties, the study offered its "fair readers" a "pretty accurate judgment of the chances they have of entering into the holy state of matrimony, and enjoying the sweets . . . of wedded life." This table only confirmed the observation of a Franklin County poet who discovered that after she turned twenty-five,

> 'tis queer, that every year
> I'm slighted more and more!
> For not a beau pretends to show
> His head within our door . . .
> And one might near as well be dead,
> As say—I'm twenty-five.[47]

Genovese has also found rebellion against marriage limited to adolescent girls: *Within the Plantation Household: Black and White Women of the Old South* (Chapel Hill: University of North Carolina Press, 1988), 255–56.

[46]Chambers-Schiller, *Liberty, a Better Husband*, 3, 68–71. See also Daniel Scott Smith, "Female Householding in Late Eighteenth-Century America and the Problem of Poverty," *Journal of Social History* 28 (1994): 83–107.

[47]Miss Horton, "Because I'm Twenty-Five," *Greenfield Gazette and Franklin Herald*, 31 May 1836; "Chances of Marriage," *The Complete New England Almanac* (Woodstock, Vt.:

Lee Chambers-Schiller has argued that in the decades between the American Revolution and the Civil War, growing numbers of New England women turned the stereotype of the forlorn spinster on its head by laying claim to the benefits of bourgeois individualism under the rubric of a "cult of single blessedness." Rejecting marriage, these women sought to cultivate an autonomous female self through spinsterhood. They chose to develop themselves and their potential by improving their education and by pursuing vocations and careers beyond the households of their kin. They also expressed the desire, however conflicted, for personal independence unchecked by the demands of their families.[48]

Despite the growing numbers of rural women who delayed or declined marriage, the towns and villages of rural New England afforded single women few opportunities to foster female autonomy through a cult of single blessedness. The relative isolation of provincial society limited women's opportunities to discover, much less follow, any kind of vocation. The relatively small populations of provincial centers such as Northampton and Brattleboro necessarily limited women's access to the varieties and quantities of volunteer and benevolent work that sustained generations of urban middle-class women. Moreover, the structure of the provincial economy made it difficult to secure wage work that was both reliable and respectable. Although women of the provincial middle class found numerous chances to earn a season's wages teaching school, teaching proved less a vocation for most of them than a job.[49] In most cases, the pursuit of a calling or career demanded that women abandon their communities. To answer the missionary's call, Fidelia Fiske, born and raised in Shelburne,

---

Rufus Colton, 1830); Sophia A. Hewes, ed., *Mother's Book*, later *Mother's Book and Lady's Companion* (Chelsea Vt.: Hewes & Howe, 1838–1842). One New England almanac offered the unmarried a view of celibacy that was only slightly more encouraging: The celibate, "like the fly in the heart of the apple, dwells in perpetual sweetness but sits alone, and is confined and dies in singularity" (*Christian Calendar and New England Farmer's Almanac for the Year of Our Lord 1827* [Boston: Christian Register Office, 1827], 47).

[48]Chambers-Schiller, *Liberty, a Better Husband.*

[49]See, for example, the Diary of a Shaftsbury [vt.] Schoolteacher, 1857, VHS; Lestina to Cyrus Wheeler, 9 May 1858, Wheeler Papers, MS-60, VHS. Elizabeth Huntington scolded her daughter for failing to appreciate schoolteaching as an opportunity to benefit society or to develop a vocation (Elizabeth Phelps Huntington to Mary Dwight Huntington, 22 March 1835, PPHFP, Box 12, Folder 12). Even women like Sophronia Grout, who viewed teaching as a means to accomplish God's work on earth, struggled to find the work rewarding. See the Diary of Sophronia Grout, 15 May 1821, 18 June 1833, and 13 June n.d. [possibly 1833], PVMA. On teaching as a job rather than as a career, see Chambers-Schiller, *Liberty, a Better Husband*, 4.

Massachusetts, traveled to Oroomiah, Persia, in 1843 and remained there for some fifteen years. Of course, not all women wandered so far to secure a career. Anne Laura Clarke of Northampton taught at academies in Georgia, Pennsylvania, and Virginia before commencing a career as a lecturer in the early 1820s. Although she returned to Northampton several times over the course of her life, her professional aspirations always drew her away again.[50]

Less ambitious women found that the realities of provincial life threw up sharp obstacles not only to the kind of personal autonomy sought by women like Fiske and Clarke but also to the more fundamental process of self-definition described by Chambers-Schiller. The social landscape of rural New England was dominated by households composed largely, if not exclusively, of kin. Accordingly, most women who avoided marriage either by chance or by choice sought their identities among siblings and cousins, nieces and nephews. With flexibility, self-acceptance, and the goodwill and financial stability of her kin, an unmarried woman might manage to carve out a place for herself within household and community. But even under the best of circumstances, this was no easy task.

For Bethia Throop Huntington, the realization that she would probably spend her life as a spinster on her parents' Hadley household provoked a painful attempt to come to terms with herself and her future. At thirty-four, she acknowledged that she had "lived beyond the time when the greater part of the matches are made" and resolved that, under the circumstances, "it is not reasonable or becoming . . . to think or talk much of such things." By forsaking her interest in marriage, Huntington hoped to gain an inner as well as outer calm. She wrote, "I have come to the conclusion that the sole way to secure peace of mind is to let the mind in her unoccupied moments dwell as little as possible on such subjects." Like many antebellum women similarly situated, Huntington determined not to fill her mind with fantasies of a husband and home but to seek her "highest happiness in the service of a Heavenly Father who can be . . . a better comforter than any earthly friend."[51]

[50]On Clarke's struggle to establish a vocation beyond the confinement of Northampton, see especially the Anne Laura Clarke Bound Letters, 1817–24, Historic Northampton, Northampton, Massachusetts. On Fidelia Fiske, see Chambers-Schiller, *Liberty, a Better Husband*, 89–90, 120–21; and Elizabeth Alden Green, *Mary Lyon and Mount Holyoke: Opening the Gates* (Hanover, N.H.: University Press of New England, 1979), 242–43, 261–62. Fiske returned to Massachusetts to serve as the chaplain at the Mount Holyoke Seminary.

[51]Bethia Throop Huntington Commonplace Book, 30 May 1839, PPHFP, Box 20, Folder 5.

When she accepted an invitation to teach "Sabbath School" in 1839, Huntington was as pleased with the chance to broaden her life as she was with the prospect of furthering God's work on earth, for she had "desire[d] for some time to be more actually engaged . . . in doing something for the good of those without the pale of the domestic circle." If one Sunday school class amounted to something less than a calling, it did allow her "the opportunity of doing <u>something</u>." Her new role also made the decorous behavior required of a spinster more palatable. It was far easier to admit that she was of an age at which "<u>extreme</u> gaiety is unbecoming," when she could add that such behavior might "dishonor her profession," a thought she found "dreadful indeed!" The prospect of teaching helped Bethia Huntington negotiate the tensions between her need to play a role in the world beyond her father's household and her deep feelings of filial obligation. After all, a Sunday school class was an irreproachable pursuit for a minister's daughter, an occupation that would have been difficult for anyone, including Bethia Huntington, to question.

If Christian duty permitted a woman like Bethia Huntington to expand her aspirations, it could also force her to rein them in. Several weeks after she commenced her new profession, Huntington's mother became ill. Elizabeth Huntington's fever prompted a deep sense of guilt in her daughter, who well understood that the first earthly duty of a Christian woman was to her family. Huntington responded to her mother's illness by vowing to be "more strict in the performance of [her] filial duties so that when sickness comes" she would have "no occasion for reproaching [herself] with neglect of duty in the slightest particular." Bethia Huntington was as good as her word. Almost two months later, a day's trip to Northampton marked the first time in "about a fortnight" that she ventured "outside the yard."[52]

Ultimately, Huntington resolved the dilemmas of spinsterhood not by forging a career in teaching but by renewing her commitment to her family. If the decision caused her any pain, she concealed it from those around her. Recalling his childhood, Theodore Huntington praised the older sister "who so supplemented the lives of each one of us that they would be hardly more than fragments without her." Bethia Huntington's "benefactions were so unostentatious, and yet so constant" that her brother could hardly recall one "word or act of hers, or even incidents connected with her." With more approval than

[52]Bethia Throop Huntington Commonplace Book, 25 July 1839, 9 June 1839, 24 May 1839, and 19 May 1839, PPHFP, Box 20, Folder 5.

accuracy, he concluded that his sister's "whole life was one of self-abnegation."[53]

Unlike her contemporary Bethia Huntington, Martha Cochran of Northampton never agonized over the conflicts between serving her family and pursuing a calling, however worthy. Strong-willed and sharp-tongued, Cochran hardly aspired to self-abnegation. But she never doubted that her primary responsibilities and her best chance for happiness lay within the Northampton household she shared with her mother and younger sisters.

Determined to accept graciously the role assigned to spinsters, Cochran nevertheless found a good measure of frustration. She readily admitted that she possessed "energies perhaps greater than are commonly given to women." Living in a community that left her with no outlet "except such as [her] own ingenuity devise[d]" and with a family who evinced "little or no sympathy" for her "employments, thoughts, or feelings," her considerable drive sometimes seemed more a burden than a gift. But Cochran assiduously refrained from self-pity, for she doubted that there was "enough in [her] circumstances to make an uncomfortable situation," much less to disturb "inward peace."[54]

Martha Cochran did not suffer for want of things to occupy her time. After moving to Northampton from Boston in the 1830s, she found her domestic duties significantly increased, for rural housekeeping entailed more work with less "help" than the Cochrans were accustomed to. In addition to providing the labor expected of every provincial woman, Martha Cochran played an invaluable role in helping her mother and sisters adjust to the mysteries of provincial housekeeping, bearing a series of domestic scrapes and adventures with remarkable good humor. When she was not needed in the kitchen or the parlor, she turned to the greenhouse, where she boarded her neighbor's plants for the winter, dabbled in mulberry speculation, and indulged her passion for fine roses and magnolias, exotic pomegranates and figs.[55]

Beyond their household, the Cochran women's "agreeable" dispositions, "well-educated tastes," and stylish hospitality created a stir in

[53]Theodore G. Huntington, "Sketches by Theodore G. Huntington of the Family and Life in Hadley written in Letters to H. F. Quincy," 55, PPHFP, Box 21, Folder 7. Tellingly, of his four sisters, Huntington remembered most vividly the eldest, Elizabeth Huntington Fisher, who left the farm at Forty Acres when Theodore was only nine. Although Theodore was certainly less familiar with Elizabeth than with his other sisters, she was the only Huntington daughter to marry.

[54]Martha Cochran to Agnes Cochran Higginson, 17 December 1837, Fuller-Higginson Papers, PVMA.

[55]See Martha Cochran to Agnes Cochran Higginson, 30 May 1836, 1 July 1836, 23 January 1839, and 10 February 1839, Fuller-Higginson Papers, PVMA.

provincial Northampton. One woman recalled that their "pretty cottage" soon became a "social centre in the village." Martha Cochran availed herself of all that Northampton's middle-class society had to offer. She attended teas, parties, and balls; she joined the walking club and organized a book club. Not merely concerned with her own amusement, she was active in Northampton's religious and benevolent societies, especially those connected with the Unitarian church. Although she had no "pretension to beauty," she won a large circle of devoted friends, for her "fine, well-trained mind, great humor" and "kindly heart . . . charmed everybody."[56]

With interests and activities in abundance, what Martha Cochran lacked was a clearly defined social role through which to structure her identity. As she observed, it was far easier to "keep in the straight & narrow way, when that path [was] hemmed in, & walled about by imperative duties." She expected that only marriage and motherhood offered women the "imperative duties" that gave life meaning. Mustering gratitude for the "many blessings" she enjoyed, Cochran acknowledged that her own life was easy enough. And she sympathized with the trials endured by married women, although her imagination did not stretch to include the difficulties faced by single women who lacked her financial resources. Still, in 1837, she wrote to her married sister, Agnes Higginson, "I know it is hard to have body & soul harrowed as yours must often be, but is it harder than to feel that body & soul might be annihilated, without being missed by a human being?"[57]

Seeking affection and purpose, Martha Cochran took in the youngest daughter of an impoverished Boston aunt in 1837. During the several years her cousin Sarah spent in Northampton, Cochran devoted much of her energy to the girl, supervising her reading, presiding over her education and her domestic training, and introducing her into her own network of kin and friends. Sarah's presence in the Cochran household seems to have provided Martha with an organizing focus; the girl may also have offered her cousin the kind of love and companionship that sustained so many nineteenth-century women.[58]

[56]Briggs, *Reminiscences*, 64. On Martha Cochran's role in Northampton society, see Martha Cochran to Agnes Cochran Higginson, 11 January 1836, 1 January 1837, 17 December 1837, 16 September 1838, and 14 January 1840, Fuller-Higginson Papers, PVMA. On Martha Cochran's efforts to organize a book club, see Mary Dwight Huntington to Frederic Dan Huntington, 20 December 1836, PPHFP, Box 20, Folder 14.

[57]Martha Cochran to Agnes Cochran Higginson, 17 December 1837, Fuller-Higginson Papers, PVMA.

[58]In her letters to her sister Agnes Higginson, Cochran explored feelings of pride, loneliness, frustration, jealousy, and passion, but the affective dimension of her relationship with her young cousin comprised the great silence in her correspondence.

Still, an informally adopted child offered only a temporary, partial solution to Cochran's dilemma. However deep the affection between the girl and her older cousin, Cochran recognized that such a tenuous relationship could not stand in for the socially recognized and legally sanctioned roles of wife, mistress, and mother. A year after adopting Sarah, Cochran acknowledged the spinster's insignificance in a letter to her sister, Agnes Higginson. In 1838, Agnes Higginson's future seemed especially bleak owing to her husbands's unsteady business and a disastrous move to Michigan. Cochran attempted to cheer her sister by rehearsing the benefits of wedded life, rightly observing that present miseries notwithstanding, Higginson would never trade her lot for that of a spinster. Singleness might occasionally appear blessed, but Cochran reminded her sister that "at some future time . . . the tables will be turned." The rewards obtained by keeping her mother's house, maintaining an active social life, and caring for her cousin would pass. Indeed, Cochran anticipated the day when her sister would be "commiserating my lonely childless old age, and I perhaps will be wicked enough in my discontent, to envy you your respected, useful, matronly, & comfortable life."[59]

Of course, unmarried women did not necessarily end their days in isolation and discontent. Particular families respected and cherished the single women who contributed to their lives and their households just as individual women managed to fashion satisfying lives for themselves outside marriage. And as Martha Cochran pointed out, marriage did not guarantee a woman happiness. In the volatile economy of the nineteenth century, it did not even guarantee security. But Cochran correctly understood that marriage offered provincial women their best chance to claim adult status—a status comprised of the interlocking roles of wife, mistress, and mother.[60]

---

[59]Martha Cochran to Agnes Cochran Higginson, 21 October 1838. The Cochran family correspondence offers little specific information about the identity of cousin Sarah, her mother's circumstances, or the duration of her stay. Although Martha Cochran volunteered to raise her cousin in 1836, Sarah apparently did not arrive until the following year. Two years later, the girl was still living in the Cochran's Northampton home, but she disappears from the correspondence after 1839. Her fate, and Martha Cochran's response to her departure, remain unclear. See Martha Cochran to Agnes Cochran Higginson, 16 August 1836, 5 September 1838, and 23 January 1839, Fuller-Higginson Papers, PVMA.

[60]As Lee Chambers-Schiller (*Liberty, a Better Husband*, 75) has noted, "Female reformers Harriet Hunt, Susan B. Anthony, and Catharine Beecher feared that many women married solely to become mistress of their own homes," believing that "their position as proprietress would bring them relief from parental domination, stature as an adult in the community, and influence as wife and mother."

Marriage and Identity

Far from precluding the development of a female self, marriage made the development of such a self possible. Brides took a special pride in the social identities they created for themselves through their marriages. Many women feared that marriage would disrupt their place within their families and towns. Once married, however, they generally found that their new status reinforced their connections to kin and community. Marriage to Dan Huntington tore Elizabeth Phelps away from her parents' Hadley household, but the homesick young woman discovered that her new status strengthened her identification with her beloved mother. When her husband paid her the supreme compliment that she was "likely to please his friends and fill [her] station with propriety," Elizabeth Phelps Huntington could boast that she truly had become her "mother's daughter." Marriage also offered women a privileged place within their communities. Arriving in Springfield as a bride in 1824, Amelia White Peabody noted with pleasure the courtesies extended by her husband's parishioners, who had been as "early as possible in their attentions to their new madam." Peabody had no illusions about the source of her authority as "madam," for she added that the congregation's calls "only prove[d] now their devotion to their <u>minister</u>." There is no reason to believe that she resented her social dependence on her husband or that it caused any friction between them. Amelia White Peabody found great happiness with William Peabody; the letters she wrote to family and friends and the sermon her husband preached after her death all reveal a loving and devoted partnership. But it was not so much the private dimension of her relationship with Peabody as her role as a minister's wife that gave her a stable and well-defined position within her community, perhaps for the first time in her life.[61]

It was not only new brides who structured their identities around their marital status. Especially for women whose husbands' occupations placed them at the core of the provincial middle class, marriage continued to anchor selfhood over the course of a lifetime. Almost ninety years old when she dictated her autobiography, Mary Palmer Tyler's self-presentation centered on her role as the wife of playwright Royall Tyler. In Tyler's narrative, her childhood and adolescence led inevitably to her marriage in 1794. Even before their marriage, Royall

---

[61]Amelia White Peabody to Moses White, 25 September 1824, Everett-Peabody Family Papers, MHS; Elizabeth Phelps Huntington to Elizabeth Porter Phelps, 11 January 1801, PPHFP, Box 13, Folder 1.

Tyler dominates the story of Mary Palmer Tyler's life. She had known Tyler, a family friend almost twenty years her senior, since she was a girl; in her autobiography, she recounts their introduction in great detail, "remembering" snatches of conversation and even the clothing she wore. From that day, she wrote, "I certainly loved him . . . although it was a purely spiritual love for years." And she notes with pride that Royall Tyler had returned her affection, calling her his "little wife." In the years between their first meeting and their marriage, Mary Palmer Tyler's own experiences and adventures serve only as a backdrop, setting the scene for Royall Tyler's next appearance in her life.

After their marriage, her relationship with her husband remained at the core of her identity. When she finally joined her husband in Guilford, Vermont, as a young wife with a new baby ("the realization of my young dream of happiness since my earliest remembrance"), Tyler claimed a matron's place in village social life. But as with Amelia White Peabody, it was Tyler's status as the wife of the town's attorney that guaranteed her social success. She found her neighbors "kind and respectful, devoted to [Royall Tyler] and for his sake disposed to like" her. She wrote of her own social circle, "A more kind, good-hearted, friendly people never lived than they all proved to be, because they were so much attached" to her husband.[62]

Although not yet forty when widowed, Mary Palmer Tyler ended the story of her life with the death of her husband in 1826. Royall Tyler's central place in his wife's autobiography stemmed partly from Mary Tyler's need to rehabilitate her husband for their children and grandchildren; on one level, her life story serves as an apology for a man whose ill-health, depression, and declining fortunes incapacitated him for the last thirteen years of his life. It is also likely that Tyler wished to avoid a painful description of the lean years before and after her husband's death, when she and her daughters struggled to support themselves, supplementing gifts from her sons and sisters with the meager income derived from plain sewing, teaching, and taking in boarders. But Royall Tyler's striking visibility in Mary Tyler's autobiography also speaks to the fundamental importance of marriage in structuring women's adult identities. Although socially prominent, the mother of eleven children, and a published author in her own right, when Mary Palmer Tyler constructed a public self for her children and grandchildren she chose to portray herself as a wife.

The significance of marriage is perhaps most poignantly demonstrated in the one of the letters that Sophia Smith wrote to Aaron Fuller

[62]Tyler, *Grandmother Tyler's Book*, 73–75, 220, 237, 243.

Jr. during their courtship in the early 1840s. Their prospects for a life together were jeopardized by the fact that both were deaf-mutes. Nevertheless, Smith resolutely pressed the case for a union of hands and hearts. She reassured Fuller that she would happily receive his suit, insisting, "I am very glad to have you." Dismissing Fuller's justifiable concerns about the obstacles posed by their shared disability, she wrote that "many both deaf and dumb married." Smith acknowledged that the larger community might scoff at such a match. For the present, she herself declined to announce their plans to her mother and sister, explaining that "they are laugh at me about beau and I and you I wont tell them." Still, Sophia Smith urged Fuller to marry her next fall, for, as she explained, "I am much happy to live with you, as the Lord, than old maid."[63]

Marginalized at once by her deafness and by her singleness, Sophia Smith was especially sensitive to the meaning of marriage. Despite his disability, Aaron Fuller, an itinerant portrait painter, could maintain a socially recognized station. As a deaf-mute spinster, Sophia Smith could not. Whatever sacrifices marriage demanded of her, it embodied her only claim to adulthood, to full selfhood, to female excellence. To publicly claim her womanhood, Sophia Smith had to claim Aaron Fuller Jr. as her husband. It is little wonder that she welcomed the chance to accept him as her "Lord."

Well into the nineteenth century, members of New England's provincial middle class defied the divisions between the public and private, the distinctions between social relations and personal attachments that characterized bourgeois society. Provincial courtships and marriages subjected men and women alike to the authority of the community, implicitly challenging the authority of bourgeois individualism. Within small towns and villages, allegiance to the values of the household economy persisted alongside the development of a market economy and the emergence of a market society. But if this allegiance bound all the members of a community, it placed different and unequal demands on men and women. Certainly, men were enjoined to marry and to marry under the guidance of their friends. But like most traditional societies, provincial towns offered men greater authority within the household and greater autonomy beyond it. The transition to a market society gradually undermined the claims of the community as it expanded men's opportunities in the world beyond towns and villages. But provincial women remained embedded in dense networks of kin

[63]Sophia Smith to Aaron Fuller Jr., 20 July 1841, Fuller-Higginson Papers, PVMA.

and neighbors, dependent on marriage for their very sense of self. Like Sophia Smith, generations of provincial women had little choice but to accept their men as their "lords." They could only echo the sentiments of Elizabeth Phelps Huntington, who wrote of her husband, "Dearest of men, with joy I bear his name, / And pay the duties which his virtues claim."[64]

[64]Elizabeth Phelps Huntington, "Acrostic on the Name of the Revd Dan Huntington," n.d., PPHFP, Box 12, Folder 23.

5

"Old people never believe in Love"

In 1845, Sarah Jane Olcutt complained to her diary, "Old people never believe in Love." For several months, Olcutt, a young woman living in Vermont's Connecticut River Valley, had been thinking about romantic love, the advantages and disadvantages of marriage, and her own marital prospects. By the fall of 1845, she was frustrated by her father's determination to involve himself in her love life—resentful of what she perceived as his overly strict control of her behavior—and baffled by the standard against which he measured her beaux and her prospects. Ignoring his daughter's desire to follow her heart wherever it might lead her, Olcutt insisted that his daughter heed her suitors' religious faith and, especially, their financial prospects. Deferential and obedient, Sarah Jane Olcutt never doubted that her father "moved with the best of motives," that he "thought himself capable of judging," that he was "more experienced in the world." Perhaps his experience had led him to see too much of the "falacity of what the world calls Love." Still, in view of her own youthful excitement, her father seemed boring, cold, pragmatic, ancient, and apparently incapable of "believ[ing] in love."[1]

There is a certain timelessness to Sarah Jane Olcutt's complaint. From one perspective, young people have always been caught up in romance, passion, and the hope of adventure while their elders have done their best to restrain them, urging them to follow the paths of cau-

[1]Diary of Sarah Jane Olcutt, n.d. [ca. autumn 1845], UVM.

127

tion and propriety. But from another perspective, Olcutt's complaint is historically located, signaling a particular moment within the intellectual and cultural history of the New England countryside. Enthralled with a distinctly romantic vision of love and courtship, Sarah Jane Olcutt condemned her father for advocating marriages based not on the sentimental stirrings of the heart but on the pragmatic concerns of the household. She condemned him for discounting love altogether. But it is more likely that the older man simply believed in love of a different sort.

Provincial Critique of Romantic Love

For much of the antebellum period, provincial New Englanders measured potential mates not against the notoriously unreliable standards of romantic love but against the values and requirements of the household economy. Wary of mere infatuation, aware that the charms of youth passed all too quickly, these men and women sought in their spouses the more enduring qualities of "virtue" and "character." Men's character and women's virtue were not abstract moral qualities. Instead, they took shape in the particular standards and practices of the household economy. Character was almost indistinguishable from the ability to provide a competency and virtue derived less from chastity than from domestic accomplishments. Tender feelings and mutual sympathy could not be dismissed, but a man's chances of providing a competency and a woman's ability to act as a helpmeet also merited considerable attention. At least until the 1840s, the persistence of these standards checked the spread of a bourgeois ideal of romantic love among provincial men and women. As numerous historians and literary critics have pointed out, the ideology of romantic love demanded that the heart rather than the head govern the choice of a spouse. According to the tenets of nineteenth-century romantic love, the heart was moved by the loved one's essence, a unique combination of personal qualities that defined each person. Far from depending on one's ability to fulfill social roles, romantic love was instead predicated on men's and women's ability to transcend and escape those roles.[2] Conceptions of romantic love compelled men and women to create and

[2]Numerous historians have emphasized the growing influence of the ideal of romantic love from the seventeenth through the nineteenth centuries. Ellen Rothman, for example, has suggested that between 1780 and 1840, middle-class men and women came to see romantic love rather than friendship as the primary requirement for marriage. She suggests that although they remained suspicious of "romantic love" and "passion" per se, they ide-

then reveal a "true" self, a self hitherto submerged beneath social conventions.[3]

Character and virtue, on the other hand, did not reside in any particular person but were more generally found in upstanding men and women. Provincial New Englanders never suggested that individuals were interchangeable, but their attitudes toward courtship and marriage reveal deep doubts that the charms of any one person, however enchanting, warranted risking one's future or disrupting the community order. In the end, of course, men and women loved each other—or not—as individuals. Yet before the 1850s, the decision to join one's fate to another's was more often dictated by the principles of what might be called reciprocal marriage than by the passions and sentiments of romantic love.[4] If men and women balked at joining hands without hearts, as Ellen Rothman has observed, they were equally reluctant to join hands without prospects—prospects best confirmed in character and virtue.

Thus William Czar Bradley of Westminster, Vermont, was glad to hear that the "industrious & useful" Miss Parker was to marry the "diligent, worthy" Mr. Deming. He urged his teenage daughter, Elizabeth, to follow their example by rejecting "the graces of youth which will soon wear away" in favor of "those estimable qualities of industry,

---

alized romantic love without naming it, choosing to define true love through an elaborate series of "negative calculations." See Ellen K. Rothman, *Hands and Hearts: A History of Courtship in America* (New York: Basic Books, 1984), 31–44. On the rise of romantic love in the United States, see Herman R. Lantz et al., "Pre-Industrial Patterns in the Colonial Family in America: A Content Analysis of Colonial Magazines," *American Sociological Review* (1968): 413–26; Nancy F. Cott, "Eighteenth-Century Family and Social Life Revealed in Massachusetts Divorce Records," *Journal of Social History* (1976): 20–43, and *Bonds of Womanhood: "Woman's Sphere" in New England, 1780–1835* (New Haven, Conn.: Yale University Press, 1977), 77–79; Laurel Thatcher Ulrich, *Good Wives: Image and Reality in the Lives of Women in Northern New England, 1650–1750* (New York: Oxford University Press, 1983), 113–25; and especially Karen Lystra, *Searching the Heart: Women, Men, and Romantic Love in Nineteenth-Century America* (New York: Oxford University Press, 1989), and Steven Seidman, *Romantic Longings: Love in America, 1830–1980* (New York: Routledge, 1991).

[3]Karen Lystra, *Searching the Heart*, 30, 270n 54, makes a similar argument. As Lystra recognizes, despite the emphasis on self-expression and romantic love as an "anti-role," the nineteenth-century self "was its own kind of role."

[4]This ideal is similar to that described by John Mack Faragher, *Women and Men on the Overland Trail* (New Haven, Conn.: Yale University Press, 1979), 180, 155–58. Finding "little appreciation of companionate values," Faragher suggested that frontier couples elevated reciprocity over romantic love, aspiring to "a dutiful and responsible partnership of labor, from which grew feelings of connection and affection." The continuity between household and homestead is suggested by Faragher's discussion of "The Young Man Who Wouldn't Hoe His Corn." The ballad, which warns young women away from lazy suitors, was carried from New England to Ohio, and from Ohio throughout the Midwest.

neatness, good sense and good temper which last long and render the evening of life comfortable and happy."[5] Young men and women generally shared Bradley's sober assumptions. Edward Dickinson lectured Emily Norcross at great length on the duties and responsibilities that accompanied marriage. Several weeks before they were to be wed in 1828, he advised, "Let us prepare for a life of rational happiness," for he did not "expect a life of pleasure, as some call it." Instead, he hoped that they would find each other "useful and successful" and that "each [would] be an ornament in society." Marcus Goodell shared Dickinson's pragmatism if not his lofty rhetoric. In 1837, Goodell recalled that after managing to buy a farm, "I thot I must git a wife and I found one I thot would do for me."[6]

Not all men approached their wedding days so coolly. The same year that Dickinson expounded rational happiness to Emily Norcross, Ebenezer Snell wrote poetry to Sabra Clark. In tiny print, delicately scrolled into the shape of an elaborate love knot, Snell wrote that although separated by distance, he and Clark were joined in mind and heart:

> . . . both of us gaze on the self-same star,
> And we bless it o'er and o'er;
> Forgetting, Alas! how lone we are,
> Thus meeting in thought once more—

The quiet astronomer had discovered, to his chagrin, that "a few hours pass . . . more pleasantly in her society than even of seeking the longitudes of sun and moon," for his fiancée could "scatter . . . the figures finely." But Snell was not drawn to Clark because she could distract him from his work; in fact, the opposite was true. He had chosen Sabra because she was "modest, amiable, tender-hearted, benevolent, . . . very retiring," energetic and "well-educated in domestic affairs," not because she was wealthy, brilliant, or beautiful.[7]

In general, provincial women recorded their assessments of

[5]William Czar Bradley to Elizabeth Bradley, 25 June 1814, Sarah Merry Bradley Gamble Papers, SL.

[6]Marcus Goodell to Ira Chafee Goodell, 30 April 1837, Goodell Family Papers, JL; Edward Dickinson to Emily Norcross, 19 March 1828, in Vivian R. Pollack, ed., *A Poet's Parents: The Courtship Letters of Emily Norcross and Edward Dickinson* (Chapel Hill: University of North Carolina Press, 1988), 196.

[7]See Ebenezer Strong Snell to Tirzah Strong Snell, 12 July 1825 and 21 July 1827, Box 2, Folder 4; "Love Knot Poem," ca. 1828, typescript, Box 2, Folder 1, Snell Family Papers, ACASC. Edward Dickinson similarly located the "excellence of female character" in "good sense, improved by reading & observation, and an acquaintance with the world, an amiable

courtship less frequently, and with less detail, than did their men. If antebellum culture granted women the authority to publish poetry, novels, and didactic literature on the subject, within particular relationships men retained the right to define the implications of courtship and the meaning of marriage.[8] Yet the surviving evidence suggests that women shared their suitors' pragmatic concerns. Women's economic vulnerability demanded that they pay close attention to a man's prospects. When twenty-year-old Lizzie Cochran agreed to marry Francis Skinner despite the considerable difference in their ages, she pointed out that "Mr. S" could tutor her in self-government, music, and drawing, that he was even tempered, of "compatible character" and "youthful in his feelings." And it did not hurt that Skinner, head of a successful Boston dry goods house, was "what the world calls, rich" and was "involved in very active and lucrative business."[9] Indeed, a woman who followed her heart without sufficient regard for a man's chances invited comment. Amelia Tyler was relieved and delighted to learn that, at the age of forty-seven, her brother William had finally proposed to a former sweetheart. Unfortunately, money was not among the many assets William Tyler would bring to his new home. Writing to welcome her future sister-in-law to the family, Tyler could not help confessing that she "could wish him richer for your sake." Other matches prompted less charitable remarks. When one Samuel Willard of Deerfield contrived to win the hand of a "lady of very respectable rank" in 1848, Hattie Fuller observed that "everyone is surprised she could fancy him."[10]

Both men and women acknowledged the connections between a man's "character," his "prospects," and his desirability as a beau.

---

disposition, & a thorough knowledge of domestic economy, and a desire to render all about her happy." Edward Dickinson to Emily Norcross, 22 October 1826, in *Poet's Parents*, 50.

[8]Ellen Rothman has found this to be true for antebellum men and women throughout New England and the Midwest, but she accounts for the difference by suggesting that men and women acted in accord with "prevailing stereotypes" that encouraged women to "embody rather than articulate the sentimental ideal . . . while men . . . felt free to offer 'learned and loving counsel on . . . womanly culture' in letters to their fiancées." On the contrary, I would argue that the explosion of antebellum women's writing on precisely these subjects suggests that "prevailing stereotypes" did grant women the authority to articulate the sentimental ideal, but that prevailing gender relations did not allow them the power to articulate that ideal to specific men within particular relationships. Rothman, *Hands and Hearts*, 11.

[9]Lizzie Cochran to Agnes Cochran Higginson, 14 July 1839, and Martha Cochran to Agnes Cochran Higginson, 19 May 1839, Fuller-Higginson Papers, PVMA.

[10]Hattie Fuller to George Fuller, 2 April 1848, Fuller-Higginson Papers, PVMA. Amelia Sophia Tyler to Miss Etheridge, 23 November 1849, Royall Tyler Collection, Gift of Helen Tyler Brown, VHS.

Again, it was Edward Dickinson, that unflagging advocate of provincial mores, who drove the point home:

> All young men commencing business, have a character to form for themselves. And tho' the opportunities of different individuals have been various, & their experience in business very unequal, and some idea can almost always be formed of a man's business talents, yet a man's success must depend on himself, and it is the safest to wait till the result is seen.[11]

As Dickinson observed, no respectable man would persuade a young woman to leave her "present happy situation" until reasonably certain that it "would not be diminished by the proposed change," and no thoughtful woman would accept such an offer.[12]

It is hardly surprising that provincial New Englanders placed so little stock in romantic love. As they understood it, the central purpose of marriage was not to secure personal fulfillment but to establish a household and reproduce the social order. Realizing themselves primarily through their social roles—roles that underscored the corporate dimension of provincial society—they found little to admire in the profound individualism that underlie notions of romantic love, with its emphasis on the discrepancy between the social and the true self. But it was provincial women, keenly aware that shared labor did not necessarily translate into shared power, who voiced the most compelling critique of romantic love.

As numerous women observed in both their public and private writings, romantic love only served to compound women's vulnerability within New England's towns and villages and within the household itself. Recapitulating the conventions of seduction novels, they worried about the vulnerability of young women in the hands of rogues and rakes. Addled by flattery and fashion, almost any woman could succumb. But the danger was not that women would succumb to illicit sexual liaisons. Instead, women worried that their daughters and sisters would find themselves seduced into disastrous marriages. Women well knew that economic dependence left them far more vulnerable

[11]Edward Dickinson to Emily Norcross, 22 October 1826, in *Poet's Parents*, 49. For Dickinson, "character" and "prospects" were indistinguishable from masculinity and the commitment to a profession. On rural New Englanders' connection of character and financial success, see the discussion of Lewis Tappan's attempt to provide New York creditors with "information about reputations in bulk and at a distance," in Christopher Clark, *The Roots of Rural Capitalism: Western Massachusetts, 1780–1860.* (Ithaca, N.Y.: Cornell University Press, 1990), 214–20.
[12]*Poet's Parents*, 49.

than their brothers to the consequences of a bad marriage. Because their power during courtship was largely defensive, enabling them to accept or reject specific suitors but denying them the freedom to extend their own offers, their ability to secure their own futures was further diminished. Accordingly, a man who wished to win a young woman's hand first had to win her confidence. This confidence was more often inspired by the kind of steadiness revealed in Edward Dickinson's references and "character" than by promises of undying affection.[13]

In fact, a man possessed by romantic love was the cause of serious concern for provincial women. Emily Norcross frowned on Solomon Warriner's attempts to woo her cousin, Olivia Flynt. At first, the young man seemed a likely candidate for marriage: He was a merchant, a militia officer, a soloist with the Springfield Handel and Haydn Society, and a good friend of her own fiancé. But as the romance progressed, his too-frequent visits to Monson and his fervent admiration for Olivia Flynt and her family gave rise to the suspicion that he pursued Flynt with more passion than wisdom.[14] Even after a man demonstrated his seriousness, the least hint of romantic sentiments could bring anxiety to the surface once again. An Enfield, Massachusetts, schoolteacher had assured herself of her beau's solemn interest before accepting his proposal. But during their engagement she confessed to "many doubts" about the "feeling which . . . prompted [his] conduct." Alarmed, she wondered whether he had felt "merely a passion or the prompting of a purer feeling."[15] From the perspective of many women, these concerns appeared entirely reasonable. The volatile and capricious passions that grew out of romantic attachments threatened the happiness and the prosperity of the provincial household. More to the point, such passions ultimately proved inimical to the stability women sought in marriage.

At the same time that they condemned romantic love's destructive power, provincial women and men conceded that it held a strong

[13]Ellen Rothman's *Hands and Hearts* describes women's reactive position in courtship. This is not to suggest that courtship posed no difficulties for men; Rothman has convincingly demonstrated men's emotional vulnerability during nineteenth-century courtship. Nevertheless, the difference between men's and women's perspective on courtship is the difference between emotional and social vulnerability.

[14]Emily Norcross to Edward Dickinson, 14 September 1827, in *Poet's Parents*, 134. Edward Dickinson shared his fiancée's assessment of Warriner's suit, which he feared was based on "wild passion" rather than "rational esteem." In Dickinson's eyes, Warriner compounded his sins by neglecting his business responsibilities to pursue Flynt. See Edward Dickinson to Emily Norcross, 10 December 1827 and 19 March 1828, and Emily Norcross to Edward Dickinson, 6 March 1828, in *Poet's Parents*, 158, 192, 195–96.

[15]Lestina [?] to Cyrus Wheeler, 6 June 185[?], Wheeler Family Papers, MS-60, VHS.

appeal for many young women. Left to their own devices, young women might be dazzled by the shallow charms of a romantic beau, overlooking the homespun virtues of the provincial suitor. *The Ladies' Monitor*, a didactic poem written by Vermonter Thomas Fessenden in 1818, cautioned young women against this danger. Written as a dialogue between a gullible country maiden fascinated by fashionable dandies and an older male mentor, the poem acknowledged the power of romantic fantasies even as it defended the plain habits of a republican yeomanry. As the young woman pointed out, the enlightened yeoman might have been the pillar of the republic, but he made an awful beau:

> His clothes of some old fashion'd taylors fangling
> Round his swart carcase shiver loose and dangling, . . .
> O could you see him at our country dances,
> Clumsy, but coltlike, how the creature prances![16]

A girl "tremble[d]" to think that the eager oaf might "pounce on her as a partner for a prance." The mentor could not deny that such men made inept suitors but observed that the same sincerity that made awkward lovers made trustworthy husbands.

Although Fessenden faulted his young listener for succumbing to the spell of fashion, provincial women were more likely to direct the blame at men. They did not doubt that their daughters and sisters could be swayed by the pleasure of romantic attachments. They suggested that young women's folly stemmed more from youthful inexperience than from some feminine predisposition to fancy. The problem was not that girlish vanity prevented women from seeing past a man's rough edges but that masculine duplicity prevented a women from measuring a man's true worth.

Several years before Fanny Negus wed Aaron Fuller, her mother worried that the high-spirited girl had been beguiled by Nathaniel Cheney, a close friend of Fanny's brothers. Full of romance, Cheney assured Fanny that she alone could "cheer" him through "every scene of fatigue and distress," for she embodied "all that my fond heart ever wished for in <u>lovely female</u>." Should his love for her ever diminish, it would be a sure sign that he had "degenerated into chill and unfeeling ideotism." Indeed, Cheney's passion was stronger than his piety. Flouting the wisdom of "learned prelates," Cheney went so far as to pro-

---

[16]Thomas G. Fessenden, *The Ladies' Monitor: A Poem* (Bellows Falls, Vt.: Bill Blake & Co., 1818), 34.

claim that there was no need of Fanny's "<u>heart being changed</u>" to render her perfect. Justifying this outpouring of passion, he wrote in 1819 that he was "not yet weary enough of this world . . . to believe there are no pleasures to be innocently enjoyed, even in this life." It is not surprising that such pretty words could dazzle a naive teenager from Petersham, Massachusetts, and Fanny Negus was impressed enough that she consented to marry Cheney.[17]

It is not clear how Fanny's family and friends regarded her courtship, but by the following summer, Cheney had exhausted the goodwill of Fanny's mother. From the perspective of Mrs. Negus, Cheney's unabashed romanticism and his reluctance to set a wedding date provoked serious questions about his intentions. Perhaps to test his sincerity, she publicly questioned Cheney's merits as a suitor and as a man, knowing that her comments would eventually find their way back to Cheney's ears. As Fanny's brother-in-law recounted, "she in her blunt way made some observations about him, and said she did not doubt but that you might have Mr. Clark of Barre and be married immediately. Your Aunt Prudence being present seconded the opinion." Acknowledging the power of provincial gossip, the brother-in-law admitted that "the above might have been told Mr. C. and perhaps a little added." When he heard Mrs. Negus's remarks, Cheney dashed off an outraged letter to the unsuspecting Fanny, who was then boarding in Greenfield, Massachusetts. Cheney's letter has not survived, but it seems to have raised substantial doubts as to the constancy of his affections. If Fanny did not share her mother's reservations before Cheney's outburst, she certainly did thereafter. Three months later, Fanny Negus commenced married life not with the impetuous Nathaniel Cheney but with the steady Aaron Fuller.[18]

Fanny Negus chanced to discover Nathaniel Cheney's true character before it was too late. Surely other, less fortunate women suffered the consequences of their ignorance. Antebellum didactic literature, popular wisdom, and village gossip all confirmed that romantic love might lead women to misfortune, trapping them in marriages with drunkards and spendthrifts or with men who were godless, lazy, or cruel. Under

[17]Nathaniel Cheney to Fanny Negus, 25 August 1819 and 18 October 1819, Fuller-Higginson Papers, PVMA.

[18]Cheney's angry letter and the incident that prompted it are discussed in a letter from Jonas Howe to Fanny Negus, 27 June 1820, Fuller-Higginson Papers, PVMA. The significance of gossip in enforcing community mores is discussed in Karen V. Hansen, *A Very Social Time: Crafting Community in Antebellum New England* (Berkeley: University of California Press, 1994), 114–36; Kathleen M. Brown, *Good Wives, Nasty Wenches, and Anxious Patriarchs: Gender, Race, and Power in Colonial Virginia* (Chapel Hill: University of North Carolina Press, 1996), 306–18; Ulrich, *Good Wives*, 55–57.

extraordinary circumstances, passionate courtships produced illegitimate children, grieving parents, and even murders and suicides.[19] But if romantic love occasionally led to disaster, it always led to disappointment, for one of the chief dangers was that it allowed women the illusion of power over men—an illusion sharply at odds with the gender relations embodied in reciprocal marriage and in the household economy generally. Whatever leverage women enjoyed as sweethearts they quickly lost as wives. In the absence of a fully developed ideology of separate spheres to grant women influence over their children and their homes if not their husbands, disillusionment was both inevitable and severe.

Such is the lesson in the song "Old Story over Again," copied by Vermonter Elizabeth Bradley into her commonplace book in 1825. In the song, a female narrator recalls that when she was young, her mother cautioned her against the duplicity of men and the false promises of romantic love. But long, tedious lectures made no impression on the girl, who was eager to find a lover. Not until after her wedding did she learn that her romantic ideal was only a fantasy, her devoted beau merely a demanding husband. Like other women, she discovered that

> The lovers forsake us, the husbands remain;
> Our vanity's check'd
> And we ne'er can expect
> They will tell us the old story over again.

The woman had ignored her mother's advice only to repeat her experience years later:

> Now teaching in turn,
> what I never could learn,
> I find, like my mother, my lessons all vain,
> Men ever deceive,
> Silly maidens believe,
> And still 'tis the old story over again.[20]

Yet the narrator did not really blame herself, or other young women, for this state of affairs. A wise mother might warn her daughter, "Never listen to men!" But, as the narrator replied, "Who should [girls] listen to then?" When approached by forlorn suitors, whose deep and tender

[19]Frances Cogan, *The All-American Girl: The Ideal of Real Womanhood in Mid-Nineteenth-Century America* (Athens: University of Georgia Press, 1989).

[20]"The Old Story over Again," in 1825 Commonplace Book of Elizabeth Bradley [Dorr], Sarah Merry (Bradley) Gamble Papers, SL.

sentiments moved them to "crocodile tears," what recourse did "poor maidens" have, "but [to] keep them alive when they swear they must die?" Reared to respect and to accommodate men, inexperienced girls found it understandably difficult to question the authority of their suitors, especially when faced with such flattering attentions. As the "Old Story" made clear, motherly wisdom and friendly supervision could not always ensure that young women choose suitable husbands or that they approach marriage with appropriate and realistic expectations. Even in New England's rural towns and villages, young women were never entirely safe from the snare of romantic entanglements.

Religion and Romance

To counter these temptations, women frequently turned time and again to the tenets of Protestant Christianity. For two hundred years, Protestant divines had equated romantic love with idolatry, even as they compared the love that joined believer and Christ to that which joined husband and wife.[21] While this vision of Christian marriage had a long history, it assumed a new urgency in the minds and writings of antebellum provincial women in the 1830s and 1840s. They reinforced the provincial ideology of reciprocal love with a complementary tradition that urged men and women to look not to each other but to Christ for solace and that yoked temporal struggles to spiritual ones. If warnings about the hazards of romantic love and the realities of provincial marriage seemed to portend a future of dreary responsibility, promises of higher purposes and rewards proved far more compelling.

Especially in the years around the Second Great Awakening, women urged one another to consider their souls before they considered their hearts. In the best marriages, men and women sustained each other through their spiritual trials, holding each other to the path of righteousness. The shared religious struggle necessary to secure eternal life mirrored the shared labor necessary to maintain the household. Provincial women happily acknowledged that work and faith could forge powerful bonds between husbands and wives. Like their ministers,

[21]See Susan Juster, *Disorderly Women: Sexual Politics and Evangelicalism in Revolutionary New England* (Ithaca, N.Y.: Cornell University Press, 1994); Richard Godbeer, " 'Love Raptures': Marital, Romantic, and Erotic Images of Jesus Christ in Puritan New England, 1670–1730," *New England Quarterly* (1994): 355–87; Seidman, *Romantic Longings*, 39–61; Amanda Porterfield, *Female Piety in Puritan New England: The Emergence of Religious Humanism* (New York: Oxford University Press, 1992); Lystra, *Searching the Heart*, 239–40; Ulrich, *Good Wives*, 106–109; and Edmund S. Morgan, *The Puritan Family* (New York: Harper & Row, 1966).

however they warned one another not to allow this intimacy to become the primary end in a marriage. In 1820, a Massachusetts woman, blessed with deep faith and a devout husband, discovered that domestic "prosperity" proved the "Christian's greatest trial." To her dismay, she found that "when a merciful God is showering upon us his richest blessings, we should be most proud to forget him."[22] The marriage infused with Christian piety, like the marriage shaped by reciprocal love, ultimately subjected the needs and desires of the individual to a larger purpose.

One Massachusetts writer extended this notion to its logical conclusion when she offered readers of the *Hampshire Gazette* a "true sketch" of Susan Burnett.[23] In this 1838 story, Susan, a girl of "fine and deep sensibilities," fell in love with Richard Bentley, a poor but lively orphan who had been her constant companion from childhood. Despite their "deep and mutual attachment," the two young people chose to delay their courtship in deference to Susan's parents, who hoped their daughter might marry into propertied respectability. Like many antebellum men, Richard was forced to leave his home to secure his fortune, and like many antebellum couples faced with separation, Richard and Susan continued their courtship through the mail, exchanging letters that only strengthened their commitment to each other. When the young man returned to the Burnetts two years later, his efforts were pronounced a success: He had acquired both capital and the approval of Susan's parents. Unfortunately, Richard had business to conclude, and he left the Burnetts again, promising to return and wed Susan at the end of the year. During this final absence, Susan received no word from Richard. Overcome by worry and grief, she wondered at the cause of his long silence: She imagined embarrassing financial setbacks, letters lost in the unreliable postal system, and even Richard's death, for she could not bear to think him untrue.

As the months passed, Susan sank into despair, roused only by the death of a close friend. Diverted from her own troubles, Susan realized "the emptiness of the world and the preciousness of humble piety," understanding for the first time that peace lay not with her lover but with her God. After her friend's funeral, Susan's faith deepened, and she began to hope that she had experienced the "change of heart" that alone "can fit the soul for heaven." Her "expectations of worldly happiness had become moderate and rational" in the years that followed, "but her hope of heaven was strong and bright." One day, Susan

[22]Eliza S. Gunnell to Weltha Brown, 17 May 1820, Hooker Collection, SL.

[23]Alphonse, "Susan Burnett—a true sketch," *Hampshire Gazette*, 25 August 1838.

received another proposal, this one "unexpected and undeserved," from a "respectable and pious gentleman" she had known since childhood. Untroubled by Susan's admission that she could never love him as she had once loved another, the unnamed gentleman persisted and the two were married. Significantly, Susan did not come to regret her loveless match, nor did she "grow to love" her husband, recognizing the value of his steady devotion measured against Richard Bentley's fleeting charms. Indeed, the author of "Susan Burnett" makes clear that the happiness of Susan's marriage is beside the point. At the conclusion of her story, "Alphonse" reminded her readers that

> [Susan's] affections are now fixed upon other and higher objects; and the gloom occasionally excited by a recollection of the past is soon dissipated by the glorious and sustaining power of religious hope. Her temper is for the most part cheerful, and her days pass smoothly in the quietude and peace of domestic life.[24]

However many women attempted to emulate Susan Burnett's serene disregard for personal happiness, few succeeded. If provincial women stopped short of setting the pleasures of this world over those of the next, even the most pious were unwilling to abandon them altogether. In ideal circumstances, religious faith could be joined to marital satisfaction. For example, Massachusetts friends Orra White, Lucy Fowler, and Betsey Parsons hoped that Christian faith and practice might also lead to marital peace. Their sentiments were summed up in a poem that the married Parsons urged "every married lady . . . to have by heart" and that White copied for Fowler as a wedding gift in 1820. The untitled poem warned that the crosses of a lifetime could not be borne by love alone: A bride should not trust her "youthful heart," for she "must divine assistance have / To act a prudent part." But given that religious devotion formed the "strongest bond" between husband and wife, a woman who wished for a happy union would do well to keep "heaven the object of [her] choice." A woman might even extend conjugal happiness into eternity, for the saved could expect to "part in death / To meet with joy again."[25]

Reminding women that the cares of marriage were fleeting but that the rewards of heaven were eternal, religion no doubt made conjugal trials easier to bear. But religion also offered women the hope of

[24]Ibid.
[25]Orra White [Hitchcock] to Lucy Fowler, 19 February 1820, Edward and Orra White Hitchcock Papers, Box 25, Folder 13, ACASC.

improving their temporal condition. Throughout the antebellum period, sermonic and prescriptive literature linked women's social status to their membership in a Christian civilization. Comparing New England women to the "heathen" women of the Middle and Far East, ministers and didactic writers argued that it was only the Christian recognition of men's and women's spiritual equality that granted women a measure of social equality and moral authority within Western culture.[26] Women extended the logic of this formulation from assessments of exotic "Hindoo" and Muslim women to the households of the Connecticut River Valley. After all, if Woman flourished only amidst the institutions and values of a Christian society, surely women would fare better under the roofs of Christian husbands. Eliza Gunnell congratulated her friend for deciding to wed a Christian, observing that "if he had not been a man of piety what a hindrance would it have been to you through this pilgrimage."[27]

A good marriage required that husbands join their wives at the feet of the Savior. Ideally, they did so of their own accord. But many men needed women's encouragement—or prodding. Women pulled their men to conversion during courtship just as they did during revivals.[28] Through courtship, the influence that women exercised over their men during the peak of revival could be extended into more ordinary seasons. On one level, conversion (and evidence of religious faith more generally) was simply another proof of a man's character, of his potential as a husband. Yet unlike the demonstration of a man's prospects, conversion was a test that could work to increase women's authority in courtship, and perhaps marriage.

Consider the courtship of Clarissa Warner and Asel Clark. Before she accepted Clark's proposal, Warner earnestly searched her heart to ensure that her decision was based on "calm judgement" rather than "imagination and passions." But after agreeing to wed the young farmer, Warner devoted far less attention to her heart than to his. She

[26]See, for example, Almira Selden, *Effusions of the Heart: Contained in a Number of Original Poetical Pieces, on Varying Subjects* (Bennington, Vt.: Darius Clark, 1820), 121. See also Cott, *Bonds of Womanhood*, 130–32.

[27]Eliza S. Gunnell to Weltha Brown, 17 May 1820, Hooker Collection, SL. Nancy Cott (*Bonds of Womanhood*, 192) has also speculated on the effect of women's increasing prominence in Protestant congregations, on the "feminization of religion," and on antebellum marriages: "In how many marriages did this difference in commitment provoke friction—diminution of respect—or despair?"

[28]On women's religious influence over their men during revivals, see especially Mary P. Ryan, *Cradle of the Middle Class: The Family in Oneida County, New York, 1790–1865* (New York: Cambridge University Press, 1983).

was deeply troubled by his failure to experience a saving grace, and perhaps more troubled still by his general indifference to conversion. She wanted him to seek Christ before their marriage; he was content to let her lead him to the Savior afterward. She saw conversion as the only guarantee of eternal salvation; he saw it simply as a way of providing her with "unspeakable pleasure."[29] In the summer following their betrothal, religion—or Clark's lack there of—became an issue of contention between the two. But it was not simply Asel Clark's soul that was at stake. Although Warner desperately wanted Clark to give himself to Christ, her insistence on the religious dimension of their marriage also served to buttress her authority to define the values expressed by marriage in general and her relationship with Clark in particular. Unless Clark could be brought to share her faith, Warner worried that their love would deteriorate into mere romance. Warner wanted a husband who would be a spiritual helpmeet. She explained to Clark, "I hope to secure in you a friend who will guide me in reference to another world, a friend who will pray for me and with me, one who will stimulate me by a holy example, warn me in temptation, and in every way assist me in my pilgrimage to the skies." But before Asel Clark could proclaim himself Warner's spiritual partner, he had to submit to Christ. By extension, he also had to submit to Clarissa Warner's "most earnest desire" that he be "brought to see clearly the love of the Savior."[30]

Warner's tenacity did not sit well with Clark. Chafing under her constant prodding, he tried to beat her at her own game. He questioned the authenticity of her faith and challenged her own emphasis on feelings as the best measure of Christian faith. Surely the Christian's "first object" was "to build up the Redeemer's Kingdom, to glorify God, & save a soul from death," he suggested. Under the circumstances, Warner's overzealous pursuit of a single soul seemed almost petty. "Justly reproved," Clarissa Warner agreed that a "true Christian" desired the conversion of all. But she refused to concede the larger point, vigorously defending her interest in Clark's conversion both as a Christian and as his prospective wife. Only if Clark actively sought the Redeemer could she be certain that "we are not building our hopes, of domestic happiness in the flowery regions of imagination but are hoping our hearts may be united in love, sanctified by grace." The message was clear. It is not certain whether Asel Clark converted before he

[29]Asel Clark to Clarissa Warner, 26 April 1834, Clark-Warner Papers, SSC.
[30]Clarissa Warner to Asel Clark, 16 July 1834, Clark-Warner Papers, SSC.

wed Clarissa Warner, but he never again challenged either her spiritual integrity or her right to define their relationship.[31]

In a context that encouraged women to assume new degrees of responsibility for their men's souls, evangelical Protestantism also offered women a way to articulate and to privilege individual aspirations.[32] Compare Clarissa Warner to Emily Norcross. When Norcross wanted to delay marriage, she cited her father's inclinations and her family's needs, invoking the values of the household economy. Although Norcross successfully postponed her wedding, her arguments rested on external sources of authority. In contrast, Warner's arguments shifted the locus of authority to her particular vision of Christian faith and duty and, ultimately, to her own subjectivity. When Clarissa Warner singled out religious rebirth as a precondition for marriage, she drew upon conventions that cast women as conduits of conversion. But in casting herself as both the judge of her fiancé's spiritual struggle and the reward for a successful struggle, she also carved out some claim to women's special moral and religious influence. As Clark discovered, the test of his faith hinged upon an examination of sentiments and subjectivity. And Warner made it clear that at least until he converted, her subjectivity trumped his. With growing frequency, provincial women like Clarissa Warner expanded religious conceptions of the "heart" to establish both temporal and religious influence, claiming authority within their households, churches, and communities as Christians and as women.

From the 1840s, women of the provincial middle class exacted new degrees of authority in their relations with men not simply on the basis of their Christian sensibilities but in the name of romantic love itself. To a large extent, this shift derived from changes and tensions within antebellum Protestantism itself, within what one historian has termed "economies of religious experience."[33] Clarissa Warner's valorization of subjectivity in general and feminine subjectivity in particular was but one manifestation of a broad series of shifts within the religious culture of the early republic. Since the eighteenth century, New England's theologians had developed a language of affections to describe

[31]Clarissa Warner to Asel Clark, 16 July 1834 and 2 May 1834, and Asel Clark to Clarissa Warner, 26 April 1834, Clark-Warner Papers, SSC.

[32]As Susan Juster (*Disorderly Women*, 180–208) points out, in the early republic, evangelical conversion required women to step outside the bonds of interdependence to establish an autonomous relationship with God.

[33]Richard Rabinowitz, *The Spiritual Self in Everyday Life* (Boston: Northeastern University Press, 1989).

the relations between God and man as well and the ties that bound communities of believers. By the nineteenth century, this language was associated with female believers, whose conversion narratives tell stories of love and betrayal and cast God as the loving father, the caring brother. This moment also marked a new gendering of religious faith. As Susan Juster has argued, as women spoke of God in the language of love, men spoke of God in the language of reason.[34] Over the first half of the nineteenth century, as the pews of Protestant churches increasingly filled with women, this emphasis on sentiment and sensibility extended beyond female believers to reshape Protestantism itself.[35]

To be sure, this shift was neither quick nor straightforward. It unfolded differently in Boston than in the remote corners of the hill country; it varied among Baptists, Congregationalists, Unitarians, and Presbyterians. And its meaning varied among generations and genders, as the legendary struggles of the Beecher clan suggest. Still, by the 1840s, this broadly based endorsement of feeling cast woman, rather than man, as the exemplar of piety. It also effectively narrowed the distance between the divine and the human. Liberal Protestants, in particular, sought to discover and cultivate the similarities between humanity and Christ rather than to map the chasm that separated them. Ultimately, they aspired to an intimate personal relationship with a God they increasingly imagined in human form.[36]

This gradual change in theology and practice was buttressed by the marriage of Protestantism and refinement. By the 1840s, as Richard Bushman has demonstrated, refinement had spread from Unitarians, Congregationalists, and Espiscopalians to more conservative, evangelical denominations. This genteel faith manifested itself in the careful cultivation of refined sensibilities as well as in gracefully designed churches.[37] Ministers not only excused but encouraged Christians'

[34]As Susan Juster (*Disorderly Women*) observes, this love was purged of the erotic power that characterized eighteenth-century evangelical women's discourse.

[35]On the "feminization" of American religion, see Lisa MacFarlane, "Resurrecting Man: Desire and *The Damnation of Theron Ware*," in *A Mighty Baptism: Race, Gender, and the Creation of American Protestantism*, ed. Susan Juster and Lisa MacFarlane (Ithaca, N.Y.: Cornell University Press, 1996), 65–80; Barbara Epstein, *Politics of Domesticity: Women, Evangelicalism, and Temperance in Nineteenth-Century America* (Middletown, Conn.: Wesleyan University Press, 1981); Barbara Welter, "The Feminization of American Religion"; and Ann Douglas, *Ann Douglas: The Feminization of American Culture* (New York: Avon Books, 1977).

[36]Rabinowitz, *The Spiritual Self in Everyday Life*, 184–85, 186, 218.

[37]Richard L. Bushman, *The Refinement of America: Persons, Houses, Cities* (New York-Knopf), 313–52.

attention to matters of taste and decorum. A refined sensibility—a sensitivity to experience and feeling—stood as both the performance and proof of Christian morality. If the move toward a theology of feeling recast God in more human form, the refinement of religious faith and practice made humans more celestial.

Cutting across denominational lines, these developments within elite and middle-class religious culture opened the door to romantic love. Members of the provincial middle class began to manipulate an extensive language of religious emotion to express their desire for lovers as well as their desire for Christ. One Massachusetts woman recalled that she and her confidantes daydreamed about husbands who would be "all perfection"; when one of her school friends became engaged, she imagined that her friend had found "all that she could pray for." In 1847, another young woman, infatuated with a man she had noticed at church, described his indifference to her after a choir sing as her "spirit's bitterest pain." Merging religious language and practice with a romantic sensibility, she relegated Christian devotion to the service of earthly love.[38]

More striking still is H. S. Kelsey's memorial of his courtship with Martha Snell. Recalling a visit before Snell's death, he fondly described their "hours of communion with each other and with God." Unlike Clarissa Warner, however, he did not cherish these "private seasons of prayer" because they brought the couple closer to Jesus. Instead, shared worship drew Kelsey and Snell closer to each other. Their prayers did not foreshadow an eternal life but the earthly life they hoped to spend together. He wrote that those hours were "earnests of what I fondly hoped would be granted us daily, night & morning, in the years to come. They were forecasts of the pure joys which must ever cluster around that centre & security of home—the family altar." Significantly, after Snell's death at the age of twenty-five, Kelsey did not honor Snell's memory by recounting her conversion, her abiding faith in Christ, and her resignation in the face of death. Instead, he created a memorial around the drama of their courtship.[39] This sacralization of the beloved and the self opened the door for the spread of romantic love in the countryside. By the 1850s, the same religious sen-

[38]Antonia to Hannah Parsons, 30 October 1847, Parsons Family Papers, SL; Nellie to Maria Wiswell Russell, March 1846, Charles Russell Papers, MHS. Karen Lystra (*Searching the Heart*, 237–57) offers an insightful discussion of the use of religious language to describe romantic love in Victorian courtship letters.

[39]"An Account of the Last Two Years of Martha Snell's Life," by her fiancé H. S. Kelsey, 12 April 1860, unpublished manuscript, Snell Family Papers, Box 3, Folder 5, ACASC.

timents that women had used to protect themselves from the excesses of romantic love and to counter the progress of individualism had contributed decisively to the triumph of both among the provincial middle classes.

Romantic Self-Fashioning

If the generation of provincial women who came of age after 1840 generally accepted the ideal of romantic love, their parents frequently failed to share their enthusiasm. Fathers particularly objected when their daughters gave themselves over to love. After all, romantic love demanded that courtships be governed not by networks of kin and friends but by the caprices of the heart. Like Sarah Jane Olcutt's father, many men correctly worried that romantic love ultimately freed daughters from their obligations to families and to households. Amherst College professor Ebenezer Snell offers a case in point. In his own youth, he had not been immune to love; during his courtship, even a brief visit from Sabra Clark was enough to "scatter" his astronomical calculations. But Snell's genuine affection for Clark occupied a circumscribed place within his life, framed by his professional aspirations, his desire for an orderly household, and his family's needs and preferences. Thirty years after his own prudent courtship, Snell was deeply disturbed by his daughter Martha Snell's romance with H. S. Kelsey, a student at Amherst College. In part, Snell opposed the match on practical grounds; because Kelsey was still in the "college course of his education," the attachment was "premature." Even if Martha Snell never consented to marry Kelsey, Snell worried that such a close connection would damage her reputation. He also feared that Martha was too easily swayed by her emotions. Granted, "feelings [were] to be cherished," but his own experiences confirmed that "judgement is given us to control them, and thus secure us from calamity."[40]

Worse, Snell suspected that his daughter's romantic connection was undermining her devotion to her parents. He expected that "parents & children should confer freely with each other on all subjects which vitally concern them." But Martha Snell, who almost certainly sensed her parents' disapproval, had been conspicuously evasive on the subject of Mr. Kelsey, and her father was dismayed that "most of what we know of your love for Mr K. is from him, and not from yourself."

[40]Ebenezer Strong Snell to Martha Strong Snell, 7 July 1855, Snell Family Papers, Box 2, Folder 3, ACASC.

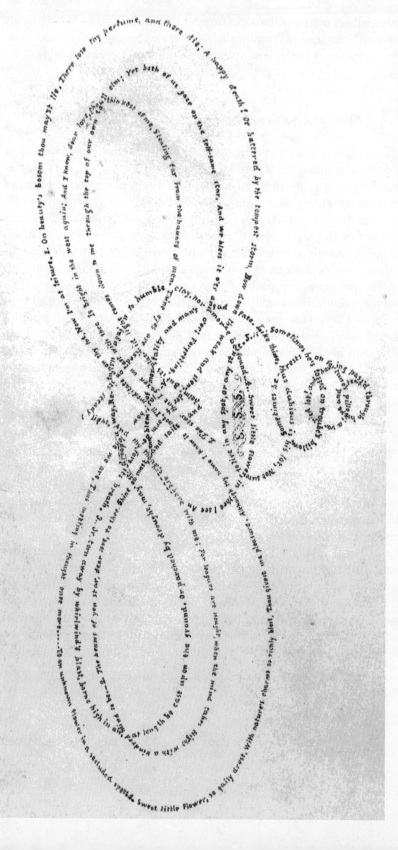

Ebenezer Strong Snell pledged his heart to Sabra Clark in 1828 with this poem, scrolled into the shape of a love knot. "Love Knot," 1828, in Snell Family Papers (Box 2, Folder 1), Amherst College Archives and Special Collections.

Attempting to shore up parental authority in general and paternal authority in particular, Snell warned his daughter that

> if a child wishes for happiness and prosperity in any course of life, let her confide in her father and mother, unless their characters are such as to render them unworthy of confidence. . . . Any checks, which you may receive from parental advice, may be grievous at the time; but they are likely to be the most important means of your safe guidance through life—I mean, so far as human help can avail.[41]

But Ebenezer Snell's cautions were lost on his twenty-year-old daughter, who maintained her connection with Mr. Kelsey and accepted his proposal in the late 1850s. After Martha Snell's death in 1860, it was not her father but her fiancé who claimed the prerogative to write her memorial.

By the end of the 1840s, a growing number of young provincial women and men subordinated the claims of kin and household to the demands of romantic love. Far from questioning the legitimacy of their romantic inclinations, they expected to fall in love, equating the jumble of feelings generated by love with emotional maturity. Especially for young women, falling in love served as a rite of passage. Although it never conferred the decisive adult status provided by marriage, the experience of romantic love did mark an end to childhood, signaling a period of ill-defined adolescence. Amherst teenager Harriett Goodell was especially anxious to fall in love. Unfortunately, she wrote in 1854, "the little God-boy who is rendering so many of my own age submissive to his sway has not yet deigned to exercise his skill in aiming at my heart." Still, she resolved to persevere, hoping "someday to win his confidence & love and thus secure the priceless gift." Goodell's eagerness to fall in love was indistinguishable from her desire to grow up.

Unlike an earlier generation of women, Goodell did not regard romantic love as a dangerous amusement, nor did she assume that her first encounter with "the little God-boy" would lead her directly to the altar. Instead, she measured her life's progress against a romantic ideal, seeking the kind of benchmark her mother and grandmother might have found in conversion. Romantic love offered Harriett Goodell and her peers a chance to assess their own lives, to measure and to cultivate a "self."[42]

[41]Ibid.

[42]Harriett Goodell to Angelo Goodell, 13 January 1854, Goodell Family Papers, JL. Karen Lystra (*Searching the Heart*, 30–37) has suggested that Victorian men and women used self-revelatory courtship letters to cultivate a "self." But as Goodell's comments suggest, the

To construct this romantic self, provincial young women looked to the sentimental language and the theatrical conventions that distinguished nineteenth-century bourgeois society. In ideal terms, romantic love may have demanded that men and women transcend the constricting roles of everyday life to encounter each other in a realm of pure sentiment. In practice, however, men and women created romantic love and the romantic self through a series of discrete roles, modeled on the heroines of sentimental fiction and didactic literature and fashioned in the parlors of an emerging middle class. To capture the essence of their romantic experiences for themselves and one another, provincial women adopted an emotional language that bespoke their identities as women and their status as "ladies," a language that drew them closer to their sisters in northern cities.[43]

Even before they entered a romantic relationship, provincial women used the conventions of romantic love to shape their self-presentation. Unrequited love, infatuations and crushes, even the anticipation of love provided the material out of which a young woman might fashion a romantic self. For example, a friend's request for romantic advice in 1847 prompted a young woman named Antonia to confess the "secret" that had "well-nigh broken" her heart, that she suffered from the "pangs of unrequited affection." For several weeks, she had been obsessed by a man who attended her church and whose "image has been omnipresent in [her] mind." Despite her attempts to catch his eye, he remained oblivious to her existence, and Antonia was becoming desperate. She expected to see her beloved that evening, and warned her friend that if he did not tell her "the story of his love" the "next news you will hear, will, in all probability, be that I am in the asylum." But Antonia's confession was hardly spontaneous. Reading back over her letter, she asked with some satisfaction, "Shouldn't I make a good novel-writer?"[44]

Sarah Jane Olcutt explicitly drew on the life experiences of sentimental writers as well as the conventions of sentimental literature to define herself. In diaries filled with romantic vignettes and provincial sketches, she marked herself as a young woman of literary talent and ambition. But Olcutt understood that the literary conventions that shaped her personal aspirations might be at odds with her emerging

creation of a romantic self was not dependent on a realized relationship with another person but could derive from fantasy as well. See my argument later in the chapter.

[43] For an insightful discussion of theatricality in middle-class culture, see Karen Halttunen, *Confidence Men and Painted Women: A Study of Middle-Class Culture in America, 1830–1870* (New Haven, Conn.: Yale University Press, 1982).

[44] Antonia to Hannah Parsons, 30 October 1847, Parsons Family Papers, SL.

identity as a writer, and she suspected that the mundane realities of married life might contradict her romantic ideal. Trying to square her personal and her literary ambitions, her fantasies and her pragmatism, she looked to her favorite writers for resolution.

Olcutt especially admired Sarah Edgarton, poet and editor of the Universalist annual *Rose of Sharon*, whose stories she read "a second & not unoften a third time." But her interest in Edgarton was not simply literary. Assuming that Edgarton's writings were an unmediated expression of her private experience, Olcutt looked to the writer for answers to her own dilemmas. When she tried to resolve her desire for romance, her reservations about marriage, and her need to write, she wondered whether Edgarton "could so delicately feel those finer feelings of the heart" if she were confined by "the plain sober every day reality." Indeed, it was possible that Edgarton's delicate, romantic sensibility might be "destroyed by the familiarity of matrimonial life." Inspired by "<u>Miss</u> Edgarton," Olcutt contemplated pursuing literary rather than personal aspirations and protecting her romantic fantasies against the realities of provincial housekeeping.[45]

A year later, in 1847, Olcutt was understandably shocked to learn that Sarah Edgarton was "Miss Edgarton no longer." Turning to her diary to sort out the implications of Edgarton's marriage, Olcutt despaired that she had "hardly time to express a thought," much less the "solitude" to give such news the consideration it deserved. She took the matter personally, for, as she explained, "we ever feel inquisitive about those that interest us." Edgarton's marriage not only challenged the fantasy Olcutt had constructed around the writer but also impinged on the young woman's vision of herself. Yet Olcutt's fantasies about Edgarton—fantasies that were shaped as much by the conventions of sentimental literature as by the young woman's literary aspirations—continued to structure her understanding of her experiences and options. Observing that Edgarton had married a man who was a "writer as well as a Preacher," Olcutt consoled herself that "Mrs. Mayo will write equally as good stories as did Miss Edgarton."[46] And after learning of Miss Edgarton's metamorphosis into Mrs. Mayo, Olcutt's own reservations about marriage disappeared from her diary.

Most provincial women never associated themselves with sentimen-

[45]Diary of Sarah Jane Olcutt, n.d. [ca. spring 1846], UVM. Olcutt's observations about Edgarton are part of a longer passage in which she compares Edgarton's treatment of romantic love to that of "*Miss* Landon" and "*Mrs*. Hale." In each case, she assumes the writer's perspective to be determined by marital status. On the career of Sarah Edgarton, see Douglas, *Feminization of American Culture*, 72–73, 406–407.

[46]Diary of Sarah Jane Olcutt, August 1847, UVM.

tal literary culture as self-consciously as Antonia or Sarah Jane Olcutt. Yet after the 1840s, even their casual depictions of their society and themselves took on the distinctly theatrical tone of sentimental litera- ture and culture. For example, Annie Storrow Higginson's 1859 description of a Deerfield wedding party infused provincial sociability with the tropes of romantic love and the studied drama of the fashion- able middle-class "affair." After carefully setting the scene (the cou- ple's new house, which "looked beautifully" and was "furnished in such good taste, simply but handsomely"), Higginson described the main characters. The bride, who looked "extremely bright and pretty," wore a white silk dress with "puffed lace" and was crowned by "the loveliest white wreath on her curls, with long drooping sprays behind." Distinguished less by his dress than by his manner, the bride- groom appeared "very happy" and behaved with "more ease and self possession" than Higginson would have expected. She noticed that "there was nothing 'doubtful' in his position on that eventful evening, he could not but feel an overwhelming certainty that he was at last [a] husband that he was in his own house, receiving the congratulations of his friends, as a bridegroom."[47]

Yet the success of this "affair" depended not only on the picture pre- sented by the bride and groom but also on the spectacle of the wedding party itself. Accordingly, Higginson credited the "inspiring" violin music, the "very magnificent" supper (two long tables of food, "bril- liantly lighted" and "loaded with dainties"), and the guests, especially the Deerfield women who were the "ornaments" of the party. The evening's emotional drama culminated when the "devoted husband" threw a "pretty crocheted white & blue shawl" over his new wife's shoulders as they went to supper. In this small and intimate gesture, the couple revealed for their guests the depth and tenderness of their feelings for each other.[48]

It is hardly surprising that the trappings of a middle-class wedding would evoke a sentimental and romantic sensibility; after all, nine- teenth-century weddings were calculated to provoke precisely the kind of sentiments that Higginson recorded in 1859. But a variety of other social occasions provided provincial men and women with the raw material for romance. Provincial society had always been distinctly heterosocial, especially compared with the increasingly separate spheres of the urban middle class. Yet by the 1850s, neighborly asso- ciation had given way to gatherings infused with the possibilities of

[47] Annie Storrow Higginson to Agnes Gordon Higginson, 9 December 1859, Fuller-Hig- ginson Papers, PVMA.
[48] Ibid.

romantic love. Between Christmas and New Year's Day 1855, Henry Hills, the twenty-two-year-old son of a prosperous Amherst mill owner, attended a bewildering round of parties, teas, dancing lessons, singing schools, fairs, and musicals. In Hills's account of the Amherst social season, however, the functions serve only as backdrops for the romantic alliances of his peers. With undisguised relish, he informed his sweetheart that Charles Russel abandoned Ellen Rust for Lottie Thayer, that Lucy still pined after Charly, and that Lucy and Susan Haskell were conspicuously escorted home from every social event by William and Porter.[49]

Certainly, earlier generations of provincial women and men viewed parties, balls, and singing schools as opportunities for courtships—courtships that led inexorably to marriage and the establishment of a household. Yet for Hills and his friends, these events and the attachments they fostered were important not simply because they might culminate in marriage but because romance itself had become an integral part of provincial middle-class sociability and identity. If Ebenezer Snell worried that his daughter's social standing and marital prospects would be tainted by a soured romance, Henry Hills thought no less of his friends for their adventures.[50] Indeed, it was precisely those adventures that helped to define his social set. Hills, Higginson, and other young men and women of their generation used this union of romantic love, peer culture, and provincial sociability to mark the boundaries of bourgeois gentility, for the stylish gatherings, the gracious manners, and the endless discourses on which their romantic sensibility depended were expressions not just of self but of class.

Love and the Making of the Middle Class

Through crushes and courtships, romantic encounters and parlor weddings, provincial New Englanders defined themselves as members of an increasingly coherent, national middle class. Shaping the rituals of love and sociability, women and men gave concrete form

[49]Henry Hills to [Mary] Adelaide Spencer, 12 January 1855, Hills Family Papers, Box 1, Folder 2, ACASC.

[50]To be sure, even in the 1850s marriage remained the ultimate goal of provincial courtship, and communities continued to register disapproval when romantic adventures appeared to preclude good marriages. Such was the case in 1852, when a young Deerfield woman rejected the hand of a man she could not love because she loved a man she could not marry. Her friend Hattie Fuller reported that Rebecca "did not have much sympathy from her friends at home, after she dismissed Mr P. for Ralph." Hattie Fuller to George Fuller, 31 October 1852, Fuller-Higginson Papers, PVMA.

to abstract bourgeois virtues such as individualism, self-cultivation, privacy, and sentimentality. If these customs helped to define what the middle class was, they also helped to define what it was not. Indeed, the social power of these rituals was found less in their capacity to elicit a precise portrait of the middle class than in their power to graphically distinguish that class from the region's laborers and farmers, to highlight the divisions riddling an increasingly stratified society.

In poetry and fiction, romantic love might bridge the distance between rich and poor, city and country. In practice, however, it served to separate the middle class from the laboring class, to distinguish the sophistication of town-dwellers and prosperous farmers from the backward rusticity of the region's yeomen and laborers. Although Henry Hills indulged the romantic foibles of his set, he was contemptuous of the affairs of those he considered beneath him. After one Leora Howard complained to Hills about the manners of a beau who had escorted her to a concert in Hadley, Hills poked fun at the girl's speech: "He <u>was so green</u>. He didn't <u>know nothing</u>." Howard's beau may have been boorish, but from Hills's perspective, Howard was little better.

Yet if Henry Hills did not consider Leora Howard as an equal, neither could he avoid her altogether. While class distinctions became increasingly rigid after the 1840s, the informality and intimacy of small-town life made exchanges like the one between Hills and Howard virtually unavoidable. In provincial towns such as Amherst, class was articulated less through the kind of spatial and social separation that marked urban class formation than by a subtle retooling of the etiquette of social proximity. Community standards obliged Hills to chat with Howard about her romantic misadventures; class affiliation demanded that he treat them with little regard.[51]

In a society that elaborated class in the context of social proximity rather than social distance and that emphasized the importance of personal attraction in selecting mates, it could prove difficult to negotiate the boundaries between classes. At fifteen, Katherine Craddoc Hodges of Oxford, Massachusetts, lacked Hills's sensitivity to the finer social distinctions. When she requested permission to correspond with "young Gilbert," a gentleman altogether worthy of her consideration, her well-to-do parents were thrilled. The prospect of such a propitious

[51]Henry Hills to [Mary] Adelaide Spencer, 12 January 1855, Hills Family Papers, Box 1, Folder 2, ACASC.

romance brought tears to the eyes of Mr. Hodges and moved Mrs. Hodges to remember her own youthful "love affairs." But several months later, Katherine's interest in "young Gilbert" was eclipsed by her fascination with another, entirely inappropriate young man. To her mother's horror, Katherine extended this man the same favors she had shown "young Gilbert." Discounting the possibility that Katherine's feelings for the young man were genuine, her mother wrote, "I presume you think because you are too young for anything of a serious nature that it is a matter of no consequence if you flirt a little with him." To be sure, Mrs. Hodges did not mind that her daughter flirted, only that she flirted with the wrong sort. She explained, "If he was one of yr equals I would let things take their own course, but on one so much your inferior both in station & education I do not like you to associate with so intimately." Urging her daughter not to disappoint her, Mrs. Hodges reminded the girl that she was destined for better things. Katherine Hodges had learned a valuable lesson about the limits of provincial sociability. A dutiful daughter, she later married William Strutt Slater, grandson of Samuel Slater.[52]

At fifteen, Katherine Hodges naively applied the same standards to everyone; at thirty-five, Elijah Cowles, a prosperous North Hadley farmer, was more discriminating. A widower with two young sons, Cowles was clearly on the lookout for a new wife. Between 1857 and 1859, he courted several women before seventeen-year-old Mary Mathews of South Bend, Indiana, accepted his hand. Problems arose when Mary Elizabeth Russell, Cowles's former housekeeper, sued him for breach of promise, claiming that she had accepted Cowles's proposal before he even knew Mathews. In his defense, Cowles measured his relationship with Russell against the standards of romantic love, arguing that it was impossible to mistake his friendly interest in the young woman for romantic passion. The trial that followed set the rituals of romance against the traditions of reciprocal love, pitting bourgeois sentimentalism against the pragmatism of the household economy. The assumptions of Cowles, Russell, and the anonymous reporter who covered the trial for readers of Northampton's *Courier* reveal the complicated intersections between romance and class, between the values of

---

[52]Mrs. S. E. Hodges to Katherine Craddoc Hodges, 18 March 1862 and 22 October 1861, Hodges Family Papers, SL. Katherine Hodges's romances took place while she was away at boarding school in Greenfield, Massachusetts. Despite the authority of a cult of romantic love, which generally served to erode parental authority, it is difficult to imagine that Hodges's flirtation could have progressed so far under her parents' roof.

the household economy and the ideals of an emerging middle class in a provincial community.[53]

To prove that Cowles had indeed courted her, Mary Russell recounted incidents that would have signaled a courtship to an earlier generation of provincial women and men. According to her testimony, their bond was cemented not by romantic sighs and tender glances but by a shared commitment to Cowles's household. Nor was the relationship marked by physical passion; as the *Courier* reporter noted, neither party testified to "acts of affection." During the nine months that Russell kept house for Cowles and his sons, the two nevertheless developed a level of intimacy remarkable even by the standards of provincial New England, where relations between employers and native-born servants remained relatively informal until the Civil War.[54] Cowles escorted Russell to evening church meetings, a picnic, singing schools, the Amherst College Commencement ceremony, and to Northampton's well-stocked shops, where he spent five dollars on earrings for the young woman. These attentions, combined with Cowles's comment that "sometime we shall be married," led Russell to believe that they were engaged. When she returned to her father's Pelham home in August 1858, she began to prepare for the wedding, throwing a quilting party, making bed clothing, and shopping for furniture. When Cowles wed Mathews several months later, Russell sued for $6,000 in damages.

In his defense, Cowles claimed that the treatment he accorded the two women demonstrated the difference between friendship and love, arguing that the courtesies he had shown Mary Russell were not proof of courtship but "were common in families similarly situated." Although he admitted proposing marriage, he insisted that the offer had been made in jest. Indeed, Cowles maintained that however cor-

---

[53]In his testimony, Cowles insisted that although he had courted several women, he pursued them in succession. When Mary Russell came to work for him, he was courting a Miss Green of Amherst. When that suit fell through, he began to look for an appropriate alternative. My account of *Russell v. Cowles* is drawn from the description of the trial that appeared in the *Northampton Courier*, 25 October 1859. Michael Grossberg discusses the significance of the case in terms of nineteenth-century breach of promise suits in *Governing the Hearth: Law and the Family in Nineteenth-Century America* (Chapel Hill: University of North Carolina Press, 1985), 56–57.

[54]Well into the nineteenth century, relations between provincial women and native-born servants resembled the flexible, unsystematic pattern of "help" that Faye E. Dudden discovered in late eighteenth- and early nineteenth-century northern households and that was supplanted by the more rigid, class-bound pattern of "domestic service" during the industrial revolution. See Dudden, *Serving Women: Household Service in Nineteenth-Century America* (Middletown, Conn.: Wesleyan University Press, 1983).

dial, his friendship with Mary Russell paled next to his ardor for Mary Mathews. With Russell, he shared the kind of companionship peculiar to men and women running a household together. But with Mathews, he shared his heart and soul. He exhibited his passion by declaring himself "smitten," conducting a voluminous correspondence, and encouraging his boarder to entertain him with renditions of the popular song "The Prairie Flower."

The differing treatments Cowles accorded the two women reflected the sort of courtship granted a country housekeeper and the kind of courtship owed to the half-sister of a congressional representative, for if a marriage to Mary Russell was not his first choice, it was not out of the question. Cowles recounted that he and Russell had discussed their options one evening as they readied his children for bed. According to Cowles, Russell had volunteered to continue as his housekeeper if he "got the mitten out West" and promised to marry her instead. Rather than rejecting her offer outright, Cowles agreed to apprise her of the progress of his suit but warned her that he could make no promises.[55] Indeed, marriage to an agreeable young woman who was respectable if not prominent and who had already demonstrated her competence as a housekeeper must not have seemed like a bad bargain. But Cowles also understood that a courtship aimed at securing a mistress for his household was not bound by the standards that governed an affair of the heart. While he pursued Mary Russell with an equanimity that recalled the emotional tenor of reciprocal love, he pursued Mary Mathews with the fervor of the sentimental beau.

For a majority of Hampshire County jurors, Cowles's explanation of his behavior toward Mary Russell stretched credulity to the breaking point.[56] Provincial men may well have carried their servants to church, but even in the most egalitarian households, masters did not routinely escort their domestic help to a social event on the scale of the Amherst College Commencement. Similarly, masters and mistresses might provide their "help" with cloth or prayer books, but they did not take them shopping for earrings. Jurors may also have questioned the depth of Cowles's passion for Mary Mathews—a woman who had been recommended to Cowles by a mutual friend aware of Cowles's predicament, a woman Cowles met only twice during an eight-month courtship. By

[55]Russell denied that this conversation ever took place; in fact, she denied ever knowing that Cowles was also pursuing Mathews. In this instance, however, the accuracy of Cowles's testimony seems less important than his admission that he had not discounted Russell's alleged proposal apparently considered it something to fall back on.

[56]At the initial hearing, eight jurors found in favor of the plaintiff; four sided with the defendant.

a margin of eight to four, Cowles's peers placed their faith in Mary Russell's account of her courtship.[57]

For the *Courier* reporter, the most compelling questions raised by the trial did not concern Cowles's guilt or innocence but the backward customs the case revealed. The marvel was not that Elijah Cowles could have succeeded in his attempt to woo two women, but that either Cowles or Russell would have participated in a courtship or contemplated a marriage without the trappings of romance. Mary Russell, and at least some of the jurors, had seen a courtship that accorded with the older standards of reciprocal love—a courtship embracing values that an earlier generation of provincial men and women believed might protect their households and communities from the chaos of market society. Yet for the reporter, "the case, from its total barrenness of those necessary attendants upon courtships . . . presented rather a cold, business-like appearance." Anything less than the sentimental fantasy of a private life completely isolated from the social dimensions of the community represented a surrender to the crassest values of the marketplace. Unwilling to assail the character of either the plaintiff or the defendant, the reporter attributed their barbarism to their provincialism, to their geographic and social distance from the cosmopolitan civility of Northampton. He smugly concluded, "It may be common to conduct courtships in that manner in North Hadley and Pelham, but it certainly isn't the fashion here."[58] The ideology of romantic love and the rituals of courtship could measure the social distance between a young woman who worked as help in someone else's home and a farmer wealthy enough to court Mary Russell. But as the anonymous reporter's comments suggest, the case could also measure the social distance between Northampton and Pelham, leaving little doubt as to which was superior.

If the triumph of romantic love revealed the hegemony of bourgeois culture, it also reinforced the gender ideology of separate spheres that stood at the heart of that culture. Within the older household economy, men had assumed primary responsibility for courtship, just as they did for most endeavors of public significance. Within bourgeois society, however, with its rigid separation of public and private, courtship was removed from the neighborhood and relegated to the parlor. By redefining courtship as a private affair, imbued with romantic love and genteel sentimentality, members of the provincial middle class associ-

[57]Elijah Cowles appealed his case to the Massachusetts Supreme Court, which ruled in his favor in 1861; see Grossberg, *Governing the Hearth*, 57.

[58]*"Miss Mary Elizabeth Russell vs. Elijah Cowles,"* Northampton *Courier*, 25 October 1859.

ated it with imaginative constructs and styles of behavior that located it squarely within the feminine sphere.

Constructing the rituals of romance as women's work, provincial communities at last granted their women a measure of socially sanctioned power over the rites that so profoundly affected their fates. For their part, provincial women aggressively manipulated this new authority to enhance their influence over their communities and their households. Alarmingly, they also used it to enhance their authority over their men. To be sure, provincial men generally welcomed women's attempts to buttress the cultural authority of their class, but male enthusiasm subsided when women attempted to broaden their sphere of influence to include not just yeomen farmers and country lasses, mill hands and Irish domestics, but middle-class men themselves. Like the rituals of genteel sociability, the rituals of courtship and romantic love were governed by protocol that required ever more exacting standards of behavior from men as well as women. By holding men not just to standards of propriety but of chivalry, provincial women appropriated an unprecedented degree of social power.

Women's attempts to impose notions of gentlemanly conduct met with varying degrees of success. In 1853, when Deerfield bachelors failed to organize a sleighing party, ignoring excellent snow and broad hints from the ladies, twenty-one-year-old Hattie Fuller could only declare in exasperation, "I think [the men] are rather stupid."[59] Two years later, Fuller confronted a more extreme version of this "stupidity" when she was plagued by the attentions of a suitor altogether ignorant of the rules governing polite society. Apparently oblivious to the etiquette of the social call, the unfortunate Mr. Taft "came in dressed up, sat down & made himself quite at home." Even after Fuller declined his request for a sleigh ride, he persisted in his bid for her affection. As Fuller recalled, "He then said, he should like to have some conversation with me some time if I had no objections. What was coming, I didn't know." What was coming was a marriage proposal, the clumsiest Fuller had ever heard of: Taft "popped the question" as Fuller was walking out of the room. Far from flattered, Fuller "wanted to call him a fool to his face." Managing to hold her tongue, Fuller nevertheless conveyed her disdain, for after begging her to keep his proposal a secret, Mr. Taft left Deerfield for "parts unknown."[60]

Hattie Fuller did not doubt that she was a young lady, yet this status

[59]Hattie Fuller to George Fuller, 30 January 1853, Fuller-Higginson Papers, PVMA.

[60]Fashion-conscious Fuller's comments about Taft's appearance suggest that whatever he was wearing was neither appropriate nor becoming. Hattie Fuller to George Fuller, 4 January 1855, Fuller-Higginson Papers, PVMA.

depended largely on the willingness of men like Mr. Taft to treat her as one, especially in a matter as serious as a marriage proposal. Because he refused to honor her as a lady, she saw no reason to honor his secret. Unlike earlier generations of New England women, whose respect for male dignity would have ensured their silence, Hattie Fuller shared the news of Taft's gaffe with everyone she knew. After recounting the story to her brother George, she explained, "Of course I could not Keep it to myself—Did you ever Know anything so perfectly ridiculous"? Fuller thought her story made for a good joke; she expected her brother would "split laughing" when he read her letter. But the ridicule she and her friends heaped upon poor Mr. Taft sent Deerfield's other young bachelors a clear message about the importance of social amenities.[61]

Other accounts show that Hattie Fuller was not the only young woman forced to fend off an unwanted marriage proposal. When a young Amherst woman named Laura found herself "trapped" with a clumsy and unwanted suitor, she dodged his attentions until the early hours of the morning when he finally managed to propose. After telling her how "smart" people thought she was, he reminded her that it "wasn't good for man to live alone." Ignoring Laura's claims that she was not in love, the young man pressed on. When an inventory of his charms failed to change her mind, he changed his tactics. Unlike Mr. Taft, who disappeared quietly into the night, this young man went on the attack. Openly hostile, he questioned Laura's right to determine the standards against which he was measured, suggesting that she entertained unrealistic expectations about romance and love. Finally, he reminded her of the dependence that ultimately awaited unmarried women in provincial society. Calling forth the specter of spinsterhood, he pointed to the "Old Maid" in their social circle and threatened that Laura's pretensions might leave her to a similar fate.[62]

By the late 1850s, from the perspective of many men, women's social demands were beginning to look less like an expression of middle-class authority than a dainty expression of feminine tyranny. In an 1858 essay for the *Hampshire Gazette*, one young man publicly objected to the ways that women manipulated their newfound power. Writing under the pseudonym Theophilus Thistle and on behalf of bachelors throughout the Connecticut River Valley, he protested that the increasing intricacy of sociability had made it impossible for young

[61]Ibid. In *Hands and Hearts*, Ellen Rothman notes the respect antebellum women accorded gentlemen's attentions, welcome or not.

[62]Henry Hills to [Mary] Adelaide Spencer, 3 October 1855, Hills Family Papers, ACASC. That this story was recounted by Hills, a friend of Laura, suggests that Laura, like Hattie Fuller, viewed discreet publicity as the best revenge.

men simply to enjoy themselves. Because all social gatherings had become opportunities for romance, any encounter with a young woman was suspect; men longed for the day when they might chat without creating the impression that they were paying a young woman "particular attentions." Worse than the notion that men were viewed only as prospective beaux was Thistle's nagging suspicion that men might not be the main attraction at these gatherings. He knew many a man who had labored to engage the attention of a young lady only to notice her "eye wandering about the room" to see how her friends were dressed.

Withal, men benefited far too little from their women's refinement. Exceedingly gracious to one another, young women failed to extend the same courtesies to their male companions. The young ladies he knew were far too quick to "make fun" of men who fell short of the genteel ideal, "laughing, and winking, and blinking at [their] deficiencies." As Thistle observed, all men could not be "splendid fellows" with "elegant manners," but they all had "human hearts and like[d] to be treated kindly."

Far from reinforcing male prestige, the intricate rituals of courtship and the gracious sociability of middle-class parlors made men little more than necessary props in a social drama constructed by and for women. As Theophilus Thistle recognized, polite society placed provincial middle-class men in a difficult position, for the same social ceremonies that trumpeted the preeminence of their class underscored the superior social skills of their women.[63] Women's mastery of bourgeois etiquette gave them a distinct advantage over their beaux. Many provincial men were dismayed by women's eagerness to press this advantage. Commanding the authority to define the boundaries of genteel behavior, provincial women appropriated the power to cut men who transgressed those boundaries.

But if their inability to meet these exacting standards led some men

[63]The demographic structure of provincial communities surely contributed to this advantage. According to Mary Jane Richards Pi-Sunyer's study of nineteenth-century Amherst, the majority of young women of marriage age lived either with their families of origin or with kin. Young men, on the other hand, were far more likely to be boarding in the households of nonrelatives. Obviously, this difference stemmed from changes in the provincial economy and occupational structure that forced growing numbers of men to pursue livelihoods beyond the family farm and outside the economic networks of kin. But it must also have given women a decided advantage in the kinds of social contests that Thistle describes. Single women circulated through a familiar network of kin and neighbors; single men remained perpetual outsiders. See Mary Jane Richards Pi-Sunyer, "Households in a Nineteenth-Century Town: A Historical Demography Study of Household and Family Size and Composition in Amherst, Massachusetts, 1850–1880" (Ph.D. diss., University of Massachusetts, Amherst, 1973).

to worry that the requirements of middle-class sociability diminished their authority as men, they did not have to look far for reassurance. Like the man who tried to bully Laura of Amherst into marriage, men could reveal their trump, threatening women with the economic and social deprivations of spinsterhood. Under duress, middle-class gentlemen abandoned polite discretion to remind ladies of their economic dependence, of the basis of male power.[64]

Ultimately, the same rituals that earlier generations had relied on to shore up reciprocal love were easily turned to the service of romantic love. Theophilus Thistle unconsciously echoed the wisdom of the mentor in the didactic poem *The Ladies' Monitor*, published forty years earlier. Both men urged provincial women not to judge men by their outward appearance, by their polish and sophistication. But for the "mentor," plainness was a virtue in itself, simultaneously protecting the republic from aristocratic pretensions and young women from the dangers of romantic love. Where the "mentor" sought to vindicate the sturdy republican yeoman, Thistle exonerated the self-made man. Plain manners did not in themselves indicate virtue; instead, they suggested that a man had risen from humbler beginnings. Far from rescuing young women from romance, Thistle worried only that women failed to extend the advantages of romance to men on the rise. Similarly, for Edward Dickinson and Emily Norcross, Sabra Clark and Ebenezer Snell, gossip signified the persistence of a corporate dimension of courtship aimed at protecting the values of the household economy. A generation later, under the pressure of an emerging market society, small talk was transformed into the stratifying gossip of Hattie Fuller and Henry Hills. Finally, by the 1840s, even the evangelical Protestantism that women had used to expose the dangers of romantic love seemed to sanctify that most earthly of connections. Strategies that had once promised to protect the household economy from the worst aspects of market society or, at the very least, to shield networks

---

[64]Karen Lystra (*Searching the Heart*, 121–56) has argued that despite inequalities in economic and social power, nineteenth-century men and women were able to escape oppressively restricting "separate spheres," encountering each other not as man and women, narrowly defined, but as individuals. In effect, she argues that romantic love and, especially, the creation of a romantic self allowed middle-class Victorians to transcend their class and gender. Certainly, within particular relationships, men and women attained different levels of reciprocity and intimacy. It is hardly surprising to learn, for example, that within romantic relationships, women sometimes assumed a dominant role while their men remained hesitant, even passive; or to discover that some Victorian couples enjoyed a freedom of sexual expression that seems "healthy" even by the standards of the late twentieth century. Nevertheless, as provincial examples make clear, as a cultural system, romantic love worked to reinforce bourgeois gender ideology.

of personal relations from the disruptive influence of individualism contributed decisively to the creation of a bourgeois culture within provincial communities.

Rather than holding social divisions at bay, rituals of courtship and romance drew new and heightened divisions within provincial society. By the end of the antebellum period, love separated class from class and town from country. Through the ideology and practice of romantic love, the women and men of New England's provincial middle class positioned themselves against their poor and rural neighbors and helped cement their alliance with middle class that dominated the region's cities. But if romantic love contributed to the coherence of the middle class, it could not rid that class of internal tensions. Through rituals that underscored the differences between male and female spheres, that emphasized the differences between men's power and women's authority, the ideology of romantic love created new divisions within the provincial middle class even as it contributed to its unity and legitimacy.

6

"Simple ideals of living"

While staying in Boston in 1804, George Bliss of Springfield, Massachusetts, was invited to dine at the Salem home of Mr. Prescott, a "brother lawyer." Bliss had heard that Prescott lived in luxury, but nothing he had heard or seen prepared him for the spectacle he encountered at the Prescott residence. More than living well, his "brother lawyer" lived in a "palace." He described the evening in a letter to his wife, Abigail Rowland Bliss.[1]

After Bliss rang the bell, a servant conducted him up a flight of stairs to a "large drawing Room," whose walls were "painted most elegantly with Landscapes & the mantle over the fireplace with fine figures." There Prescott sat, awaiting his guests. Bliss spent nearly an hour chatting with the Prescotts and their twenty-odd guests before the company adjourned to the dining room for a "superb & elegant feast." The dinner included soup, roast and boiled mutton, roast venison "alamode," beef, chickens, roast and boiled turkeys, pies, pastries, apples, raisins, nuts, and wines, "besides many other dishes which [he] did not see or dont recollect." He was especially impressed with the venison, which was cooked at the table "by means of Dishes having under them a blaze made I think by burning spirits." More remarkable than the feast was Mrs. Prescott herself. He wrote his wife that "what I noticed was that

[1]The Prescott party is described in George Bliss to Abigail Rowland Bliss, 31 January 1804, Bliss-Morris Archives Collection, CVHM.

162

Mrs. Prescott gave no order at the table." Nor had she left the drawing room to supervise the kitchen staff. Instead, she achieved the remarkable feat of "appear[ing] otherwise as a guest" at her own party. Charged with presiding over an enormous dinner, Mrs. Prescott managed the evening with more ease than Bliss, who concluded "such a feast is a hard job—I hope & trust I shall have no more of that work to perform before my return."

In the past ten years, historians have served up adventures such as George Bliss's to explain society and culture in the early republic. In particular, they have looked to such anecdotes as part of a larger exploration of sociability, of the myriad gatherings and networks that simultaneously pulled people together and set them apart. No longer the stuff of antiquarian cataloges and antiques magazines, dinner parties, parlor socials, and neighborly visiting now seem to reveal more than the broad outlines and the fine details of bygone days. Instead, these occasions have assumed a new significance as part of the informal, extrapolitical processes through which men and women delineate distinctions of class, gender, and political affiliation. From this perspective, seemingly private patterns of sociability no longer stand in opposition to the world of political parties, voluntary associations, and public rituals. Private and public no longer figure as opposite and oppositional worlds but as points along a single continuum.

More recently, sociability has captured the imaginations of historians of rural life. Looking at neighborly visiting, work parties, and community organizations, these scholars have been struck by patterns of sociability that they correctly associate with the mutuality of the household economy and that persisted well into the nineteenth century. Informal, inclusive, and decidedly heterosocial, the style of rural sociability seems to confound the conventions of bourgeois culture—conventions that placed the stamp of respectability on members of the urban middle class. Holding the befuddled, mildly disapproving George Bliss up against the self-confident elegance of Mr. and Mrs. Prescott, these scholars have concluded that provincial sociability served as a bulwark against the encroachments of bourgeois culture and even against capitalist social relations.[2]

---

[2]On rural sociability, see Mitchell Snay, "How the Country Folk Frolic: Sociability in Late Eighteenth-Century Rural New England," paper presented at Society for Historians of the Early American Republic 1994; Karen V. Hansen, *A Very Social Time: Crafting Community in Antebellum New England* (Berkeley: University of California Press, 1994); Jane Marie Pederson, *Between Memory and Reality: Family and Community in Rural Wisconsin, 1870–1970* (Madison: University of Wisconsin Press, 1992); Nancy Gray Osterud, *Bonds of Community: The Lives of Farm Women in Nineteenth-Century New York* (Ithaca,

If provincial New Englanders never cast aside the sociability of their parents and grandparents to ape cosmopolitan civility, sociability hardly served as the last bastion of the household economy. A closer examination of the experience and cultural meaning of sociability reveals it as a far more contested, contradictory terrain. Between 1800 and 1860, provincial women and men developed a hybrid sociability, one that moved between the high fashion of the Prescotts and the plain style of George Bliss. On the one hand, rural New Englanders increasingly incorporated elements of cosmopolitan, genteel culture into their own patterns of sociability. Many antebellum provincials appropriated the manners, customs, and entertainments of the urban middle class, undermining the religious dimensions of women's self-presentation in the process. On the other hand, even the most casual nineteenth-century observers agreed that provincial sociability retained a special tenor, derived from translating community spirit into practice. Provincial gatherings were certainly less formal and less exclusive than their urban counterparts; less obviously, a persistent localism and a lasting suspicion of urban gentility contributed to the sense of community.

But at least as important as what women and men did was what sense they made of it. And when provincial New Englanders considered sociability as a social process rather than as an individual diversion, they generally overlooked the increasing gentility of provincial culture to emphasize the persistence of older forms of social interaction that derived from the household economy. Exaggerating the distinctiveness of their world, they constructed a vision of village sociability that served to distance them from both the urban middle class and the social relations that characterized a market society. But while provincial sociability retained its unpretentious, inclusive, and increasingly old-fashioned flavor, it served to obscure class differences and to articulate the ambitions of an emerging rural middle class.

N.Y.: Cornell University Press, 1991); Barbara Karsky, "Sociability in Rural New England," in Barbara Karsky and Elise Marienstros, eds., *Time and Work in Pre-Industrial America* (Nancy: Presses Universitaires de Nancy, 1991). Although all of these historians suggest that sociability served as a check against bourgeois culture, Osterud (*Bonds of Community*, 280) extends this argument the furthest, suggesting that the kin-based mutuality and the heterosociability of Nanticoke Valley served as a "bulwark" against capitalist social relations.

Contours of Sociability

During the first half of the nineteenth century, growing numbers of northern, urban, middle-class women and men laid claim to something of the Prescotts' style, elaborating new and increasingly complex patterns of sociability. Mirroring the increasingly intricate and arcane rules governing commercial transactions, the manners described in countless etiquette books testified not simply to new kinds of entertainments but to new styles of interaction. Middle-class men and women worked hard to approximate the apparently effortless elegance of the Prescotts. In Boston, New York, and Philadelphia, ladies and gentlemen moved through parlors and promenades with grace and precision. Approaching one another with a studied sincerity, they fashioned new emblems of class and self.[3]

Provincial New Englanders tended to observe this transformation in much the same way as George Bliss. As a rule, they disapproved of such extravagant display. More often than not, they were intimidated by the unfamiliar splendor of urban sociability. After all, they came from communities whose grandest occasions merged work and sociability. There was neighborly visiting aplenty, but the most memorable gatherings—barn raisings, huskings, quilting parties—were tied to the work rhythms of the agricultural calendar and more fundamentally to the reciprocity of the household economy. Work-based sociability did not disappear in the antebellum era. Women, in particular, continued to look to sewing circles to relieve the tedium of needlework. But as Bliss's letter suggests, provincial women and men were also fascinated

[3]See Richard L. Bushman, *The Refinement of America: Persons, Houses, Cities*: (New York: Knopf, 1992); David Scobey, "Anatomy of the Promenade: The Politics of Bourgeois Sociability in Nineteenth-Century New York," *Social History* 17 (May 1992): 203–27; John F. Kasson, *Rudeness and Civility: Manners in Nineteenth-Century America* (New York: Hill & Wang, 1990); and Karen Halttunen, *Confidence Men and Painted Women: A Study of Middle-Class Culture in America, 1830–1870* (New Haven, Conn.: Yale University Press, 1982). Stuart M. Blumin (*The Emergence of the Middle Class: Social Experience in the American City, 1760–1900* [New York: Cambridge University Press, 1989], 179–91, 184–85) argues that while the parlor etiquette described by Halttunen was aimed at "the wealthiest and most socially ambitious middle-class families," the rank and file of the urban middle class also "found that the parlor made demands on their deportment." I suspect that historians of the urban middle class, who have relied heavily on antebellum prescriptive literature for their discussions of bourgeois social life, might well have exaggerated its formality, just as other historians have overemphasized its domesticity, its rigid separation of public and private, and so on. Still, contemporary observers agreed that the style of sociability was far more formal, elaborate, and theatrical in the city than in the hinterland. For an extended discussion of the ways in which provincial New Englanders elaborated these differences in style, and the significance they found in those differences, see later in this chapter and Chapter 8.

by people like the Prescotts and by patterns of sociability that seemed so different from their own.[4]

Between 1820 and 1860, provincial women and men adopted something of the Prescotts' style. The etiquette governing social occasions became more intricate and less flexible; teas, parties, and dances conformed to increasingly complicated conventions. Especially in provincial centers such as Springfield and, later, Northampton or Brattleboro, impromptu, neighborly gatherings gradually gave way to planned "affairs" requiring elaborate confections, tasteful decorations, and fancy gowns. As early as 1830, Mrs. John Howard of Springfield, Massachusetts, dazzled her friends with a lavish ball in honor of a new bride. Amelia White Peabody, who had seen the best of Salem society before moving to Springfield, noted with approval that the Howards "received the company in one parlour, danced in the other, and had supper up stairs." More remarkable than the scope of the entertainment was the care that had gone into embellishing it. Peabody reported that one Margaret Emery, charged with arranging the supper table, had produced "astonishing decorations." Peabody asked her sister, who was tucked away in Lancaster, New Hampshire, "Would you believe that she carves out of beets, carrots and turnips, the most natural roses in the world, that stuck on green leaves, will deceive a person unless examined very closely?" Nor was Mrs. Howard the only woman in Peabody's circle to entertain elaborately. One Betsey Howard aspired to host a "similar party," boasting that there was "no house in town so well fitted for the purpose as her's." Committing her entire home to the festivities, she planned to use her "north parlour for a supper table, the other for her company to sit in, her kitchen for dancing, and bedroom for refreshments." Another of Peabody's friends, Sophia, knew that she could not hope to rival these parties in scale. Instead, Peabody expected that she would impress her guests with the "great simplicity but real richness" of her furnishings.[5]

---

[4]Daniel Vickers, "Competency and Competition in Early America," *William and Mary Quarterly*, 3d ser., 47 (1990): 3–29; Laurel Thatcher Ulrich, "Martha Ballard and Her Girls: Women's Work in Eighteenth-Century Maine," in *Work and Labor in Early America*, ed. Stephen Innes (Chapel Hill: University of North Carolina Press, 1988); Jack Larkin, *The Reshaping of Everyday Life, 1790–1840*, (New York: Harper Perennial, 1988), 266–71; Karsky, "Sociability in Rural New England"; Hansen, *A Very Social Time*; and Osterud, *Bonds of Community*.

[5]Amelia White Peabody to Mary Jane White, 16 January 1830, Everett-Peabody Family Papers, MHS. Older women occasionally commented that the cooking at such affairs had also become more elaborate. Describing a Northampton dinner that she attended in 1840 with her son and daughter-in-law, Elizabeth Phelps Huntington commented that "our dinner was very good of course two or three fashionable dishes, and a cup of coffee to finish

Ebenezer Snell painted the parlor of his family's house "from memory." For all the room's plainness, the wallpaper, clock, and "Family Record" above the hearth reveal the family's efforts at middle-class refinement. Drawing, Snell family living room "from memory," by E. S. Snell, 1838, in Snell Family Papers (Map Case 1, Drawer 12). Amherst College Archives and Special Collections.

By the end of the antebellum period, even residents of distinctly rural towns could enjoy entertainments that approximated the leisure of city people. Twenty-five years after Amelia White Peabody described Springfield's social season, sisters Agnes Gordon Higginson and Annie Storrow Higginson found comparable opportunities in Deerfield, a small farming community some forty miles up the Con-

off with." Elizabeth Phelps Huntington to Frederic Dan Huntington, 18 March 1840, PPHFP, Box 12, Folder 8. For a more detailed account of the transformation of provincial sociability, see my " 'The New England Fashion': Sociability, Social Networks and the Creation of a Provincial Middle Class," *Journal of the Early Republic* (forthcoming, Fall 1999).

By the end of the antebellum period, the standards of provincial refinement demanded far more elaborate furnishings and decoration. Surely handpainted wallpaper and a graceful sofa helped make the Hanover, New Hampshire, parlor of Ira Young and Eliza Adams Young a setting for gracious sociability. Courtesy of Dartmouth College Library.

necticut River. Despite their mother's worries that rustic Deerfield offered the young women few advantages, the two managed to piece together a social life that exceeded Peabody's both in show and in pace, although they had to travel some to do so. The sisters regularly availed themselves of the parties, dances, and book club meetings held in the homes of the town's better families. They also rode to Northampton to dance away the long winter nights at balls held in the town's hotel and rounded out their social life with frequent train rides to visit kin in Brattleboro, Vermont, where they enjoyed parties, cotillions, and especially the parlor theatricals in which Annie Storrow Higginson took special pleasure.[6]

[6]See Agnes Cochran Higginson to Stephen Higginson II, 18 December 1855, 28 December 1855, and 21 February 1856, and Agnes Gordon Higginson [Fuller] Diary, 1855–56, Fuller-Higginson Papers, PVMA.

If entertainments such as balls and theatricals eventually supplanted older, work-oriented forms of sociability, they also contributed to the reshaping of women's self-presentation. For much of the antebellum period, the gatherings described by Amelia White Peabody and the Higginson sisters occupied only a modest place in provincial women's diaries and letters. Certainly, these occasions offered women and girls a welcome respite from work and a chance to visit with neighbors and kin, but they rarely stood at the center of women's self-presentation. The rhythms of Christian practice marked the routines of their lives; the struggle for faith stood at the core of self. By the end of the antebellum period, however, leisure played a far more significant role in shaping the boundaries of the female self.

In the journal she kept from the 1810s through the 1840s, Mary Tyler dutifully noted the outlines of her social life. She recorded callers, tea parties, and dinner invitations in the same plain style she used to describe the number of candles made, pies baked, and shirts hemmed. She devoted considerably more attention to the triumphs of her adult sons on whose financial support the family depended; less frequently, she praised the selfless labor of her two daughters. But she reserved her most elaborate and graceful prose to mark the rare occasions when she contrived to travel the two miles from Brattleboro to Guilford to worship in the Episcopal church, where she could experience the "happiness of again listening to the effusions of true Piety breathed in language Simple yet Elegant." Inspired by the beauty and power of one especially "excellent" sermon, Tyler described her hunger for grace, comparing herself to the fertile earth waiting for seed: "May the Infinite Being who saw and knows with what joy I receive this portion of the good deed, grant it may take root as in good ground well prepared, and spring up & bear fruit a hundredfold!" The solace Tyler found in faith, as well as the pleasure she took in the liturgy, dominated her presentation of herself. Social activities had their place in the routines of everyday life, but opportunities to praise God in the church of her first choice constituted life's grand occasions.[7]

Elizabeth Phelps Huntington, who kept several concurrent journals, used her writing almost exclusively as a vehicle for secret prayer. Like Tyler, she described trips to church and moving sermons. She also made careful note of the many anniversaries that measured her years;

[7] 15 July 1821, VHS; 18 August 1822, Royall Tyler Daybook, 1817–21, Document 45:15, Royall Tyler Collection, Gift of Helen Tyler Brown, VHS; Mary Palmer Tyler Diary, 1821–43, Document 49:1, Royall Tyler Collection, Gift of Helen Tyler Brown, VHS.

the births and deaths of loved ones, her wedding day, the date she was admitted to church, the dates on which her children experienced a saving grace—all warranted special prayers and dutiful fasting. In Huntington's journals, leisure hardly makes an appearance, and the everyday routines of family and household figure only as a heuristic device, providing inspiration for prayer. Although religious themes dominated the scores of letters she wrote to her children in the 1830s and 1840s, she also included a good measure of family news, including occasional descriptions of her social milieu beyond the family farm. Like Tyler, Huntington enjoyed tea parties and visits with old friends, but she was unnerved by anything grander. Although she was rarely troubled by uncertainties about proper decorum, she struggled to negotiate between the behavior required of a congenial guest and the behavior demanded of a pious Christian. The rigors of a large Northampton party in the late 1830s completely undermined her ability to gauge her self-presentation. She confessed that "it required some discretion, and much of the 'fear of the Lord, which is the beginning of wisdom,' to resist the temptation to levity on the one hand and to avoid the appearance of severity and moroseness on the other." Uncertain that she managed to strike the proper chord, she retreated to the moral high ground; at the very least, such "occasions offer as good an opportunity as any to honour religion before the tho'tless." Far from reinforcing her sense of self, the demands of secular sociability compromised Huntington's sense of self.[8]

This tension between the sacred and the secular could prove especially troubling for young women, who faced the temptations of society more frequently than did their mothers. How was a young woman to demonstrate "that love which the christian is required to feel towards the people of this world" when so many of those people conspired to draw her away from Christ? When nineteen-year-old Eliza Adams found herself caught in this dilemma, her friend Delia Willis reminded her of the Christian's final accounting. "Were one of our dear companions to be brought to a serious deathbed what would be her language in regard to parties and the manner in which professing christians had treated them"? Willis asked. "Would she not say it was time spent worse than in vain"? These were not abstract questions. Willis pointed to "a lady of my acquaintance" who spent the past "25 years accustomed to the society of those who were fond of parties." Although the

[8]Elizabeth Phelps Huntington to Frederic Dan Huntington, n.d. [ca. 1838], Box 12, Folder 8 PPHFP; Diary of Elizabeth Whiting Phelps Huntington, *passim*, PPHFP, Box 13, Folders 7–10.

older woman had been plagued by the same doubts that troubled Eliza, she admitted that simply by attending parties "she gave her sanction and when all was over she had done little different from them who went freely." But even Delia Willis was not immune to the lure of society. Several months later she confessed that she attended a "social visit" only to discover that "there was not in that whole group a heart which beat in unison" with hers. Returning home at the evening's end, Willis concluded that she "enjoyed more heartfull pleasure in one solitary half hour" of prayer than in "years of the 'happy confusion' " that characterized so much of society.[9]

It was one thing for a woman to encounter "happy confusion" among her neighbors and friends, another to confront it within her own home. When Adaline Young returned from a term at Mary Lyon's Ipswich school in 1833, she was mortified that her family received calls on the Sabbath. On the one hand, Young believed that "we ought not to separate ourselves from those that think different from what we do," especially when the heterodox included one's immediate family. On the other hand, "a person who intends to regard the Sabbath, does not wish to be disturbed." When family and friends ignored her gentle hints that "it was not a proper time to call," Young found that in "endeavouring to please the world" she had offended her "Maker." Turning to her older brother for guidance, she asked, "What shall I do? any thing that I can see is duty, I will gladly do, though it may be painful. . . . I . . . do not know what step to take."[10]

For a subsequent generation of women, the commotion of society posed no problem at all. Far from figuring as moral dilemmas, social affairs commanded detailed descriptions, eclipsing accounts of inspiring sermons and spiritual struggles. These women lavished attention on the kinds of gatherings that Mary Tyler had only cursorily described and that Eliza Adams, Delia Willis, and Adaline Young had found so bedeviling. In the newsy letters she wrote to her daughter in the early 1860s, Mrs. Hodges of Oxford, Massachusetts, sporadically reminded the girl to pray and once described a memorable Boston sermon in which the reverend upbraided his wealthy flock for napping in church. In general, however, Mrs. Hodges chose not to explore questions of faith, turning instead to her own busy social life. She recounted Boston vacations, family visits, and one particularly memorable dinner party at which she served "potted pigeons with paste cakes, & roast chicken

[9]Delia Augusta Willis to Eliza Minot Adams, 11 October 1829 and 2 April 1829, Adams Family Papers, DCL, MS 420, Box 5, Folder 13.

[10]Adaline Young to Ira Young, 12 January 1833, Adams Family Papers, DCL, MS 420, Box 5, Folder 55.

with cauliflower, first course including of course all the minor vegetables. For dessert, apple slump pies and grapes, splendid ones . . . from Boston."[11]

Relaying the local news to a friend who was teaching in Boston in 1859, a young Deerfield woman named Rebecca commented not on recent sermons but on recent parties. Unfortunately, the town was "not gay." A last dance proved "so disagreeable" that she had "determined not to attend another." Reversing the pieties of Elizabeth Phelps Huntington, Rebecca urged her friend to thank God that she was wintering among "better pleasures, more salutary influences." She wrote " 'Rejoice & be exceedingly glad' for great is yr joy in Boston—You must have much to amuse and instruct your youthful mind."[12]

Endowing their social lives with the significance that an earlier generation would have reserved for their spiritual lives, such women might also extend the language and imagery of parlor sociability to events of religious importance.[13] Receiving word in 1856 that her friend Elwarder had died, Agnes Gordon Higginson went to view the body. Recalling the incident in her diary, she drew on the same conventions she used when describing the appearance of her living friends at parties and dances. Ignoring Elwarder's prospects for grace, she wrote only that her friend looked "<u>lovely beautiful</u>"; with a funeral wreath round her head, the dead woman even looked "very natural." The year before, learning that "Sophie Harris of Brattleboro" had died, Higginson chose to memorialize her not as a Christian but as the kind of young woman who proved an asset at parties, "a lovely girl whom everybody liked."[14]

By the end of the antebellum era, women and amusements that would once have been condemned as "tho'tless and gay" no longer threatened the standards of Christian piety, much less respectability. Indeed, gentility, made manifest both in manners and in temperament, assumed an increasingly significant role in women's depictions of

[11]Mrs. Hodges to Katherine Craddoc Hodges, 22 October 1861, 17 December 1860, and 15 March 1860, Hodges Family Papers, SL. Significantly, Hodges was as worried about the appearance of her daughter's prayers as she was about their content; in a letter dated 15 March 1860, she urged Katherine to "be as careful about being ostentatious about it as you would be of acting as though ashamed of it." On the connections between inculcating religious faith and inculcating gentility, see Richard Bushman, *Refinement of America*, 319–26.

[12]Rebecca to Agnes Gordon Higginson [Fuller], 11 January 1859, Fuller-Higginson Papers, PVMA.

[13]On the intersection of church, parlor, and gentility, see Bushman, *Refinement of America*, 313–52.

[14]Diary of Agnes Higginson [Fuller], 7–8 March 1856, and 19 March 1855, Fuller-Higginson Family Papers, PVMA.

themselves and those closest to them. But if the elaborate conventions of bourgeois sociability took on new prominence in women's self-fashioning, they never dominated their everyday lives.

Women accustomed to the rigid ritual of the city call quickly learned that provincial society defied many of their assumptions about visiting and sociability in particular. On a trip through Vermont in 1820, Julietta Penaimen was "not a little terrified" to arrive at her New Fane lodgings during tea. To her surprise, her hostess overlooked the gaffe, receiving the party with "smiles and many a welcome." Penaimen was more baffled still the next morning when her hostess indicated her displeasure that Penaimen's party had failed to rise and dress until long after the other boarders had assembled for breakfast. For Penaimen, a world in which the protocols of tea might be disrupted while the morning meal remained sacrosanct was topsy-turvy indeed.[15]

When Amelia White Peabody assumed the role of minister's wife in 1824, she expected to treat the Springfield congregation according to the etiquette that had prevailed in Salem, Massachusetts. Scheduling parish calls, she and her husband tactfully arranged afternoon visits for "such as are too humble to make morning calls." Unfortunately, the ladies of her husband's parish were unaware that even women without sufficient help to allow "morning calls" should be prepared to accept formal calls later in the day. To their horror, the couple surprised one woman who calmly "opened the door with a handkerchief over head & dressed in washing style, & a mop in her hand just in the act of cleaning the floor." The Peabodys beat a hasty retreat, promising to return later.[16]

The nicest provincial women never mastered the decorous social call described in antebellum advice books. The same ladies who paid one another the compliment of a "formal" call were just as likely to drop in at odd times. The diaries and letters of town women, especially, abound with improvised tea parties honoring unexpected guests. For example, the Cochran women were hardly prepared to receive guests the day they moved into their Northampton home in 1836. The poor repair of their unrenovated cottage was compounded by the clutter of moving crates and scattered furniture. During a makeshift tea in the cellar (one of the only rooms that was not "littered up"), Martha

[15]Julietta Penaimen to Jonathan Dorr Bradley, 18 February 1820, Bradley Family Papers, SL. E. Goddard, a young woman traveling through New Hampshire with her father in the early nineteenth century, was less charitable than Penaimen in her assessment of provincial hospitality. See E. Goddard Diary, [n.d.], 1976–58, NHHS.
[16]Amelia White Peabody to Eliza White, 4 November 1824 and 30 September 1824, Everett-Peabody Family Papers, MHS.

Cochran and her mother were surprised by the sound of guests "on the piazzas above." If their disarray embarrassed the Cochrans, it did not faze "the Hardings, Mr. Willard and Sue Flint." Unlike the Peabodys, these guests did not volunteer to return at a better time: There was nothing to do but entertain them. Martha Cochran dryly observed that after she showed them "the beauties of our lovely cottage," the entire party "sat down in the midst of shavings & plants" to play the piano and sing.[17]

Some twenty-five years later, Deerfield residents exhibited even less regard for the proprieties of the social call. One evening in 1859, twenty-seven-year-old Hattie Fuller, her twenty-one year-old brother John, and a boarder named Matty decided to amuse family and friends with a "masquerade." With the two women "dressed up as young men" and John decked out in "a hooped skirt and bonnet," the spectacle was "too funny for anything." Not content to remain at home, the company took off on a series of unannounced visits. Still in costume, they stopped at "Baxter Stebbin's & made a call, & afterwards went over to the Clary's."[18]

Even when provincial women and men sought to emulate the gracious sociability of an urban middle class, they never quite succeeded. It was one thing to identify with the rituals of cosmopolitan gentility, another to reproduce them. The realities of rural New England quickly deflated grand schemes. Royall Tyler, who never forgot his Boston beginnings and never lacked for social pretension, once insisted that his wife host an elegant soiree for his business associates and their "ladies." Ignoring their rustic "parlor" and primitive kitchen, oblivious to the untrained country "help" and the small children, he ordered up a dinner of "a roast and a boiled turkey, a fine ham, roast chickens, and a pair of very fine ducks, oyster sauce and cranberries" with nuts and apples for dessert.[19]

Mary Palmer Tyler struggled valiantly to fulfill her mission. She hired two extra women to help with the cooking, serving, and child care. She borrowed plates, dishes, knives, forks, glasses, and a cake for tea. At the last minute, she fussed with her appearance, for her hus-

[17]Martha Cochran to Agnes Cochran Higginson, 30 May 1836, Fuller-Higginson Papers, PVMA.

[18]Annie Storrow Higginson to Agnes Gordon Higginson, 9 December 1859, Fuller-Higginson Papers, PVMA.

[19]The dinner party is described in Mary Palmer Tyler, *Grandmother Tyler's Book: The Recollections of Mary Palmer Tyler (Mrs. Royall Tyler), 1775–1866*, ed. Frederick Tupper and Helen Tyler Brown (New York: G. P. Putnam's Sons, 1925), 284–91; quotation is from p. 288.

band "was naturally anxious that I should look and behave well on the occasion." Despite her best efforts, dinner was an hour late, the service was clumsy, and the baby shrieked throughout the meal. Insisting that they had had a marvelous time, the guests fled immediately after dinner, taking Royall Tyler with them. Years later, Mary Palmer Tyler recalled that

> this was the first and last time we attempted a dinner party, but contented ourselves with social tea parties with our intimate friends; there were but few in those days, and we could enjoy them without perplexity or more expense than we could afford, and in that way we avoided much unhappiness.[20]

Royall Tyler's pretensions had been crushed by the frontier conditions of early nineteenth-century Vermont. But even later in the century, circumstances could conspire to squelch social ambition. In 1858, a North Hadley family resolved to celebrate a wedding in grand style. Without considering that their house had been constructed for other purposes, they invited one hundred guests, a small orchestra, and a handful of singers to mark the occasion. As the orchestra and singers began the piece that preceded the vows, the floor collapsed and the entire party fell four feet. Rumpled and dirty but unhurt, the party reconvened at the minister's house, where they managed to execute the ceremony, if not the elegant affair.[21]

Sociability and Social Networks

Comical weddings and spoiled dinner parties, impromptu masquerades and neighborly visits—these were the aspects of social life that provincial New Englanders commented on when they turned their attention to sociability. As we have seen, women's diaries and letters offer abundant evidence of a growing gentility; those same sources suggest the ways in which that gentility reshaped not only patterns of provincial sociability, but provincial women's identities. But when men and women contemplated the broader significance of sociability, they ignored the refinement that they cultivated so conscientiously. When they considered sociability as a system of association rather than as the mere effect of individual preference, they affirmed the survival of "old-time" ways in New England's villages and towns. Diaries and

[20]Ibid., 290, 287.
[21]*Hampshire Gazette*, 27 April 1858.

letters that testify to the growing refinement of provincial life also insist upon the endurance of older patterns of interaction and association. Published accounts, in particular, paid scant attention to the growing formality of social life, to parties, theatricals, and balls. Instead, both published and unpublished accounts stress the survival of older patterns of sociability—patterns derived from the household economy.

To demonstrate the persistence of old-time ways, provincial New Englanders could draw on their own experiences and on those of their neighbors and kin; judging by the experiences of Hattie Fuller and Martha Cochran, they did not have to look far for evidence. But if a relatively informal style of sociability lasted through the antebellum period, that same style took on new significance in the context of changing class and gender identities. In their diaries and letters, their memoirs and imaginative literature, provincial women and men elaborated new meanings for old practices. They drew on the rhetoric of republicanism and the conventions of sentimental literature to clarify and magnify the significance of sociability in general and the merits of provincial sociability in particular. Playing simplicity against fashion, authenticity against pretense, and especially country against city, they exaggerated the distinctiveness of provincial sociability. They also conflated the style of provincial sociability with the structure of provincial social relations.

Trying to explain the "peculiarity" of antebellum provincial sociability, Theodore Bliss suggested that "simple ideals of living made it unnecessary to assume an external gloss that did not belong to our everyday existence." This distinctive simplicity fostered an equally distinctive egalitarianism. Looking back at antebellum Northampton, Bliss insisted that social relations and social life were marked by "a certain tone of sincerity and self-respect" that enabled the "butcher, the baker, and candlestick maker" along with the "minister, teacher, and lawyer" to meet in a "large community of intelligent, thinking people."[22]

---

[22]Arthur Ames Bliss, ed., *Theodore Bliss, Publisher and Bookseller: A Study of Character and Life in the Middle Period of the XIX Century* (1911), 37–38. In 1886, Susan I. Lesley (*Recollections of My Mother* [Boston: privately published, 1886], 84) recalled that when she was a girl, "there were no very rich people in Northampton; but many persons of elegant culture, refined and aristocratic manners, and possessing a moderate competence, lived there in much ease, envying no one, really believing themselves highly favored, as they were, and practising a generous hospitality at all times." Although less enamored of provincial society, Francis H. Underwood (*Quabbin: The Story of a New England Town* [Boston: Lee & Shepard Publishers, 1893], 99) similarly argued that (relatively) widespread

Self-serving and nostalgic, his comments nevertheless contain an element of truth. Yet the openness Bliss celebrated owed less to "simple ideals" than to the complex material realities that shaped provincial social networks.[23] The distinctive cast of sociability derived in no small measure from the social structure of rural towns and villages. On the most basic level, community size reinforced the flexible social networks that Bliss remembered. Because the relatively small populations limited the numbers who might be included within a local middle class, all but the most intimate gatherings necessarily encompassed a variety of men and women.[24]

The distinctive class structure of provincial communities played an even larger role in shaping social networks. Numerous social and economic historians have traced a rise in economic inequality from the eighteenth century to the eve of the Civil War. As Christopher Clark has demonstrated, rural New Englanders were also increasingly divided by the "quantity of property that people held, the forms that it took, and the ways they could use it."[25] But if this inequality early produced a recognizable rural working class, it was far slower to produce a recognizable middle class. As students of the New England countryside are discovering, the rural middle class resists the categories of wealth and occupation that social historians have developed to trace middle class formation in cities such as Boston, Philadelphia, and Utica and Rochester, New York.[26] Middling and middle-class provincial townsmen defy straightforward distinctions between manual and nonmanual labor, artisan and entrepreneur, farmer and merchant, as Christopher Clark and Jonathan Prude have demonstrated. By their

---

property ownership placed the "smith or the joiner who owned his house and shop . . . on equal terms with the farmer, his customer, and could hold up his head with the best."

[23]My thinking here is influenced by Stuart Blumin, who defined social networks as "the arrays of interactions characteristically experienced by the members of specific groups of people in their daily rounds—within the home, at work . . . and in whatever other public and private spaces people confront and interact with one another." See his *Emergence of the Middle Class*, 264–65.

[24]Compare Nancy Grey Osterud, *Bonds of Community* 244–48, who credits dense kin networks rather than social class for creating similar patterns of informality and openness within a small rural community later in the nineteenth century.

[25]Christopher Clark, *The Roots of Rural Capitalism: Western Massachusetts, 1780–1860* (Ithaca, N.Y.: Cornell University Press, 1990), 264.

[26]Classic studies of urban middle-class formation include Paul E. Johnson, *A Shopkeeper's Millennium: Society and Revivals in Rochester, New York, 1815–1837* (New York: Hill & Wang, 1978); Mary P. Ryan, *Cradle of the Middle Class: The Family in Oneida County, New York, 1790–1865* (New York: Cambridge University Press, 1983); Blumin, *Emergence of the Middle Class.*

lights, the butcher and lawyer of Bliss's memoir may have had more in common than we initially expect.[27]

Compared with its urban counterpart, the provincial middle class appears to have been far more flexible. It may also have been more divided. Christopher Clark has revealed significant tensions among Connecticut River Valley wealthholders, whose access to the benefits of a national commercial and financial marketplace varied considerably. These same farmers, artisans, merchants, and manufacturers were separated by more than economic opportunity: They were divided by the extent of their adherence to the ethos of the household economy, marked by either a commitment to "older patterns of family support and neighborhood assistance" or by the decision to heed the call of the market by relying on institutionalized finance and diversifying their property holdings.[28] From this perspective, provincial social networks derived not simply from the permeability of the middle class at its upper and lower margins but also from its internal contradictions.

These hazy class distinctions combined with the intimacy of small-town life to preserve the kind of familiar, face-to-face interactions that had all but disappeared from city streets by 1820. Francis H. Underwood recalled that, among Massachusetts yeomen, "it was the custom to salute on the highway or in public places; to pass even a stranger without some recognition would have been considered rude." Indeed, he explained, "one of the reasons city people were so disliked" was their refusal to bow, or "pass the time o'day."[29]

These social obligations extended beyond farmers to bind men and women of different ranks. Underwood described a comic confrontation between a rustic church deacon and a wealthy townsman, Mr. Grant, whose daughters, two "pert minxes," had raised the ire of the pious villagers with their worldly piano-playing. To demonstrate the virtues of piano playing in general and his daughters in particular, Grant invited the deacon and his wife to tea. Underwood, who deplored the vulgarity of provincial life, played the scene for full comic effect. The "pert minxes," coached by their father, were tastefully dressed and "on their good behavior." In contrast, the deacon's wife took off a "calash" of green silk only to reveal "a tufted turban of lemon-colored batiste" that

---

[27]Clark, *Roots of Rural Capitalism*; Jonathan Prude, *The Coming of Industrial Order: Town and Factory Life in Rural Massachusetts, 1810–1860* (New York: Cambridge University Press, 1985). Significantly, although Clark and especially Prude describe the emergence of a rural "working class," they never use the terms "middle class" or "bourgeoisie" when referring to the elites of their communities; instead, they refer to coalitions of merchants, manufacturers, artisans, farmers, and the odd professional.

[28]Clark, *Roots of Rural Capitalism*, 264.

[29]Underwood, *Quabbin*, 73–74.

called to mind the "headgear of an oriental prince." The urbane and tolerant Mr. Grant provided a foil for the deacon.

In Underwood's telling, the "pyanner" triumphed. By the end of the visit, Deacon Rawson agreed that the piano, like so many other symbols of secular gentility, was good or bad "accordin' to th' yeuse thet's made on't." Mrs. Rawson overturned her earlier conviction that the girls were "high-flyers and praoud," declaring, "I don't want ter see better behavin' gals, nor modester dressed than they was." Although the story's humor depended on the deacon and his wife, its moral extended to the Grant family. The girls "were apparently softened and calmed" by their encounter with rustic folk. Once contemptuous of farm life, they respectfully inquired about "cheese-making, and promised to go out and see the dairy, the calves, the poultry, and all the delights of the farm." And if Grant had been amused by the deacon's audacity and his old-fashioned piety, he could not afford to dismiss him.[30]

Compared with Theodore Bliss's description of village egalitarianism, Underwood's comedy of manners betrays an acute awareness of the subtle, even petty, hierarchies of village life. But these divisions did not translate into a strict segregation of classes. In both accounts, men and women of different classes moved across the same provincial landscape, accommodating one another with more or less grace. This pattern of social acknowledgement and accommodation seems to have prevailed in life as well as literature. To be sure, social standards and social inclusiveness varied greatly among communities and within them, depending on the size and sophistication of the town as well as the resources available to particular families and the closeness of their connections to urban culture. Still, both the tone and the structure of provincial society allowed for considerable interaction between classes, linking an increasingly genteel middle class to uncultured farmers and even to the very respectable poor. Unlike the good citizens of Boston and Philadelphia, who grappled with the problems posed by rough-looking strangers, provincial men and women hammered out an etiquette of social proximity that allowed them to coexist with poorer neighbors whose names and histories they knew all too well.[31]

[30]Ibid., 202–206.

[31]Stuart M. Blumin (*Emergence of the Middle Class*, 231) argues persuasively that the shift from the "personalized, face-to-face hierarchies of the eighteenth century . . . to the more distant, categorical hierarchies of the nineteenth century" was central to the experience of class in the nineteenth-century city, notwithstanding his puzzling conclusion that this process represents a shift from a "pre-class" to a "class" society. On the threatening presence of strangers in northern cities, see Halttunen, *Confidence Men and Painted Women* and Kasson, *Rudeness and Civility*.

Theodore Bliss himself came from a family that had been destitute almost since his birth. After an ill-advised loan destroyed his father's finances and his reason, young Theodore was shuttled from one relative to another until he was finally apprenticed to a Northampton printer and bookseller. Such a young man could hardly be said to have traveled in the best circles. But when Mary Wright, whose family was prominent if not wealthy, began to attract his "respectful attention on the street," Bliss had no difficulty befriending her; he quickly became a regular visitor at the Sunday evening musicals hosted by Wright and her sister.[32]

Caroline Clapp Briggs, a contemporary of Bliss, found religion to be more important than wealth in drawing the boundaries of her social circle. During her youth, she recalled, "my acquaintances were mostly Unitarians. I had no intimate acquaintance with any family in the Orthodox church." Yet within her congregation, Briggs befriended members of Northampton's best families. In the 1840s, after her father lost his job as the town jailer, the young woman and her sister "did sewing, copying, or anything our hands could find to do, as well as taking in boarders" to help support the family. Scrambling to help support her family, Briggs was a regular visitor in the homes of her betters. She benefited from the "large hospitality" of the wealthy Hunt family, whose house "was more tasteful than any other in the village, better furnished, with ornaments and pictures, and always decorated with tastefully arranged flowers"; she relaxed in silk manufacturer Samuel Whitmarsh's conservatory, with an "atmosphere so summer-like that one could easily forget all the frost and snow outside." She particularly enjoyed the Cochrans' society, taking great pleasure in Martha Cochran's keen wit.[33]

There were limits to the liberality of Northampton's better families. While Theodore Bliss found Mary Wright easy to meet and easier still to love, marrying her proved far more difficult. His concerns about his future deterred him from proposing marriage until he had begun to make his fortune in Philadelphia. If Caroline Clapp Briggs often enjoyed afternoon teas, charitable sewing, and perhaps even cotillion parties at the homes of Northampton's elite, she was almost certainly not included among their intimates. Briggs idolized the rather formidable Martha Cochran, describing her as "one of the rarest women I ever met." But the young woman failed to make an equal impression

[32]*Theodore Bliss*, 45.

[33]Caroline C. Briggs, *Reminiscences and Letters of Caroline C[lapp] Briggs*, ed. George S. Merriam (Boston: Houghton Mifflin, 1897), 58–59, 60, 65, 77.

on Cochran. Indeed, the Cochran women's newsy letters ignored the Clapp family altogether. Caroline Clapp Briggs remained at the edges of the Cochrans' vision, one of the nameless women who regularly appeared in their parlor for meetings of the sewing society and the reading club.[34]

Still, the intimacy of provincial society gave both Briggs and Bliss an entrée that would have been denied them in a larger city. More important, it encouraged a mutual identification. By allowing Deacon and Mrs. Rawson, Theodore Bliss, and Caroline Clapp Briggs a stake in the world of their betters, provincial sociability softened the harshest edges of class distinction. The growing awareness of class was muted by a shared sense of community.

This sense of community was also reinforced by a valorization of the local, the particular. Gathering together as friends and neighbors, provincial women and men shared an affinity for one another not simply as individuals but as members of particular towns and villages. The same expansive social landscape that allowed Theodore Bliss to court Mary Wright and that gave Caroline Briggs entrée into the parlor of Martha Cochran was hemmed in by an entrenched localism. Indeed, the style of provincial sociability worked to intensify local identities. This is not to suggest that provincial New Englanders had no interest in the world outside their households and towns. Both the influx of urban newspapers and the eclectic national stories reprinted in provincial papers speak to the growing ties between the North's cities and its hinterland.[35] For women like Mary Palmer Tyler and Amelia White Peabody, who boasted close ties to Boston and Salem through their kin, the city and the society it represented could seem closer still. But when cosmopolitanism threatened to leave the printed page and intrude on

[34]Briggs, *Reminiscences*, 58; Bliss's courtship is described in *Theodore Bliss*, 45–47 and in my Chapter 5. It is useful here to compare Briggs's perceptions of Unitarian fellowship with those of Elizabeth White Peabody, whose husband presided over Springfield's Unitarian congregation. In 1842, the Peabodys hosted a series of parties to "establish a more intimate" relationship with the poorer members of their congregation. In planning the parties, Peabody invited groups of the working men and women who were "in the same circle among themselves, & then add half a dozen or so of our own circle, of such as are disposed to make themselves agreeable to [the working-class congregants]." Peabody's claim that "we never had pleasanter parties" notwithstanding, the degree of division is obvious. In general, the smaller the town, the more democratic and flexible the sociability. Elizabeth White Peabody to Mary Jane White, 22 March 1842, Everett-Peabody Family Papers, MHS.

[35]Richard D. Brown, *Knowledge Is Power: The Diffusion of Information in Early America, 1700–1865* (New York: Oxford University Press, 1989), esp. 132–59. For the effect of this diffusion of information on provincial women, see Catherine E. Kelly, "Between Town and Country: New England Women and the Creation of a Provincial Middle Class, 1820–1860" (Ph.D. diss., University of Rochester, 1992).

provincial lives and communities, women, especially, could respond with a profound parochialism.

Reserving their deepest affinities for men and women whose faces and histories they knew almost as well as their own, women often distanced themselves from the unfamiliar. While visiting kin in Roxbury, fourteen-year-old Mehab Ann Bradley was invited to call on "Mr. Tom Williams." Bradley did not regard the occasion as a social opportunity, a chance to broaden her circle of acquaintances. On the contrary, she wrote, "I spent a very dull afternoon, they being strangers to me." And this was not simply the attitude of an awkward and self-absorbed adolescent.[36]

During a year-long stay with her sister in Hamilton, New York, twenty-eight-year-old Sophronia Grout found that the hospitality of her sister and brother-in-law did not fully compensate for the strangeness of her new surroundings. Grout had grown up as the daughter of a Hawley, Massachusetts, minister; when she traveled from home, she moved through a network of kin and friends who claimed some connection either to Hawley or the Grout family. In Hamilton, she was cut loose from her social network; despite her sister's presence, she felt isolated from people who shared her associations and identity. The experience was deeply disorienting. As she explained to her parents, "to be in the midst of a people whose customs are new to one, & not one female associate who I ever saw before or who is acquainted with one person that I have ever known personally places me in a situation that I have before been a stranger to."[37]

Like so many other single women who found themselves far from home, Sophronia Grout took refuge in the church. She managed to attend church three times on Sundays and once during the week, relying on Bible classes to acquaint herself with like-minded "females." To deepen her sense of belonging, she requested a letter of dismission from her father's parish that she might formally join the Hamilton parish. "I think I should feel more interested in them & more at home with them if I belonged to the same body & they probably would take a deeper interest in my spiritual welfare," she reasoned. But if Grout had demonstrated her commitment to the Christian community of Hamilton, the community was far slower to declare a commitment to her. Coming out of one church meeting, Grout saw a woman she recognized from her Bible class and suggested they walk home together. The woman "appeared somewhat surprised at my freedom" but con-

[36]Mehab Ann Bradley to Jonathan Dorr Bradley, 7 August 1820, Bradley Family Papers, SL.

[37]Sophronia Grout to John Grout and Polly Taylor Grout, 23 June 1828, Sophronia Grout Papers, PVMA.

sented to accompany Grout. Others were not so charitable. After another meeting, she found herself walking alongside two "ladies" from her new parish. When Grout attempted to begin a conversation, "they began to slacken their pace & appear rather amazed that I should take such liberty." Generally, Grout tried to "amuse" herself at the "shyness" of her new neighbors. But after this snub, she wrote, "I crossed the street & hastened home almost determined to make no more efforts." The people of Hamilton were "cautious about forming hasty acquaintances," even with so exemplary a young woman as Sophronia Grout.[38]

This caution was not peculiar to Hamilton, New York. Encountering unfamiliar women, however respectable in appearance and manner, provincial women did not see sisters with a shared gender identity; they saw strangers. On a long stage ride from Salem to Worcester in 1822, Amelia Peabody found herself alone in the coach with three other women, "all equally unknown to each other." Without "protector[s]," she boasted that the group "exhibited an instance of independence" that was "not often to be met with." Although the women were "too polite to seek . . . a general acquaintanceship," they gradually "discovered enough of one another's "condition & character to put [them] on a very sociable footing." Significantly, the stories through which the women revealed their "condition and character" had less to do with class or personality, narrowly defined, than with provincial networks. Peabody was delighted to learn that one of her companions, whose name she never did learn, was a "neighbor" from Bradford, Vermont, a town "some forty miles below" her Lancaster, New Hampshire, hometown. The two knew Vermonters in common and shared many friends in Springfield, Massachusetts. This knowledge only confirmed what the anonymous woman's "manners, style of conversation & appearance" had already suggested. Locating her companion in a social network that intersected with her own, Amelia White "conceived her to be a <u>Lady</u>."[39]

Like Amelia White and Sophronia Grout, provincial women knew

---

[38]Sophronia Grout to her sisters, 29 June 1828, and Sophronia Grout to John Grout and Polly Tarble Grout, 23 June 1828, Sophronia Grout Papers, PVMA.

[39]Amelia White [Peabody] to Daniel A. White, 8 October 1822, Everett-Peabody Family Papers, MHS. Peabody was more confident among strangers than many provincial women. On a visit to Boston in 1797, Elizabeth Phelps reported her terror at the prospect of introducing herself to her brother's landlady; see Elizabeth Phelps [Huntington] to Elizabeth Porter Phelps, 20 August 1797, PPHFP, Box 13, Folder 1. See also the Diary of Mary Hoyt Wilson, 15 September 1826, PVMA. Grieving over the death of Amelia Lyman, she wrote, "What makes it doubly aggravating is, that this child" died "in a land of strangers . . . a hundred miles from home with no kindred save but a sister to weep over her grave."

themselves and their associates not simply as individuals or as embodiments of abstract concepts of "class" and "gender" but as members of networks that were embedded in and dependent on particular households and towns. Sizing up the men and women around them, they valued the shared histories of families and communities over the vagaries of personal experience. Such was the case in the spring of 1848, when the Parsons family of Gilmanton, New Hampshire, received an unexpected visit from "Joseph Haines of Lynn & his brother Andrew from Galena," former Gilmanton residents. The Haines brothers had hardly played a large role in Sarah Jane Parsons's childhood. Although it was "very pleasant to meet them," she "had no recollection of either of them." But several weeks later, recalling the good talk and gossip her family had enjoyed with the prodigals, Parsons commented, "How much pleasanter such old friends seem than new ones."[40] Parsons did not need to know the brothers themselves. She needed only to know that they knew her household and her kin, her neighbors and her community. Sharing a past with her townsmen, her kin, and, by extension, Parsons herself, the Haines brothers provided a reassurance that "new" friends could not. For some time, Sarah Jane Parsons had been unsettled by Gilmanton's shifting population, by the absence of familiar faces and the sudden appearance of new ones on the town's streets. It is in this context that she found the Haines brothers so comforting. These two strangers, these two "old friends," reinforced her identity—an identity shaped by the history of a particular community and anchored in the relations of a particular family.[41]

Town versus Country

The "peculiarity" of provincial sociability did more than ease tensions between classes and shore up a sense of community. The

[40]Sarah Jane Parsons to Elizabeth Parsons Hidden, 28 June 1848, Parsons Family Papers, SL.

[41]This localism extends beyond personal relations to shape abstract questions of Christian salvation. When Elizabeth Phelps Huntington's son Frederic Dan Huntington, a minister, was called to proselytize at the Massachusetts state penitentiary, she was delighted; few men had an opportunity to perform a more necessary service. But although she understood both the depth of his commitment and the scope of his mission, she subsumed them beneath loyalty to the fortunes of his hometown. Mindful of the larger world in which her son moved, she could not resist urging him to make a special effort to "instruct the young men from Hadley, who have been sent to State's Prison." Elizabeth Phelps Huntington to Frederic Dan Huntington, 21 April, n.d. [ca. 1842], PPHFP, Box 12, Folder 9.

same patterns of sociability that seemed to narrow the distance between members of an emerging middle class and their poorer farming and laboring neighbors, binding them together as a single community, also served to emphasize the cultural distance between country and city. Indeed, the sociability that prevailed in New England's towns and villages allowed men and women to construct a middle-class culture that owed less to urban, middle-class style than to its disavowal. Visits to the urban center regularly provided provincials with ample fodder for comparison. But even distant reports about city entertainments could prompt provincial women, especially, to comment on the distance between town and country.

Marianne Cochran, for example, relished the society meetings and musicals that kept her away from her Northampton home three nights out of seven. In her letters, however, these homely diversions stand in sharp contrast to the extravagant affairs of prosperous Bostonians with whom she had a passing acquaintance. With disapproval only slightly checked by envy, she contrasted the modest dimensions of her own social life with a "dinner & ball where a bouquet was placed at every plate & after meats &c all adjourned to another room & table for the dessert!"[42] Distancing themselves from the elaborate conventions of bourgeois civility, Cochran and her contemporaries simultaneously constructed and took refuge in the respectability of New England's morality—a morality increasingly at odds with the show and display of bourgeois culture. One woman recalled that even at Northampton's largest parties "everything . . . was managed after the most economical fashion." Disdaining "confectioners' commodities," guests contented themselves with simple fare—apples, walnuts, and a basket of oranges, or cake and wine. Reproaching a younger, more sophisticated generation, she boasted that "all the food was good, because it was homemade; and it was not the New England fashion to despise good, well cooked food."[43]

Such comments surely testify to the human propensity to censure others and to praise the good old days at the expense of the present.

[42]Marianne Cochran to Agnes Cochran Higginson, 10 February 1839, Fuller-Higginson Papers, PVMA.

[43]Briggs, *Reminiscences* 66. Hard times could make hospitality simpler still. During the 1857 depression, the "gentlemen" of the Brattleboro's Lawrence Water Cure Establishment recast their Wednesday-night socials. As Mary Tyler reported, "They are not to have any refreshments—and the Ladies are to agree to have no new dress—but wear such as they have and it is called the 'Hard times club.' " Mary Tyler to Thomas Pickman Tyler, 1 December 1857, Royall Tyler Collection, Gift of Helen Tyler Brown, VHS.

But they also reveal the ways in which provincial women and men participated in the construction of the New England village ideal, with its images of an organic social order based on widespread property ownership and maintained through neighborly society.[44] The homemade props of rural sociability kept it free from the taint of the urban market, just as social networks kept provincial New Englanders free from the corrupting divisions of bourgeois social relations. Sentimental and nostalgic, this construction of the "New England fashion" and the New England village ultimately cut against the localism that had marked provincial society. It was one thing to belong to a specific community with a specific history, another to inhabit a village ideal that owed less to the attributes of any one town than to the putative differences between New York City and Hadley. To celebrate an idealized New England village, women and men had to flatten out the differences between real ones.

Through the structure of social networks and the discourse surrounding sociability, middle-class women and men depicted New England's towns and villages as standing outside of bourgeois class relations and transcending bourgeois culture. Their increasingly elaborate style of sociability revealed their deepening identification with genteel habits of the urban middle class. But to the extent that sociability recalled the corporate social relations of earlier generations, members of the emerging middle class could abstract their communities and themselves from social change and bourgeois social relations. Far from serving as a bulwark against the encroachments of bourgeois culture,

[44]My thinking on the connections between the idealized vision of the New England village and nineteenth-century bourgeois culture has been influenced especially by Joseph S. Wood, *The New England Village* (Baltimore: Johns Hopkins University Press, 1997); Stephen Nissenbaum, "New England as Region and Nation," in *All over the Map: Rethinking American Regions*, ed. Edward L. Ayers, et. al. (Baltimore: Johns Hopkins University Press, 1996); Robert A. Gross, "The Confidence Man and the Preacher: The Cultural Politics of Shay's Rebellion," in *In Debt to Shays: The Bicentennial of an Agrarian Rebellion*, ed. Robert A. Gross (Charlottesville: University of Virginia Press, 1993), 297–324; Lawrence Buell, "American Pastoral Ideology Reappraised," *American Literary History* 1 (Spring 1989): 1–29, and *New England Literary Culture: From Revolution to Renaissance* (New York: Cambridge University Press, 1986); Sarah Burns, *Pastoral Inventions: Rural Life in Nineteenth-Century Art and Culture* (Philadelphia: Temple University Press, 1989); and John R. Stilgoe, *Borderland: Origins of the American Suburb, 1820–1939* (New Haven, Conn.: Yale University Press, 1988). Daniel Walker Howe, in *The Political Culture of the American Whigs* (Chicago: University of Chicago Press, 1979), also offers suggestive evidence of the importance of a pastoral vision of New England for the nineteenth-century Whig project. See also my " 'The Consummation of Rural Prosperity and Happiness': New England Agricultural Fairs and the Construction of Class and Gender, 1810–1860," *American Quarterly* 49 (1997): 574–602.

social styles derived from the household economy could be turned to the needs of an emerging middle class. By contributing to the New England village ideal, the influence of this same sociability spread beyond provincial New England to shape northern bourgeois culture, for the sentimentalized picture of village life that loomed large in nineteenth-century literary culture and political discourse sprang not simply from the imaginations of urban intellectuals and canonical writers but from the experiences, strategies, and texts of provincial New Englanders themselves as they negotiated the transition from household economy to market society.

7

"All the artificial barriers which society sometimes erects, appeared to be thrown down"

When Theodore Bliss recalled his youth in antebellum Northampton, Massachusetts, he fondly summoned up a public culture that was both unpretentious and decidedly masculine. Provincial New England fostered a "sincerity and self-respect" that enabled the "butcher, the baker, and candlestick maker" along with the "minister, teacher, and lawyer" to meet in a "large community of intelligent, thinking people." Northampton and villages like it stood as a reproof to northern cities, whose public spaces were increasingly segregated by the social divisions of class, ethnicity, religion, and gender. If Bliss deplored the false distinctions that separated the butcher and the lawyer in the nation's cities, his account of provincial sociability reproduces the distinctions that banished women from antebellum public culture. In the Northampton of his memory, it was only virtuous *men* who mingled on streets and in bookstores without regard to rank or wealth. Women, virtuous or otherwise, were nowhere to be found.[1]

Bliss's memory owed less to reality than to nineteenth-century gender ideology. Merchants and mechanics did pass the time of day on provincial streets. But so did their daughters and wives. The most cursory reading of diaries, letters, and newspapers demonstrates that

---

[1] Arthur Ames Bliss, ed., *Theodore Bliss, Publisher and Bookseller: A Study of Character and Life in the Middle Period of the XIX Century* (1911), 37–38.

throughout the antebellum period, provincial sociability persistently defied the rigid separation of spheres that nineteenth-century observers and twentieth-century social historians have posited as the sine qua non of middle-class society. Provincial women were confined neither to the privacy of the home nor to homosocial networks. At private gatherings, women encountered, sought out, and even enjoyed the company of their men. And they laid claim to the public culture of antebellum New England in two senses—staking out a physical presence in public space and a symbolic one in civic life.

On one level, there is nothing extraordinary in the discrepancy between Bliss's account and the picture of provincial society that emerges from diaries, letters, and newspaper accounts. Historians of all stripes have frequently cautioned against mistaking prescription for practice. And feminist historians, in particular, have recognized for some time the discursive nature of the nineteenth century's separate spheres.[2] Yet if we now accept that women and men did not inhabit separate worlds—if we agree that ideology did not serve as a mirror held up to experience—we are far less certain about the relation between gender ideology and experience. More to the point, although we now agree that middle-class women and men of the nineteenth century did not inhabit separate worlds, we still know relatively little about the world they created together.[3]

We know far less about the broader social, political, and cultural implications of heterosociability, the ways in which it might have shaped the construction of private and public spheres. Although several recent studies have examined the ways in which neighborly visit-

[2]For overviews of these developments in feminist historiography, see especially Joan Wallach Scott's Introduction to *Feminism and History*, ed. Wallach Scott (New York: Oxford University Press, 1996), 1–13; Carolyn Steedman, "Bimbos from Hell," *Social History* 19 (1995): 57–67; Linda K. Kerber, "Separate Spheres, Female Worlds, Woman's Place: The Rhetoric of Women's History," *Journal of American History* 75 (1988): 9–39; Nancy A. Hewitt, "Beyond the Search for Sisterhood: American Women's History in the 1980s," *Social History* 10 (1985): 299–321, esp. 300–304. The classic feminist analysis of the gendered division between public and private remains Michelle Zimbalist Rosaldo, "Women, Culture, and Society: A Theoretical Overview," in M. Z. Rosaldo and Louise Lamphere, eds., *Woman, Culture, and Society*, (Stanford, Calif: Stanford University Press, 1974), 17–42.

[3]The bulk of the scholarship exploring the heterosocial dimensions of nineteenth-century life has focused on courtship and romantic love. Certainly, these studies have proved a valuable corrective to the notion that women inhabited a "female world of love and ritual," but they hardly illuminate the whole range of heterosocial experience. See, for example, Steven Seidman, *Romantic Longings: Love in America, 1830–1980* (New York: Routledge, 1991); Karen Lystra, *Searching the Heart: Women, Men, and Romantic Love in Nineteenth-Century America* (New York: Oxford University Press, 1989); and Ellen K. Rothman, *Hands and Hearts: A History of Courtship in America* (New York: Basic Books, 1984).

ing and community organizations drew nineteenth-century women and men together, these studies have assumed that patterns of heterosociability reveal not only the defiance of separate spheres but the defiance of middle-class hegemony.[4] Seen this way, women's presence in the public sphere signifies a bold transgression of nineteenth-century gender conventions, while heterosociability serves as a noisy challenge to middle-class hegemony. Perhaps. But provincial heterosociability was shaped by men as well as women and was elaborated by prosperous town residents as well as rustic farmers and the laboring poor. Far from defying the dominant conventions of gender and class, it helped to constitute them. How, then, can we make sense of provincial heterosociability?

Questions about the intersection of gender, sociability, and social order have been enlivened by recent debates about the boundary of the public sphere and the relation between public and private spheres. Building on Jurgen Habermas's formulation of the "authentic public sphere," scholars have begun to conceptualize the public as that portion of society which negotiates between the private concerns of families and households and the interests of the state and that encompasses the social spaces and processes through which public opinion is formed.[5] More recently, scholars have made a compelling case for the value of public sphere for historians of gender. Habermas's "authentic" public sphere developed within and emerged out of the private sphere. More to the point, as David S. Shields and Dena Goodman have demonstrated, this public sphere was constituted through a variety of discursive institutions, some constructed by women and many more constructed by men and women together.[6]

[4]See Karen V. Hansen, *A Very Social Time: Crafting Community in Antebellum New England* (Berkeley: University of California Press, 1994), and especially Nancy Grey Osterud, *Bonds of Community: The Lives of Farm Women in Nineteenth-Century New York* (Ithaca, N.Y.: Cornell University Press, 1991).

[5]Jurgen Habermas, *The Transformation of the Public Sphere: An Inquiry into a Category of Bourgeois Society* (Cambridge, Mass: MIT Press, 1989). For critical discussions of Habermas's concept of the public sphere, see, for example, the essays collected in Craig Calhoun, ed., *Habermas and the Public Sphere* (Cambridge, Mass: MIT Press, 1992). For Americanists' attention to and interventions in these debates, see David Waldstreicher, review of Craig Calhoun, ed., *Habermas and the Public Sphere, William and Mary Quarterly*, 3d ser., (1995): 175–77; David S. Shields, *Civil Tongues and Polite Letters in British America* (Chapel Hill: University of North Carolina Press, 1997); Kathleen M. Brown, *Good Wives, Nasty Wenches, and Anxious Patriarchs: Gender, Race, and Power in Colonial Virginia* (Chapel Hill: University of North Carolina Press, 1996); and David Scobey, "Anatomy of the Promenade: The Politics of Bourgeois Sociability in Nineteenth-Century New York," *Social History* (1992): 203–27.

[6]See, for example, Dena Goodman, *The Republic of Letters: A Cultural History of the French Enlightenment* (Ithaca, N.Y.: Cornell University Press, 1994) and "Public Sphere

By challenging the rigidly gendered, categorical opposition of public and private in this way, the notion of a public sphere can help us to move beyond the static opposition between the masculine domains of state and market and the feminine domains of parlor and kitchen. This reframing broadens the definition of politics and civic life beyond citizenship and voting to include the literary societies, coffeehouses, salons, and civic rituals that influenced political values and behavior. In the process, it reveals a public world in which women created social and cultural meanings not simply through their absence but also through their presence. Finally, the concept of a public sphere enables us to see beyond the ability of particular women to gain access to political power in order to think about broader meaning of patterns of female presence and absence in the public sphere.

Provincial New Englanders proved reluctant to cast the public sphere as male and the private sphere as female, much less to draw impenetrable boundaries between the two. The private sociability and the public culture that developed in rural New England from the late eighteenth century through the antebellum period are better understood as parts of a continuum rather than as separate, much less oppositional, spheres. A single word—"society"—signified the company of friends and neighbors, the sociability of voluntary associations, and the public assemblies that accompanied civic rituals. For the most part, this "society" was conspicuously heterosocial. Unlike the public culture of antebellum cities that increasingly emphasized the exclusive fellowship of white men, both as citizens and as property owners, the public sphere of New England's countryside accorded space to women as well as men.[7] At the levels of both symbol and practice, cultural associations and public rituals demanded the presence of women and men. Indeed, during the antebellum period, provincial women *in-*

---

and Private Life: Toward a Synthesis of Current Historiographical Approaches to the Old Regime," *History and Theory* 31 (1992): 1–20; David S. Shields, *Civil Tongues and Polite Letters*. For an overview of feminist critiques of Habermas, see Belinda Davis, "Reconsidering Habermas, Gender, and the Public Sphere: The Case of Wilhelmine Germany," in *Society, Culture, and the State in Germany, 1870–1930*, ed. Geoff Eley (Ann Arbor: University of Michigan Press, 1996), 397–426.

[7] On the urban public sphere, see Mary P. Ryan, *Women in Public: Between Banners and Ballots, 1825–1880* (Baltimore: Johns Hopkins University Press, 1990). For a discussion of the role of men's cultural associations in the creation of an urban middle class, see Stuart M. Blumin, *The Emergence of the Middle Class: Social Experience in the American City, 1760–1900* (New York: Cambridge University Press, 1989), 206, 211–18. Blumin argues that despite the significance of cultural associations for middle-class culture, they have been underrepresented in discussions of nineteenth-century middle-class volunteerism, mostly because they left few records. But he also contends that such associations played no public role—an analysis that differs greatly from my own.

creased their visibility in public culture. In provincial communities, members of an emerging middle class deployed *heterosociability* to negotiate new gender and class identities and to construct both public and private spheres. Their experiences shed new light on the dynamic relationship between gender, sociability, and the development of public and private spheres.

Everyday Heterosociability

From the time they were old enough to join in parties and socials, provincial girls and boys were thrown together. Mary Palmer Tyler of Brattleboro, Vermont, delighted in entertaining her children's friends at parties that included both boys and girls. One winter afternoon in 1819, she invited twelve "little girls" to take tea with her ten-year-old daughter Amelia; the party was later joined by "some boys" for an evening of dancing. Two years later, after a party for her eldest daughter, Tyler found "a good store of good things left" and told Amelia that she could make the leftovers into a party if it would "suffice for winter." "Greatly delighted," Amelia Tyler "mustered 17 misses"; her brother Joseph, "quite inspired," rounded up "7 young lads and they had quite a jovial time." Tyler's parties do not suggest an ungendered sociability. After all, her daughters took responsibility for inviting the neighborhood girls while her sons summoned the boys. Still, the parties brought boys and girls together to eat, drink, dance, and sing.[8]

The heterosociability enjoyed by the Tyler children and their friends persisted throughout the lives of most provincial women and men. After moving to Deerfield, Massachusetts, in the 1850s, Agnes Cochran Higginson received a warm welcome from her neighbors. She was promptly visited by Mr. and Mrs. Lincoln, Mr. and Mrs. Smith, and Mr. and Mrs. Moores. Helen Mills Huntington, wife of a Northampton attorney, received calls from both male and female friends in the 1840s. Her in-laws, Dan and Elizabeth Phelps Huntington, generally visited their friends as a couple. One fall day in 1835, the Huntingtons received two invitations: The same morning that "widow Maj. Smith" invited the Huntingtons to drink tea "in company with Doct. Brown and lady," "Mrs. Doct. Porter sent a note, requesting [their] company and Bethia's at their house to meet friends at tea today." Surveying this embarrassment of riches, Huntington declared the conflict "a pity, as

[8]16 December 1819, 16–17 December 1817, and 11 June 1818, Royall Tyler Daybook, 1817–21, Document 45:15, Royall Tyler Collection, Gift of Helen Tyler Brown, VHS.

calls of this kind are so rare." The number of invitations may have been unusual, but the makeup of the parties was not. In Hadley, Massachusetts, even the smallest gatherings included both men and women.[9]

Provincial women and girls spent a good deal of time in the company of male kin and friends. Treasuring the hours they spent with mothers, sisters, and female friends, women took equal pleasure in the company of their men. Hattie Fuller described one "merry" evening spent with her good friend Rebecca. The two young women "sat up 'till two o'clock, ate mince pies & gingerbread apples &c." With such good food and fine conversation, the young women agreed that they lacked only the company of Hattie's brother, George. She wrote him that "we would have been pleased to have you steped in while we were enjoying ourselves."[10]

Such frequent and familiar contact afforded particular men and women the opportunity for friendship. Royall Tyler's elegant and urbane manners earned him the favor of Guilford and Brattleboro women. Something of a ladies' man, he enchanted the wives of lawyers, farmers, and mechanics alike. But this charm was not an empty exercise, for Tyler counted at least some of these women among his dearest friends. After the death of his "truely valued Friend Madam Denison" in 1822, Tyler's precarious health took a turn for the worse; mourning his loss, he became "very unwell—and depressed in spirits."[11] Martha Cochran, who was Theodore Bliss's Northampton contemporary, was especially close to her neighbor, Judge Lyman. Although easily irritated by the foibles of her friends (including the meddlesome Mrs. Lyman), Cochran never lost patience with the judge. Instead, she welcomed his unplanned visits, enjoyed his company at whist, and took his opinions seriously. Deeply suspicious by nature, she also trusted him. When squabbles between her sisters, brother-in-

[9]Elizabeth Porter Huntington to Frederic Dan Huntington, 8 October 1835 and 18 March 1840, PPHFP, Box 12, Folder 8; Agnes Cochran Higginson to Stephen Higginson II, 20 April 1854, Fuller-Higginson Papers, PVMA. Compare Mary Palmer Tyler (*Grandmother Tyler's Book: The Recollections of Mary Palmer Tyler (Mrs. Royall Tyler) 1775–1866*, ed. Frederick Tupper and Helen Tyler Brown (New York: G. P. Putnam's Sons, 1925), 270) who wrote that the rhythms of the agricultural calendar determined the makeup of Vermont tea parties; in the summer, male guests included only the host, the physician, a minister, and a lawyer.

[10]Hattie Fuller to George Fuller, 4 January 1855, Fuller-Higginson Papers, PVMA. See also Agnes Cochran Higginson to Stephen Higginson II, 18 December 1855, Fuller-Higginson Papers, PVMA. Elizabeth Phelps Huntington to Frederic Dan Huntington, 8 October 1835, PPHFP, Box 12, Folder 7; Bethia Throop Huntington Commonplace Book, 24 May 1839, PPHFP, Box 20, Folder 5.

[11]9 December 1822, Mary Palmer Tyler Diary, 1821–43, Document 49:1, Royall Tyler Collection, Gift of Helen Tyler Brown, VHS.

law, and mother left her own future especially unstable, she turned to the judge for advice and support. Her confidence, and her friendship, was returned. Never questioning either her discretion or her intellectual capacity, Lyman relied on Cochran to relay information to her brother-in-law, Stephen Higginson II, regarding their shared business transactions.[12] If these two friendships were not exactly common, they differed from the experiences of other men and women more in degree than in kind.

Historians have correctly noted the privileged role of friendship in the early republic. In the decades following the Revolution, friendship was celebrated as a political metaphor, held up as a badge of refinement and elaborated as a daily practice. Yet, for the most part, friendship figures as though it were inherently homosocial.[13] If the friendships between Royall Tyler and Madame Denison and Martha Cochran and Judge Lyman confound prevailing assumptions about the homosocial nature of friendship, they revise our understanding in other ways. The intimate, eroticized female friendships described by Carroll Smith-Rosenberg and the romantic male friendships described by Anthony Rotundo signaled the triumph of bourgeois culture not simply in their validation of men's and women's separate spheres but in their self-conscious creation of interiority. In contrast, friendships between provincial women and men were fostered by a broad pattern of sociability that derived from the household economy and that undergirded provincial society throughout the antebellum period. Like the connections that joined Hattie Fuller and George Fuller to their friend Rebecca, the bonds between Royall Tyler and Madam Denison and Martha Cochran and Judge Lyman were extensions of relations within and between households. As neighbors and as Unitarians, members of the Cochran and Lyman households socialized regularly in a

[12]Martha Cochran to Agnes Cochran Higginson, 23 January 1839, 10 February 1839, and 14 January 1840, and Marianne Cochran to Agnes Cochran Higginson, 6 January 1839, Fuller-Higginson Papers, PVMA.

[13]On friendship as a homosocial construction, see especially Carroll Smith-Rosenberg, "The Female World of Love and Ritual: Relations between Women in Nineteenth-Century America" and "Hearing Women's Words: A Feminist Reconstruction of History," both in her *Disorderly Conduct: Visions of Gender in Victorian America* (New York: Oxford University Press, 1985), 11–52, 53–76, and Anthony Rotundo, "Romantic Friendship: Male Intimacy and Middle-Class Youth in the Northern United States, 1800–1930," *Journal of Social History* 23 (1989): 1–25. See also Carol Lasser, " 'Let Us Be Sisters Forever': The Sororal Model of Nineteenth-Century Female Friendship," *Signs* 14 (1988): 158–81; William R. Taylor and Christopher Lasch, "Two 'Kindred Spirits': Sorority and Family in New England, 1839–1846," *New England Quarterly* 36 (1963): 23–41. For an extended analysis of one eighteenth-century male-female friendship, see Edith B. Gelles, *Portia: The World of Abigail Adams* (Bloomington: Indiana University Press, 1992), 57–71.

variety of settings. Tyler's connection with Denison was one part of a more general friendship between two families: Mary Tyler counted Mrs. Denison among her dearest friends, and Royall Tyler's affection for Mrs. Denison was matched by his regard for her husband. The relations between the two families were reinforced by common business interests; attorney Tyler worked regularly with Denison, a Brattleboro judge. For provincial New Englanders, particular friendships were located within the larger networks that connected men and women within their communities.[14]

The hetersociability of provincial society extended well beyond the confines of particular families and households to shape the development of provincial public culture. In the decades following the Revolution, ambitious and often itinerant publishers, educators, artists, and peddlers moved books, portraits, and ideas into the northern hinterland, sparking what one historian has called a "Village Enlightenment."[15] By the 1820s, expanding cultural and intellectual interests and opportunities encouraged many provincial New Englanders to busy themselves in a variety of classes, cultural associations, and voluntary societies. This marriage of commerce and culture enabled rural people to partake of some of the texts, props, and practices that had signaled gentility for earlier generations of New Englanders. Part of a national democratization of refinement, these efforts at self-improvement—or, more accurately, at self-fashioning—mark the flowering of provincial culture. But they also reveal the ways in which the development of the provincial public sphere derived from the practices of private sociability, particularly its heterosociability.

Especially during the long winters, provincial New Englanders looked to dancing and singing schools to foster sociability. Virtually every New England village, no matter how small, boasted some sort of singing school after 1820. Originally aimed at taming the cacophonous

[14]For a similar discussion of friendships between rural men and women in late nineteenth-century New York, see Osterud, *Bonds of Community*, 247.

[15]David Jaffee coined the term "Village Enlightenment" to describe the interconnection of commerce and culture that transformed rural New England in the hundred years before the Civil War; he has done more than any other historian to explore this process of cultural change. See Jaffee, "The Village Enlightenment in New England, 1760–1820," *William and Mary Quarterly*, 3d series, 47 (July 1990); 327–46; "One of the Primitive Sort: Portrait Makers of the Rural North, 1760–1860," in eds., *The Countryside in the Age of Capitalist Transformation: Essays in the Social History of Rural America*, ed. Steven Hahn and Jonathan Prude (Chapel Hill: University of North Carolina Press, 1985), 103–38; and "Peddlers of Progress and the Transformation of the Rural North, 1760–1860," *Journal of American History* 78 (September 1991); 511–35. See also Jack Larkin, *The Reshaping of Everyday Life, 1790–1840* (New York-Harper Perennial 1988), 208–9; William J. Gilmore, *Reading Becomes a Necessity of Life* (Knoxville: University of Tennessee Press, 1989).

noise of singing congregations into sounds more pleasing to God and man, singing schools quickly assumed a central role in rural social life. Theodore Huntington recalled that because the "the social element shared largely" with pedagogy, the schools "afforded a fine opportunity for the young people to get acquainted."[16] As countless diaries and letters suggest, singing schools fostered neighborliness, sustained friendships, and occasionally launched romance. Dancing classes and parties served much the same function. Although dancing withered under evangelical criticism after the 1830s, dancing classes had regained their appeal by the 1850s. In 1857, Milton Reed reported that half of his household, including his father, had decamped for the Surry, New Hampshire, Hall, "for it is one of the dancing school evenings and besides that the Young folks are intending to dance after School." In very small villages, or towns that lacked a central meeting place, classes rotated from place to place to attract and accommodate students. In 1850, Mary Hopkins carefully recorded the numbers of "couples" who braved the weather to attend a biweekly "Evening Dancing School" that moved between Sunapee and Newport, New Hampshire; by her count some thirty to forty men and women turned out to learn and practice the latest dance steps. Especially among younger men and women, dancing classes held out the promise of refinement and the prospect of a sweetheart.[17]

Mixing sociability and courtship, singing schools and dancing classes depended on the presence of men and women for obvious reasons.[18] But lyceums and literary societies drew men and women

[16]"Sketches by Theodore G. Huntington of the Family and Life in Hadley Written in Letters to H. F. Quincy," 47–50, PPHFP, Box 21, Folder 7. See also the Diary of Mary Hoyt Wilson, 26 November 1826, PVMA; Julia Dutton to Lucretia Wilson Dutton, 26 September 1847 and 18 December 1847, Lucretia Wilson Dutton Papers, UVM; Emmeline Flint to Mary Ann Tarble Flint, 25 February 1839, Haile Papers, VHS; Diary of Mary Hopkins, 22 February 1851, NHHS; Martha Rhoda Willson Diary, 13 January 1851, Cheshire County Diaries, HSCC; Harriet Holkins to Eliza Minot Adams, 14 May 1824, DCL; Sarah Hazen to Eliza Adams, 20 March 1830, Adams Family Papers, DCL, MS 420, Box 5, Folder 12. On the religious origins of singing schools, see Larkin, *Reshaping of Everyday Life*, 252–56.

[17]Marion Hopkins Diary, 20 February 1850, 25 February 1850, 4 March 1850, 7 March 1850, 10 March 1850, and 17 March 1850, Mary Hopkins Diary, 1976–53, NHHS; Milton Reed to Missouri Reed, 26 November 1857, 13 December 1857, and 11 February 1858; and Jackson Reed to Missouri Reed, 10 January 1858, in Reed Family Papers, HSCC. On nineteenth-century dancing, see Larkin, *Reshaping of Everyday Life*, 239–44.

[18]On cultural associations as opportunities for courtship, see Huntington, "Sketches," 47–50, PPHFP, Box 21, Folder 7; Harriet Holkins to Eliza Minot Adams, 14 May 1824, Adams Family Papers, DCL, MS 420, Box 5, Folder 13. But even dancing schools could not always guarantee equal numbers of men and women. Milton Reed complained in 1857 that "there is only nine or ten girls that attend [dancing school], while at the same time there is

together to share in the life of the mind. Provincial women who attended lyceum lectures enjoyed readings "from some Particular portion of Shakespeare," inquiries into the "Object of Loyalty," and discussions of whether the pen or the sword "has won the greatest laurels." Angelina Bodman attended one lyceum debate in which women not only observed but also judged the proceedings; two two-man teams had debated the question before the audience, and a "Lady committee" decided the winner.[19] Women's interests extended beyond displays of literary cultivation and questions of moral probity, which might be encompassed within the feminized culture of sentiment. At lyceums they could satisfy their curiosity about topics that historians, at least, have relegated to the masculine sphere of scientific inquiry. For example, in 1821, Mary Palmer Tyler was "greatly amused" by effects of the "exhilerating gas," nitrous oxide, on some young men at a chemical lecture. Some thirty years later, a female schoolteacher in Shaftsbury, Vermont, attended a chemistry lecture and "enjoyed it much."[20]

If lyceums invited provincial women to partake of the "Village Enlightenment" alongside their men, reading clubs and literary societies encouraged them to play a more active role in shaping that enlightenment and public culture generally. Throughout the nineteenth century, provincial New Englanders met in reading clubs and literary societies to develop and display their intellectual cultivation. These groups varied widely in size and in membership. Some were aimed at young people, and probably served as informal extensions of their schooling in academies and seminaries.[21] Other groups included only adults, and some groups included everyone from adolescents to the aged. Whatever the group's composition, participants read and discussed contemporary literature. They also produced and circulated essays, stories, letters, and occasional verse of their own. Literary societies certainly encouraged and fostered individuals' identities as writers; Cincinnati's famous Semi-Colon Club, which nurtured the literary careers of Catharine Beecher and Harriet Beecher Stowe, provides the

---

some fifteen or twenty boys. Not very proportioned you see." Milton Reed to Missouri Reed, 26 November 1857, Reed Family Papers, HSCC.

[19]Angelina Bodman to Oliver B. Bodman, 10 January 1845, Bodman Family Papers, SSC; Hannah Fulton Reed to Lyman Reed, 19 November 1851, Reed Family Papers, NHHS; Martha Rhoda Willson Diary, 25 September 1850, Cheshire County Diaries, HSCC.

[20]Diary of a Shaftsbury Schoolteacher, 5 February 1857, MSC-165, VHS; 18 April 1821, Royall Tyler Daybook, 1817–21, Document 45:15, Royall Tyler Collection, Gift of Helen Tyler Brown, VHS.

[21]See, for example, Mary Hoyt Wilson Diary, 30 August 1826 and 28 September 1826, PVMA; Sarah Hazen to Eliza Minot Adams, 16 November 1829, Adams Family Papers, DCL, MS 420, Box 5, Folder 13.

most obvious example.[22] But if these societies shaped the identities and careers of particular writers, they also influenced antebellum intellectual life. As Joan Hedrick has cogently argued, "parlor literature" mediated between oral and print culture and helped to create a national literary culture by shaping communities of readers.[23]

The overwhelming majority of these groups counted women and men among their members. When Thomas Tenney was a student at Dartmouth College in the 1820s, he joined a weekly reading society composed of four men and five women. He reported that the group "contrive[d] to pass the eve wonderfully well; have read the life of Franklin he is a pattern for dilligence. We are now reading the life of Quincy, a noble character, one of first lights of the revolution." And the society fostered an appreciation for more than history. Tenney conceded that, at least in Hanover, "the young ladies have much more of a taste for what is solid and sensible than is generally supported. I make these remarks because I have sometimes done them injustice."[24] Tenney may have been surprised at the high-mindedness of Hanover's "young ladies," but women were hardly a marginal presence in provincial literary clubs. After the first meeting of the Northampton Reading Club in 1855, secretary W. S. B. Hopkins reported that fifteen young ladies "departed, under the escort of two solitary gentlemen," complaining that this was "no anomaly for Northampton!" Poetry (read by females) and criticism (read by males) apparently held little appeal for the town's bachelors; after the first meeting, even the club's president resigned. Rejecting the notion of a feminized club, the group hoped that readings of comic plays might attract more men. After a reading of Sheridan's *Rivals* drew ten men, "a fabulous number for staid Northampton," the Reading Club regularly scheduled comedies, ranging from *A Midsummer Night's Dream* to *She Stoops to Conquer*. The club's commitment to heterosociability outweighed their dedication to sober themes.[25]

To say that women and men participated in literary societies is not

[22]On the Semi-Colon Club, see Nicole Tonkovich, "Writing in Circles: Harriet Beecher Stowe, the Semi-Colon Club, and the Construction of Women's Authorship," in *Nineteenth-Century Women Learn to Write*, ed. Catherine Hobbs (Charlottesville: University Press of Virginia, 1995), 145–75; and Joan Hedrick, *Harriet Beecher Stowe: A Life* (New York: Oxford University Press, 1994), 76–88.

[23]Hedrick, *Harriet Beecher Stowe*, 76–82.

[24]Thomas Tenney to Bezaliel Smith, 3 November 1825, 825603, DCL.

[25]Northampton Reading Club Records, vol. 1, 3 December 1855 and 22 October 1855, FL. Deerfield's reading club also attracted a disproportionate number of women; one meeting attracted "30 intelligent women and a few men." See Agnes Cochran Higginson to Stephen Higginson II, 21 February 1856, Fuller-Higginson Papers, PVMA.

to say that they participated on equal terms. Voluntary associations, however heterosocial, were hardly free from the gender conventions that dominated the rest of provincial society. The Hanover "Pickwick," which met during the 1840s, included select students and faculty along with the faculty wives and daughters. After convening in the parlor of "one of the citizens a lecture [was] read by another." Only after the "gentlemen" exhausted their discussion of the lecture did the "conversation become more general between the ladies and gentlemen."[26] Women's participation in the Pickwick and other literary societies was constrained by gender conventions that cast them as readers rather than writers, as listeners rather than as speakers.

Women's Associations

The singing schools and literary societies that drew women and men together in the pursuit of cultivation were countered by benevolent associations that assembled them separately to perform God's work on earth. Conforming to the conventions of separate spheres, religious and reform associations gathered women together without their men to pursue distinctly female agendas.[27] In New England towns and villages, as in northern cities, benevolent associations offered women an unusual and gratifying degree of autonomy. Between 1830 and 1860, thousands of provincial women joined a myriad of voluntary organizations generated by the "evangelical united front."[28] Many enlisted in the "ladies' auxiliaries" of temperance and anti-slavery societies. Many more joined the sewing circles that formed the backbone of antebellum Protestant benevolent and missionary work. In 1836, Northampton's Congregational churches alone boasted eleven benevolent sewing circles, which "embrace[d] most of the Ladies in the two orthodox congregational churches." The women of Franklin County, Massachusetts, contributed their time and monies to an education society, a tract society, and a Bible society; they also supported

[26]Henry Willard to the Hon. John Willard, 17 February 1849, 849167, DCL.

[27]On the connections between the development of women's sphere and women's benevolent work, see especially Nancy F. Cott, *The Bonds of Womanhood: "Woman's Sphere" in New England, 1780–1835* (New Haven, Conn: Yale University Press, 1977); Carroll Smith-Rosenberg, *Disorderly Conduct: Visions of Gender in Victorian America* (New York: Oxford University Press, 1985); and Mary P. Ryan, *Cradle of the Middle Class: The Family in Oneida County, New York, 1790–1865* (New York: Cambridge University Press, 1989).

[28]The term *evangelical united front* originated with Charles I. Foster, *An Errand of Mercy: The Evangelical United Front, 1790–1837* (Chapel Hill: University of North Carolina Press, 1960); quoted in Blumin, *Emergence of the Middle Class*, 193.

both foreign and domestic missions. Between 1833 and 1844, almost sixty mothers formed a maternal association in Millbury, Massachusetts, a small Worcester County town whose economy was dominated by manufacturing and the trades. Like urban women who responded to social and economic dislocation by tightening the maternal bond, each member of the Millbury association considered herself "sacredly bound to pray daily for her children, and with them practicably . . . urging them immediate repentance"; each prayed that "by the influence of her daily example," she might win her children's "hearts to the love and service of their redeemer."[29]

As numerous historians have observed, middle-class women found both gender solidarity and a rare measure of autonomy in nineteenth-century benevolent organizations.[30] Even the editor of the *Hampshire Gazette*, who condescendingly described the societies' proceeds as small "streams of charity," recognized that sewing circles offered pious women a special community. "By the means of these circles," he

[29]Constitution of the Maternal Association in Millbury, Massachusetts, Millbury, Mass., Papers, AAS. In the 1840 Census, Millbury, with a population of 2171, listed 296 males employed in agriculture and 496 employed in manufacturing and the trades. Information about Northampton and Franklin County women appeared in the *Hampshire Gazette*, 15 March 1842 and 21 September 1836. My discussion of provincial women's participation in benevolent work is based on Elizabeth Phelps Huntington to Catherine Carey Huntington, 18 February 1829, PPHFP, Box 12, Folder 2; Angelina Bodman to Joseph Bodman, 10 May 1846, Angelina Bodman to Oliver B. Bodman, 10 January 1845, and Philena Hawkes Bodman to Luther Bodman Jr., 1 June 1845, Bodman Family Papers, SSC; Elizabeth Parsons Hidden to Emily Parsons Tenney, 20 June 1847, and Emily Parsons Tenney to Elizabeth Parsons Hidden, 29 March 1847, Parsons Family Papers, SL; Sophronia Grout Diary, [n.d.] September 1825, [n.d.] November [ca. 1830], and scattered references 1828–29, PVMA; Sophronia Grout to parents, 23 June 1828, Sophronia Grout Papers, PVMA; Julia Dutton to Lucretia Wilson Dutton, 19 December 1845 and 18 December 1847, Lucretia Wilson Dutton Papers, UVM; Nancy Avery White Diary, vol. 6, 3 March 1836, 13 December 1837, and 9 April 1840, White-Forbes Diaries, AAS; Records of the Northampton Martha Washington Temperance Society, FL; Records of the Northampton Anti-Slavery Society, FL; Records of the First Congregational Church Ladies' Benevolent Society, JL. But see also Bathsheba Crane (*Life, Letters, and Wayside Gleanings for the Folks at Home* (Boston: James H. Earle, 1880), 115–16) who praised a Vermont woman who eschewed the "principles and measures" of the Moral Reform Society in favor of exerting her influence through "humbler duties" that kept her close to home.

[30]Studies emphasizing women's organizational autonomy include Carroll Smith-Rosenberg, "Beauty, the Beast, and the Militant Woman," *American Quarterly* 23 (1971): 562–84; Keith Melder, *The Beginnings of Sisterhood: The Women's Rights Movement in the United States, 1800–1840* (New York: Schocken Books, 1977); Barbara J. Berg, *The Remembered Gate: Origins of American Feminism; the Woman and the City, 1800–1860* (New York: Oxford University Press, 1978); Nancy A. Hewitt, *Women's Activism and Social Change: Rochester, New York, 1822–1872* (Ithaca, N.Y.: Cornell University Press, 1984); and Lori D. Ginzberg, *Women and the Work of Benevolence* (New Haven, Conn.: Yale University Press, 1990).

wrote, "visiting is accomplished, the signs of the times are observed, intelligence is diffused, [and] good feeling is cultivated."[31]

Of course, what the editor failed to notice was that within these communities, women claimed an authority denied them in other situations. Single-sex Christian organizations allowed even the most proper lady to accept a position of formal leadership with an easy conscience. At the first meeting of the Northampton Reading Club, women who had been nominated for executive offices declined "on the ground that the office should be filled by a gentleman." But in benevolent organizations, women were honored to accept elected office. In 1838, nineteen-year-old Lizzie Cochran was invited to serve as treasurer of Northampton's Unitarian sewing society. Although "the remembrance of her account book impelled her to decline," she consented to direct the society's "fancy work" department. Cochran approached her new station with a deep sense of pride. Shortly after accepting the position, she wrote that the office required seven hours "of devotion" every other week and a "good deal" of other labor and responsibility besides. Although the Millbury maternal association elected a superintendent, secretary, and treasurer, leadership responsibilities were shared among the members; each woman took a turn conducting monthly meetings and selecting readings.[32]

As a minister's wife, Amelia White Peabody took an exceptionally active role in Springfield's reform community. Unlike the majority of provincial women, whose participation was hemmed in by the demands of family and household, Peabody found a ready-made career in benevolent work. Shortly after moving to Springfield in 1824 with her new husband, Peabody joined the local Charitable Society. To her surprise, she was appointed treasurer at the first meeting she attended. The following summer, Springfield's Unitarian women formed a larger society; by "taking in work & making 'articles,' " Peabody hoped "to give those an opportunity to do good who have all the disposition but who cannot so easily give money as their time." Accustomed to her new role as minister's wife and benevolent woman, she matter-of-factly noted her appointment as the new society's secretary. Fifteen years later, near the end of her life, her enthusiasm for good works continued unabated. Developing a passionate interest in colonization, she wrote, "I always keep some Liberia work on hand, and really feel as if I had

[31]*Hampshire Gazette*, 21 September 1836.

[32]Constitution of the Maternal Association in Millbury, Massachusetts, Millbury, Mass. Papers, AAS; Lizzie Cochran to Agnes Cochran Higginson, 16 December 1838, and Marianne Cochran to Agnes Cochran Higginson, 28 October 1838, Fuller-Higginson Papers, PVMA; Northampton Reading Club Records, vol. 1, 22 October 1855, FL.

not done quite all I ought to do, unless I do something on it every day." The next year, she added temperance to her list of causes. After serving for several months as "one of the managers" of a society aimed at assisting the families of "reformed drunkards," she concluded that "nothing could have been pleasanter than such a duty, which besides the ordinary pleasure of doing good, brought us personally acquainted with the families which were changed from the deepest misery to happiness."[33]

Benevolent work granted women like Lizzie Cochran and the members of the Millbury maternal association an unprecedented degree of authority and autonomy. Occasionally, it offered a woman like Amelia Peabody the chance to expand her identity beyond the walls of her household and the needs of her family. But if benevolent societies offered nineteenth-century women a measure of power, provincial communities checked that power at every turn.

Women's participation was constrained both by life cycle and geography. Not surprisingly, the most active members and officers were frequently single women or middle-aged matrons—women who shouldered the lightest responsibilities for housework and child-rearing. Even Amelia Peabody's activism seems to have fallen off during the years in which she found herself most burdened with the care of four small children.[34] Geography also have played a decisive role in shaping women's organizational activities. Living in Northampton proper, with more help than many provincial women, the Cochran sisters had no difficulty attending the biweekly meetings of the Unitarian sewing society. Similarly, sixteen-year-old Angelina Bodman of nearby Williamsburg counted on regular and large attendance at her sewing society. She was disappointed when a "great deal of illness" reduced the meeting she hosted to a mere twenty women. But women whose households were removed from town centers or whose budgets made help scarce participated far more sporadically. For example, as a single

[33]Amelia White Peabody to Mary Jane White, 22 March 1842 and 21 January 1841, and Amelia White Peabody to Eliza White, 24 July 1825 and 19 December 1824, Everett-Peabody Family Papers, MHS.

[34]On the relationship between women's life cycles and their participation in benevolent societies, see Anne M. Boylan, "Timid Girls, Venerable Widows, and Dignified Matrons: Life Cycle Patterns Among Organized Women in New York and Boston, 1797–1840," *American Quarterly* 38 (1986): 779–98. Benevolent work was hardly the only activity that waxed and waned with the rhythms of women's life cycles. Laurel Thatcher Ulrich has demonstrated that Martha Ballard's eighteenth-century obstetric practice depended in large measure on the presence of her daughters, who shouldered the burden of household tasks. See "Martha Ballard and Her Girls: Women's Work in Eighteenth-Century Maine," in Stephen Innes, ed., *Work and Labor in Early America* (Chapel Hill: University of North Carolina Press, 1988), 70–105.

woman living in her parents' rural household, Catherine White Forbes of Westborough, Massachusetts, occasionally managed to attend meetings of her church's sewing society. But as a young wife with two small children, she found her activities more sharply confined. In the late 1840s, she recorded in her diary that her husband had attended a "Young People's Prayer Meeting," as well as temperance, antislavery, mechanics', and agricultural association meetings. But except for frequent visits to her mother, Catherine White Forbes stayed home. Over the course of a lifetime, a provincial woman could expect to assemble with female neighbors and kin to contribute to the benevolent work of her community. Yet one must be careful not to exaggerate the importance of those hours measured against the routines of women's everyday lives.[35]

If individual women moved in and out of voluntary associations, the associations themselves maintained a consistent presence within community life. But it is not clear that even the most established provincial associations provided women with a genuinely autonomous social space. Nancy Grey Osterud has persuasively argued that within one postbellum farming community, small-town familiarity undermined the independence of community organizations. At political clubs and lodges, mutual-aid societies and ladies' auxiliaries, she contends, "people placed one another in terms of their family status, kin-group membership, and neighborhood, as well as in terms of their economic position."[36] The same may well have been true of antebellum provincial women's organizations. Particularly in smaller communities, women probably viewed one another not as deracinated individuals or members of an abstract middle class but as representatives of dense networks of kin and neighbors, as women whose connections to other women, children, and men were well known.

Gender and Public Rituals

The structure and culture of provincial communities also constrained provincial women's ability to cast themselves as Woman, to depict their charitable mission as a separate and distinctly female endeavor. Just as women could never forget that their charitable work was yoked to a larger cause, they could never forget that their organi-

[35]See Catherine White Forbes Diary, vol. 9, Nancy Avery White Diary, vol. 6, White-Forbes Diaries, AAS; Angelina Bodman to Joseph Bodman, 10 May 1846, Bodman Family Papers, SSC.

[36]Osterud, *Bonds of Community*, 249.

zations were embedded within causes and communities dominated by their men. This connection became especially clear during the public fairs held to sell the fancy work women had made at countless sewing circles. In 1834, alarmed by the frivolity of many benevolent fairs, Hadley women barred men from attending. Disregarding the women's pious motivations, Hadley men complained loudly, insisting that a male presence would have increased profits and "the more money received the better." The women's decision was supported by the editor of the *Hampshire Gazette*, who praised the "Ladies of Hadley" for managing a "quiet fair among themselves, without resorting to the usual display, artifice and foolery."[37]

But single-sex fairs were the exception; most fairs made special arrangements to attract men. Several years later, following a "Ladies Fair" in Northampton, the same editor who credited Hadley's women for their discretion complimented Northampton's women for a fair that proved especially pleasing to a masculine sensibility. To be sure, he praised the women for the $250 the event raised, as well as for the artful arrangement of their tables. Yet rather than describing the women themselves as capable organizers, or even as devoted Christians, he emphasized their personal connections, and their subordination, to the town's men: "The ladies never appeared to greater advantage, and if some of the crusty old bachelors did not become warmed in their affections, they deserve to be consigned to the polar regions."[38]

Nor were such sentiments confined to men. Amelia Peabody described a particularly successful antislavery fair that had been organized to appeal to male visitors: "We had a fine entertainment of hot oysters, coffee, and ice creams, beside cake, &c, so that gentlemen could take their suppers there, and they staid and chatted and passed the evening, very much as they would at a party." The event raised more than $400. Fairs existed primarily to raise money for charitable causes and secondarily to show off ladies' taste and accomplishments. But fairs were also expected to please and acknowledge men.[39]

In part, these fairs accommodated men because of their ability to

[37]*Hampshire Gazette*, 16 April 1834.

[38]*Hampshire Gazette*, 8 January 1840.

[39]Amelia White Peabody to Mary Jane White, 21 January 1841, Everett-Peabody Family Papers, MHS. This interpretation differs from that of Lee Chambers-Schiller, who argues that abolitionist fairs, especially the Boston Anti-Slavery Fair, cast "men as supplicants for female favor" in a feminized setting. See her essay " 'A Good Work among the People': The Political Culture of the Boston Anti-Slavery Fair," in *The Abolitionist Sisterhood: Women's Political Culture in Antebellum America*, ed. Jean Fagan Yellin and John C. Van Morne (Ithaca, N.Y.: Cornell University Press, 1994), 273.

buy the fancy work their women had produced. And if men were not members of the particular societies that sponsored the fairs, they surely counted themselves as part of the larger causes that the fairs sought to advance. Finally, as public ceremonies, benevolent fairs also depicted the common good and the social order, both of which depended on men as citizens and heads of households. The same logic prevailed at other provincial ceremonies. Similar to the parades of nineteenth-century New York, New Orleans, and San Francisco studied by Mary Ryan, the public rituals of provincial communities consistently paid homage to men's political, economic, and social power. But Ryan argues that urban ceremonies, reflecting the transformation that relegated middle-class women to the private sphere, acknowledged women only as genteel spectators or as "Liberty" or "Columbia"—mute, depoliticized symbols of a republican order.[40] Provincial rituals, on the other hand, idealized the social order not as a bourgeois society but as a corporate community made up productive households. Precisely for this reason, provincial ceremonies included women. If the different elements of communities and households were hardly equal, they were all essential and all accorded a place in public rituals. Indeed, women maintained a visible presence in the symbolic lives of their communities for most of the antebellum period.

Just as men demanded attention at ladies' fairs, provincial women laid claim to a measure of recognition at other public ceremonies. Cattle shows provide the most obvious example. Agricultural festivals marked an important milestone in the rural calendar, gathering entire families to display the fruits of their labor, to learn about agricultural improvements, and to socialize and celebrate the harvest. Reminding Hampshire County residents of the significance of cattle shows after an uncharacteristically poor turnout in 1840, Edward Dickinson described the fairs as "the great holiday, of not only farmers, but of *all the people.*" The entertainments and exhibitions marked "a time of general rejoicing at the common prosperity, and the general improvement in all arts of industry and economy, that render life happy." As Dickinson's comments suggest, the fairs played an important symbolic role within provincial communities. The cattle show not only celebrated the "arts of industry and economy" but also represented them. In the same way that early nineteenth-century parades symbolized the disparate elements of the polity, agricultural fairs embodied the ele-

[40]Ryan, *Women in Public*, 31.

ments of the rural economy.[41] Exhibits of fat cattle and swine, wheat and "paris pumpkins," woolen blankets, and cheese all testified to the labors of men and women.[42]

This is not to suggest that men and women found equal recognition at the fairs. The most popular events—speeches, races, and ploughing contests—celebrated the rhetorical prowess of the republican gentleman and the physical strength of the New England yeoman. The exhibitions themselves testified to the differences and the inequalities between men and women. Premiums made clear the inequalities that structured the sexual division of labor: In 1839, a good bull could earn eight dollars; the same year the prize-winning "rose blanket" was awarded only three dollars. Women's contributions were further diminished after the department of "domestic manufactures" was transformed into an incongruous combination of fancy work and commercially produced goods. Translating "domestic" into domesticity and "manufacture" into factory, cattle shows ultimately obscured the continuing importance of farm women's productive labor beneath a mountain of embroidered hunting scenes, carved card baskets, and wax flowers. Although the shows continued to pay tribute to the values of the household economy, they were not immune to the pressures of an emerging market society. But if the fairs transformed the productive mistress into the leisured lady, they resisted the bourgeois conceptions of public and private that banished urban women from public ceremonies.[43]

[41]*Hampshire Gazette*, 21 October 1840. See also *Hampshire Gazette* 14 October 1835, 16 October 1839, 14 October 1840, 12 October 1841, and 19 October 1841. For an extended discussion of the construction of gender and class at cattle shows, see my " 'The Consummation of Rural Prosperity and Happiness': New England Cattle Shows and the Construction of Class and Gender, 1810–1860," *American Quarterly* 49 (1997): 574–602. Mark Mastromarino similarly emphasizes the importance of cattle shows in encouraging community solidarity and reinforcing the corporate dimension of agricultural societies, but he does not view the fairs as ceremonies, nor does he acknowledge the presence of women at fairs, except as spectators. See his " 'Cattle Aplenty and Other Things in Proportion': The Agricultural Society and Fair in Franklin County, Massachusetts, 1810–1869," *UCLA Historical Journal* 5 (1984): 50–75.

[42]Mary P. Ryan argues that parades reproduced the polity in "The American Parade: Representations of the Nineteenth-Century Social Order," in *The New Cultural History*, ed. Lynn Hunt (Berkeley: University of California Press, 1989), 131–53.

[43]"Fancy work" is described in the *Hampshire Gazette*, 14 October 1856; the premiums were listed in the *Hampshire Gazette*, 16 October 1839. Christopher Clark (*The Roots of Rural Capitalism in Western Massachusetts, 1780–1860* [Ithaca, N.Y.: Cornell University Press, 1990], 278–79) also suggests that the growing emphasis on fancy work at agricultural fairs trivialized women's work relative to men's, "allowing men to congratulate themselves on the importance of their own work." But Clark may have overemphasized the respect accorded women's work by earlier generations of provincial men and women, as the difference in premiums suggest. Nancy Grey Osterud provides an excellent discussion of the ways in which women's agricultural work was valued (*Bonds of Community*, 202–79).

Academy examinations played a similar role in the ceremonial calendar. At the close of each term, a visiting committee made up of leading townsmen attended the oral examination of the student body.[44] But these examinations were also attended by the public—by the neighbors, friends, and kin of the students, teachers, and visiting committee members. If the presence of local notables certified the intellectual quality of the education and contributed a certain gravity to the proceedings, the presence of the community turned the examination into a public ceremony. Open examinations at private academies underscored the civic importance and public obligations that accompanied even expensive private educations at the same time that they underscored the authority and the prestige of those families who could afford to purchase such an education.

Reinforcing both corporatism and hierarchy, the examinations also reinforced the heterosocial dimension of provincial life. Both men and women turned out to watch the examination of male and female students, who were generally taught by female teachers. Mary Hoyt Wilson concluded her stay at the Deerfield Academy with an examination that "lasted all day" and was attended by a "numerous audience." She proudly recorded that by the afternoon, the examination hall was full. To be sure, it was the "young men" who were accorded the honor of closing the ceremony with "speaking and orations." But young women also captured a measure of recognition.[45] And although women could hardly aspire to sit on visiting committees, they could and did levy their own assessments of student ability. When Bethia Throop Huntington attended the examination of a Hadley academy in the 1820s, she remarked that whereas she had missed her brother's exam, she had heard both Abby White and a student named Whitney examined and judged Whitney's composition and oration "both excellent."[46]

The same patterns of heterosociability that distinguished benevolent fairs, cattle shows, and academy examinations—patterns that required women's participation even as they reinforced men's preeminence—prevailed at explicitly political events. Ceremonies orchestrated to honor republican citizens and advance the cause of party politics included

[44]In 1830 and 1832, for example, the visiting committee for Catherine Fiske's Keene Academy included two ministers, one judge, one doctor, and three colonels. See *Catalogue of the Young Ladies Seminary in Keene, N.H., for the Term Ending October, 1830* and *Catalogue of the Young Ladies Seminary in Keene, N.H., for the Term Ending October, 1832*, HSCC.

[45]Diary of Mary Hoyt Wilson, 24 October 1826, PVMA. Lavinia Bailey Kelly honored her classmates at the "young ladies school kept at Mr Hills" who were publicly examined by recording their names in her diary. Diary of Lavinia Bailey Kelly, 30 July 1828, NHHS.

[46]Bethia Throop Huntington to Mary Dwight Huntington, n.d. [before 1830], PPHFP, Box 20, Folder 4.

women as well men. But far more than other community events, political celebrations joined heterosocial ritual to the rhetoric of bourgeois gender roles and relations. Provincial ceremonies stopped far short of recapitulating the ideology of separate spheres, which categorically excluded women from the public sphere, much less the political arena. Yet civic rituals did prompt rural New Englanders to take special notice of women's uplifting, harmonizing influence. This was especially true of Fourth of July celebrations, where women manipulated dramatic spectacle and lofty rhetoric to stake out a striking public presence.

In her study of nineteenth-century women's attempts to create a public space for themselves, Mary Ryan noted women's absence from urban, antebellum July Fourth celebrations. Although "images of femininity fluttered over and around all the holidays," city women did not begin to "poach" upon July Fourth celebrations until after the Civil War. Indeed, she suggests, urban women generally evinced little interest and less identification with the national holiday. Yet even during the antebellum period, provincial women never dismissed July Fourth as a singularly masculine holiday, devoid of meaning for their daily lives. Instead, they viewed the anniversary of independence as a holiday worthy of public ceremonies and celebrations, rituals in which they were entitled to share.[47]

At times, provincial women used the holiday to create an audience for events that directly reflected women's special interests as Christians and reformers. Fusing female benevolence with civic pride, the Baptist women of Westfield, Massachusetts, scheduled their 1842 charity fair to coincide with the Fourth of July festivities. In 1843, Northampton women helped to organize a ceremony that simultaneously honored the Fourth of July and advocated temperance. Along with a band of between 700 and 800 children, and a "Cold Water Army," women paraded to a picnic area, where the entire company enjoyed cakes (prepared by the women) and speeches (delivered by the ministers). Such events allowed women to recast the meaning of the Revolution, binding the future of the republic to the progress of evangelical Protestantism.[48]

But many more women appreciated the holiday simply for its civic importance. Mary Tyler, whose father and grandfather had served in the Continental Army, took personal pride in the Fourth. In 1821, she and her family celebrated national independence with a house "full of

[47]Ryan, *Women in Public*, 24, 41–42, 43, 54.

[48]Anne Marie Hickey, "The Celebration of the Fourth of July in Westfield, 1826–1853," *Historical Journal of Massachusetts* 9 (1981): 42; *Hampshire Gazette*, 11 July 1843.

Folks from morning till night." She happily noted that "all the first Ladies of our Village" assembled to watch as the Brattleboro parade passed in front of the Tylers' house, affording their guests "the best view of any place in the Vicinity."[49]

While Tyler and her friends observed the festivities from upstairs windows, other women played an active role in civic celebrations. In 1839, Northampton women organized an enormous outdoor tea party. As a woman who wrote using the name Tabitha reported in the *Hampshire Gazette*, the attractions included food, dancing, music, fireworks, the French tricolor, an aerial balloon, and the women themselves. Arranging themselves and their feast beneath an arbor decorated in "excellent taste," the ladies "constituted the center of attraction that they succeeded in *managing* so vast a multitude." But Tabitha insisted that this was not simply a parlor social on a grand scale, a private entertainment turned out of doors for a special occasion. Like the cattle shows, the tea party symbolized the organic unity of provincial life. She wrote that at the women's hands, "all the artificial barriers which society sometimes erects, appeared to be thrown down, and all denominations and parties were represented." Young and old, male and female "congregated pell mell, to give and receive pleasure." The "return of this national jubilee" demanded that men and women "all meet as fellow citizens," reminding members of an increasingly divided community that they were "indeed members of the same family."[50]

The following year, the "Ladies of South Deerfield" claimed the "sacred right and privilege" of "celebrating the anniversary of their country's Independence." To commemorate the occasion, the women threw a tea party for some two hundred men and women on the bank of the Connecticut River, offering their guests a "repast" that bore "ample testimony to the domestic education of those who provided it." After the meal, the women inverted the standard program of such occasions. As their men listened, they passed a series of resolutions. The "Ladies of South Deerfield" hailed the "virtues and heroism" of the founding fathers and thanked the "kind Providence" that was responsible for the founders' success. Invoking women's special morality, they pledged themselves to "act against every vice, which would injure

[49]Mary Palmer to Amelia Sophia Tyler, 4 July 1821, Royall Tyler Collection, Gift of Helen Tyler Brown, VHS. Tyler's grandfather, Joseph Palmer, was a general; her father, Joseph Pearse Palmer, was a brigade major and later a quartermaster general. In her autobiography, Tyler describes and embellishes her family's war experience. See Tyler, *Grandmother Tyler's Book*, "During the Revolution."

[50]Tabitha, "The Tea Party," *Hampshire Gazette*, 10 July 1839.

and degrade our own sex, or unman and debase the other." But the women also declared themselves "highly interested" in the nation's liberties because the "rights, mental and moral judgement, usefulness, respectability and enjoyment of females rise or fall with the liberty of any country." Accordingly, they endorsed Gen. William Henry Harrison for the presidency, "rejoic[ing] in the prospect of his being placed in the chair of state." The celebration concluded with the usual rounds of cold water toasts. Although men's toasts dominate the published account of the tea party, the Greenfield *Gazette and Mercury* reported that several "Ladies" took the floor, leading toasts to "Our Puritan Mothers," who possessed the power to "incite as to the performance of good and noble deeds" and "Our Social Meetings," which were "hallowed by all that is good and pure in our natures."[51]

It is tempting to interpret these resolutions as a backhanded radicalism, a covert assertion of women's right to formal political participation. After all, as a generation of women's historians has made clear, the ideology of separate spheres and antebellum political culture combined to cast electoral politics as the quintessential male pursuit.[52] And, indeed, the "Ladies of South Deerfield" did foreshadow the mixture of gender difference and liberalism that informed the nineteenth-century woman movement. Yet such political pronouncements do not necessarily betoken a proto-feminism, nor do they demonstrate a transgression of "woman's sphere."

Antebellum women of all political stripes cultivated fierce political loyalties. Lori Ginzberg has pointed out that with the growing importance of electoral politics, women became "increasingly visible" partisans in political campaigns, "reflecting both their growing concern with electoral power and the assumption that—even unenfranchised— women would participate in the political efforts of their class or cause."[53] If the Deerfield women were not extraordinary in their enthusiasm, neither were they extraordinary in their choice of candidates. Several historians, especially Elizabeth R. Varon, have observed that

[51]"Celebration at South Deerfield," *Greenfield Gazette and Mercury*, 14 July 1840.

[52]The case for a masculinization of antebellum politics was most forcefully summarized and extended by Paula Baker, "The Domestication of Politics: Women and American Political Society, 1780–1920," *American Historical Review* 89 (1984): 620–47, esp. 626–30. See also Michael McGerr, "Political Style and Women's Power, 1830–1930," *Journal of American History* 77 (1990): 864–85, esp. 866–68.

[53]Ginzberg, *Women and the Work of Benevolence*, 71–72. For examples of party loyalties and political partisanship among provincial women, see the correspondence of Mary Tyler (Royall Tyler Collection, Gift of Helen Tyler Brown, VHS), Elizabeth Phelps Huntington (PPHFP), and Elizabeth White Peabody (Everett-Peabody Family Papers, MHS).

William Henry Harrison was especially successful in attracting crowds of committed, energetic female partisans.[54]

What distinguishes provincial women is not their political partisanship but the form it took. Varon's women partisans attended stump speeches and rallies in droves, demonstrating both their allegiance to and the moral superiority of the Whig party. And Ginzberg's reformers fought hard for the candidates of their choice, men who would play an increasingly important role in the business of reform. But the scrappiest reformers and the fiercest partisans generally did not make speeches in front of their men. The special slant of the Deerfield tea party owed as much to the special dynamics of provincial ceremonies as to broader patterns of antebellum women's political activism.

On the one hand, women's active role in civic rituals and partisan spectacles placed these events on a continuum with other provincial ceremonies—ceremonies that ascribed an organic unity to New England's towns and villages. When Northampton women reminded their neighbors in 1839 that they were "indeed members of the same family," their authority depended less on their gender, on their essential femininity, than on their participation in a ceremonial tradition that served to remind men and women alike of the reciprocal obligations that structured households, communities, and polities. At a time of heated partisanship and deepening class divisions, women's participation in civic rituals may well have called to mind a more orderly, if less democratic, political process. On the other hand, occasional references to women's shared identities as Woman allied provincial women and men with the interests of a northern middle class. And, of course, their repeated references to themselves as daughters, wives, and mothers— as "females"—reminded their audiences that they were dependents, creatures who were by definition barred from the political arena. Reminding their townsmen that their only connection to formal politics obtained through their relations with their men, they assuaged anxieties about their political aspirations and their propriety. The "Ladies of South Deerfield" could lay claim to the rhetoric of electoral

[54]The most thoughtful exploration of Harrison's appeal to women is found in Elizabeth R. Varon, "Tippecanoe and the Ladies, Too: White Women and Party Politics in Antebellum Virginia," *Journal of American History* 82 (1995): 494–521. Randolph A. Roth (*The Democratic Dilemma: Religion, Reform, and the Social Order in the Connecticut River Valley of Vermont, 1791–1850* [New York: Cambridge University Press, 1987], 250) also found that Vermont Whigs made a special effort to enlist the support of reformist women, "praising their involvement in the petition campaigns against liquor licenses and slavery in the District of Columbia and inviting them as observers to party rallies." See also Ginzberg, *Women and the Work of Benevolence*, 71–72.

politics and remain "ladies" precisely because they did so as part of a ritual that located them not as political players pursuing their interests but as women anchored within the households of their husbands and the communities of their fathers.[55]

From this perspective, civic rituals and partisan political ceremonies hardly stood in opposition to private sociability, much less the other forms of social interaction that constituted the provincial public sphere. Cattle shows, academy examinations, and even partisan July Fourth celebrations resonated among provincial New Englanders precisely because they echoed other forms of sociability. Public society did not counter private society so much as amplify it. Along with dancing classes, lyceum lectures, reading clubs, and the ubiquitous singing schools, civic rituals pulled the heterosocial styles and practices of provincial sociability out of private networks and into public spaces.

This heterosociability derived not simply from some abstract or universal private sphere but from the practices that obtained in the household economy. The presence of women and men at tea parties, voluntary associations, and civic holidays bespoke the reciprocal obligations that bound kin, neighbors, and households in the late eighteenth and early nineteenth centuries. Reciprocity, of course, is not synonymous with equality. At the same time that men's and women's participation in "society" reminded New Englanders of men's and women's contributions to their households and communities, innumerable distinctions elevated men over women, underscoring women's cultural, economic, and political subordination. Indeed, women's visibility in the public sphere may well have served to magnify their men's power. Standing alongside their neighbors, their kin, and their women, some provincial men could appropriate power not simply on the basis of their gender but also through their status as members of particular families, households, and communities.

While the heterosociability of rural New England recalled the values and practices of the household economy, it also gave shape to an emerging middle class. Singing schools, dancing classes, and literary societies united women and men in the project of self-fashioning and the performance of gentility. And although a variety of public rituals and celebrations depicted provincial towns as organic, corporate communities, women's roles in those events allowed them to elaborate

[55]But compare Varon ("Tippecanoe and the Ladies Too," 504–506), who argues that the Virginia Whigs embraced women as partisans precisely because their presence conjured up bourgeois constructions of Woman and, concomitantly, of Woman as the embodiment of innate female moral superiority.

identities as middle-class "ladies," as Woman. The fancy work that came to dominate displays of domestic manufactures at cattle shows celebrated the fiction of women's removal from the realm of production; the rhetoric of the "Ladies of South Deerfield" articulated the fiction of women's special moral sensibility. Withal, provincial women's striking visibility in public ceremonies served both to announce the emergence of a rural middle class and to cast the creation of that class as the natural evolution of the household economy.

At parlor gatherings and July Fourth celebrations, through the friendships of individual women and men and the capacious fellowship of literary societies, provincial New Englanders created a middle class that owed far more to the close association of women and men than to their separation. Certainly, heterosociability shaped relations between women and men in ways that defy our assumptions about the centrality of "separate-spheres" ideology to middle-class culture of the nineteenth century. Moreover, heterosociability shaped the relation between public and private spheres in surprising ways. To explore the public and private spheres of rural New England is to discover continuity where one least expects it. It is also to see the ways in which provincial New Englanders manipulated gender conventions, sociability, and a broad public sphere to fashion new identities of gender and class. To square the Northampton of his youth with the middle-class gender ideology of his adult years, Theodore Bliss banished women from city streets and from the story he chose to tell about public life. Historians have committed the opposite mistake. Discovering women on the streets, occupying public space, they have imagined the women defying separate spheres and challenging middle-class hegemony. To square heterosocial experience with nineteenth-century gender ideology, they have banished the middle class from the story. But the experiences of provincial New Englanders suggest the need to tell more complicated stories about gender, sociability, the public sphere, and the middle class.

8

"Joining anon in fashion's noisy din"

Between 1838 and 1841, Vermont writer and magazine editor Sophia Hewes tried to alert Connecticut River Valley readers to an alarming new presence prowling the streets of New England's provincial towns and villages. The lady of fashion had arrived. In a series of original and reprinted essays, Hewes spelled out the dangers fashion posed for rural New Englanders as well as for the vulnerable and empty-headed young women who were its special prey. An 1841 essay made the consequences explicit. The anonymous writer admonished young women for their aversion to labor and their appetite for fashion. These fine creatures might boast of their skills in "the fine arts and polite accomplishments, in music, painting and dancing," but the writer doubted their ability to manage household affairs "in a judicious, prudent and economical manner." Putting on airs to attract likely beaux, would-be "ladies" eventually made disastrous wives for young mechanics and merchants, men whose prospects depended on a close supervision of the family's budget.[1]

But these young women posed a threat that extended well beyond the households of their unfortunate husbands. Idleness and fashion had created an artificially inflated market for consumer goods and services. Sharp-eyed merchants and tradesmen were quick to take advan-

[1]"Can She Spin," *The Mother's Book and Young Lady's Companion*, September 1841, 50–51. Versions of this essay appeared in a number of antebellum magazines. I have been unable to determine either the origins of the essay or the extent of any revisions Hewes might have made before reprinting it.

214

tage, charging exorbitant prices not only for luxuries but also for life's "necessaries." The writer tartly concluded that "it is not a little inconsistent to hear parents complain about the price of provisions while they bring up their daughters to walk the street and expend money."

One hundred and fifty years later, these complaints retain their familiar ring. Well before she reappeared to preside over expansion of consumer culture in the twentieth century, the specter of the fashionable young woman was a central figure in economic morality tales.[2] From the 1700s, she haunted the pages of magazines and sermons, novels and treatises, embodying and exacerbating the rise of consumer culture. Prefiguring Thorstein Veblen's critique of social emulation, writers on both sides of the Atlantic offered up cautionary tales in which a grasping, mindless, and usually female consumer simultaneously undermined the social order and launched the consumer revolution.[3]

More recently, this woman and these texts have shaped the work of scholars exploring the origins of consumer culture. In the last ten years, historians, economists, sociologists, and anthropologists have overturned the familiar story of the industrial revolution. In the old story, an increase in the supply of manufactured goods (made possible by mechanization and the reorganization of labor) led automatically to an increase in the demand for manufactured goods. It now seems clear that it was an increase in demand for manufactured good that quickened the pace of production. The consumer revolution gave rise to the the industrial revolution. This research into the timing, nature, and dimensions of the consumer revolution has generated a rich, growing, and sometimes contentious literature. Yet despite significant disagreements over the chronology and meaning of the consumer revolution, scholars have generally accepted the assumptions about social emulation that colored eighteenth-and nineteenth-century discussions of consumption in general and fashion in particular. The industrial revolution may have been born of the consumer revolution, but the con-

[2]See Victoria de Grazia, Introduction to *The Sex of Things: Gender and Consumption in Historical Perspective*, ed. Victoria de Grazia and Ellen Furlough (Berkeley: University of California Press, 1996), 1–10, for a thoughtful discussion of the ways in which fashion and consumption are gendered female.

[3]Thorstein Veblen, *Theory of the Leisure Class: An Economic Study in the Evolution of Institutions* (New York: Macmillan 1899). On Veblen's influence on late nineteenth-century views of consumer culture and consumer behavior, see Simon J. Bronner, "Reading Consumer Culture," in *Consuming Visions: Accumulation and Display of Goods in America, 1880–1920*, ed. Simon J. Bronner (New York: Norton, 1989). For a critique of Veblen's influence among historians of postbellum America, see Jackson Lears, "Beyond Veblen: Retinking Consumer Culture in America," in *Consuming Visions*.

sumer revolution was born of men's and especially women's desire to outshine their neighbors and match their betters.[4]

American historians, especially, have relied at least implicitly on theories of social emulation both to describe and explain the spread of consumption and the development of capitalism. Indeed, the presupposition of social emulation is so pervasive that historians as different as Alan Kulikoff and Gordon Wood have invoked it to buttress their (conflicting) accounts of the transition to capitalism in rural New England and in North America generally. In Kulikoff's marxian analysis, northern farmers occupied "contradictory class positions." "Neither exploiter nor exploited," northern yeomen resisted the logic of a bourgeois worldview until at least the middle of the nineteenth century. When farmers did succumb, women were never far from the scene. It was the desire for "household amenities," Kulikoff asserts, that fueled the "embourgeoisment of farm women" and "accelerated the spread of rural capitalism in the North."[5] For Wood, the triumph of the middle class comes hand in hand with the American Revolution. And in his account, both the rise of capitalism and the spread of democratization turn on "emulative consumption": It was the desire to purchase new goods that led farmers to increase production and the availability of those goods that loosened the bands of social hierarchy. As Wood points out, when Benjamin Franklin's wife replaced his pewter spoon and earthen bowl with silver and china, "she was both raising her family's standard of living . . . and contributing to this consumer revolution."[6]

---

[4]The literature on the consumer revolution is large and growing quickly. For overviews of the debates, see Jean Christophe Agnew, "Coming up for Air: Consumer Culture in Historical Perspective," in *Consumption and the World of Goods*, ed. John Brewer and Roy Porter (New York: Routledge, 1993), 19–39; Lisa Tiersten, "Redefining Consumer Culture: Recent Literature on Consumption and the Bourgeoisie in Western Europe," *Radical History Review* 57 (1993): 116–59. On the eighteenth-century consumer revolution, see Colin Campbell, *Romantic Ethic and Spirit of Modern Consumerism* (Oxford: Basil Blackwell, 1987); Neil McKendrick, John Brewer, and J. H. Plumb, *The Birth of a Consumer Society: The Commercialization of Eighteenth-Century England* (Bloomington: Indiana University Press, 1988); Carole Shammas, *The Pre-Industrial Consumer in England and America* (New York: Oxford University Press, 1990); Cary Carson, Ronald Hoffman, and Peter J. Albert, eds., *Of Consuming Interests: The Styles of Life in the Eighteenth Century* (Charlottesville: University Press of Virginia, 1994). On consumption and gender, see de Grazia and Furlough, eds., *The Sex of Things*.

[5]Allan Kulikoff, *The Agrarian Origins of American Capitalism* (Charlottesville: University Press of Virginia, 1992), 49.

[6]Gordon Wood, "Inventing American Capitalism," *New York Review of Books*, 9 June 1994. See also his *Radicalism of the American Revolution* (New York: Vintage Random House, 1993). T. H. Breen's recent work on eighteenth-century consumption further illustrates the ways in which American historians have relied on notions of social emula-

Historians exploring the emergence of rural capitalism have rightly observed that the increasing density of market relations signaled by consumption bound the economic fate of the northern hinterland to that of the region's cities, although they generally imagine consumption simply as a series of economic transactions. But as Kulikoff and Wood suggest, it was also central to the process of imaginative identification that narrowed the social and cultural distance between town and country. Yet this process was hardly as straightforward, as inexorable, as their analyses assume.

New Englanders left abundant evidence of the ways in which consumption reshaped the provincial landscape over the course of the antebellum period. Store records, newspaper advertisements, and individual account books document both the growing quantity and variety of consumer goods that became available; the same records point to an acceleration of trade. From the 1830s, the number of rural stores increased significantly, as did their stock in trade. This was true not only for a town like Northampton, which had long served as a commercial center, but also for smaller towns that lacked Northampton's commercial heritage. In addition to stocking goods that rural households families had always purchased, these stores offered cloth, flour, butter, and produce—goods that would once have been produced within individual households or traded among them. But the stores also routinely sold goods that would have been rare luxuries for earlier generations of provincial New Englanders. By the 1830s, middle-class families were buying more and were buying more often.[7]

Consider the household of Ebenezer Strong Snell, a professor at Amherst College. From the 1820s, Snell kept a careful and consistent accounting of his family's income and expenditures, sorting his expenses into categories for food, clothing, and "misc." In 1828, the week of his marriage to Sabra Clark, Snell paid a Brookfield cabinetmaker $77.66 for furniture to set up housekeeping. The two began married life with seventeen chairs, including two rocking chairs and two armchairs, a bird's-eye maple bureau, a French bedstead, and several

---

tion. See his "An Empire of Goods: The Anglicization of Colonial America, 1690–1776," *Journal of British Studies* 25 (1986): 467–99, and "The Meanings of Things: Interpreting the Consumer Economy in the Eighteenth Century," in Brewer and Porter, eds., *Consumption and the World of Goods*, 249–60.

[7] See Christopher Clark, *The Roots of Rural Capitalism: Western Massachusetts, 1780–1860* (Ithaca, N.Y.: Cornell University Press, 1990), 159, 170; Randolph A. Roth, *The Democratic Dilemma: Religion, Reform, and the Social Order in the Connecticut River Valley of Vermont, 1750–1850* (New York: Cambridge University Press, 1987), 120, 268–70; Mary P. Ryan, *Cradle of the Middle Class: The Family in Oneida County, New York, 1790–1865* (New York: Cambridge University Press, 1983), 199–201.

tables. Over the next twenty-five years, the Snell family routinely purchased cloth, including a variety of calicos, ginghams, merinos, and delmines. They bought new shoes and paid to have old ones repaired. They purchased meat, butter, flour, molasses, and apples by the bushel. They subscribed to a variety of religious periodicals and contributed to missionary societies and, in later years, to the colonization society. But they also spent sums large and small on things that would have seemed recklessly extravagant to their parents. They fashioned a dining room for themselves, complete with purchased furniture, casings, wallpaper, and looking glass. They invested $20 in a portrait, probably of Ebenezer, and another $1.50 for a "picture in a frame." They purchased a "centre lamp" and an "air-tight" for their parlor. They ordered a printing plate and calling cards for Sabra Snell, so that she might visit in style. And they spent small sums on family entertainment, including 50 cents to view a "mastodon."[8] Along with countless other New England families, the Snells did their share to further the consumer revolution.

But what are we to make of this evidence? It is one thing to know what the Snells bought. It is another to know what sense they made of those purchases and still another to know what they thought about consumption and fashion writ large. Did they view their purchases as the genteel props of upward mobility, as symbols of a self-conscious cosmopolitanism? It is hard to imagine that Sabra Clark Snell, who was repulsed by the "noise and confusion" of New York City, would have had much desire to emulate the style of urban elites. As David Jaffee has observed, the expansion of rural consumerism in the early nineteenth century was "no simple diffusion of urban goods but a wider cultural movement in a new age of abundance."[9] A close reading of provincial New Englanders' published and private accounts of consumption, fashion, and especially social emulation reveals a far more complicated story. Treated as a problematic rather than a given, such discourses move us beyond simple narratives of capitalist development, beyond stories that turn either on women's natural passion for finery or on the inevitable movement of goods and styles from the city to the hinterland.

[8]This description of the Snells' purchases is drawn from Ebenezer Strong Snell Accounts, 1828, 1834, 1840, 1845, and 1850, Snell Family Papers, ACASC, Box 7, Folders 1–2.

[9]David Jaffee, "One of the Primitive Sort: Portrait Makers of the Rural North, 1760–1860," *The Countryside in the Age of Capitalist Transformation*, ed. Steven Hahn and Jonathan Prude (Chapel Hill: University of North Carolina Press, 1985), 113.

Ideologies of Fashion

Throughout the first half of the nineteenth century, provincial writers and editors drew on the conventions of bourgeois and republican ideologies to frame their discussions of consumption and, especially, fashion. In their hands, "fashion" was a remarkably elastic word. Occasionally, it was an innocuous noun, signifying nothing more that the current style, usually the current style of women's clothing. But far more frequently, fashion was a loaded word. Defying moral and especially religious sensibilities, fashion was all that was both false and fleeting. Used in this broader way, fashion could and did signify an enormous range of commodities and behaviors. If it encompassed clothing, cosmetics, and household furnishings, it also encompassed education, sociability, speech, and even attitude. "Fashion" obtained less in the use or misuse of any particular commodity than in a particular way of being in the world. It suggested both the worldly pleasures of the very wealthy and the pretentious attempts of the lower classes to claim those pleasures for themselves. Fashion was not synonymous with either consumption or social emulation, but it was fashion that bound the two together.[10]

Like other Western thinkers, provincials sought to convey the dangers of fashionable consumption and social emulation through a series of binary oppositions. They juxtaposed production against consumption, saving against spending, thrift against extravagance, and country against city. Recalling America's special political history, they also juxtaposed republican simplicity against aristocratic decadence. But if the broad outlines of provincial discourse conformed to the conventions of transatlantic and national discourses, tensions and shifts within it spoke less to the consumer revolution writ large than to its implications for the New England hinterland.

Until the mid-1830s, discussions of fashion turned on the sharp distinctions between republican and patrician cultures. For example, Almira Selden's 1820 play, *Irish Exiles in America*, nominally centered on Evelina Balfour and her mother, impoverished Irish gentlewomen who await the outcome of Ireland's struggle for freedom in the New

[10]On the meaning of fashion for the nineteenth-century middle class, see Karen Halttunen, *Confidence Men and Painted Women: A Study of Middle-Class Culture in America, 1830–1870* (New Haven, Conn.: Yale University Press, 1982), 60–64; Richard L. Bushman, *The Refinement of America: Persons, Houses, Cities* (New York: Knopf, 1992), 302–306.

England countryside.[11] But the heart of the five-scene play, significantly set on the Fourth of July, pits Miss Armyne, a "young Lady of Fortune," against Emily Merton, the virtuous daughter of a virtuous yeoman, and considers which of the two young women can claim to be the true "Daughter of Columbia."

Both American women seek the friendship of Evelina Balfour. At first Evelina, who had enjoyed wealth and position in Ireland, felt drawn to Miss Armyne. But Miss Armyne, a "sport of fashion" whose passions were "whirled by every gale that blows from the grand point," was drawn to the Irish women only by curiosity and a thirst for novelty. From Miss Armyne's perspective, the depleted Balfour fortunes necessarily limited her association with Evelina, who would have been markedly out of place at the balls and parties that took up so much of the wealthy girl's time. As Miss Armyne explained, "If, without a breach of politeness, I could have introduced Miss Balfour to the gentry of my grade in life, I should have been quite happy too. . . . But this . . . was next to impossible."[12] Much to their surprise, the Balfours found true friendship in Emily Merton and her family.[13] The country girl, "incapable of art," remained devoted to the Balfours throughout their trials, and the genteel refugees came to appreciate her for more than her loyalty, for Emily proved a charming companion. No mere rustic, Emily embodied the best aspects of the emerging middle class and of the traditional countryside, infusing rural simplicity with education and culture. To celebrate the Fourth of July, she planned an elaborate garden pageant, complete with classical motifs and floral garlands, and wrote songs and poems for the day's ceremonies, which included a graceful ode to Irish and American liberty. Mrs. Balfour rightly attributed Emily's accomplishments to her republican origins: "We never should have dreamed of finding such refinement of manners . . . in a simple peasant's hut in Ireland—But so it is. . . . Liberty refines the cottage as well as the palace."

At the play's close, the Balfour fortunes and the Balfour scion are miraculously restored. Even after Evelina regains wealth and position, she recognizes that her true companion remains the farmer's daughter: It is Emily, not Miss Armyne, who "henceforth must be the friend of

---

[11]Almira Selden's *The Irish Exiles in America: A Drama in Five Scenes* appears in her *Effusions of the Heart: Contained in a Number of Original Poetical Pieces, on Various Subjects* (Bennington, Vt.: Darius Clark, 1820), 134–52.

[12]Ibid., 150, 148.

[13]Family is central to Emily's existence. Selden endows her with a loving and thoughtful mother, a brother and sister, and a father who fought in the Revolutionary War. Significantly, Miss Armyne's family is neither seen nor mentioned.

[her] heart."[14] Predictably, Emily Merton, whose polestars are innocence and simplicity, triumphs over Miss Armyne and her aristocratic pretensions. For her part, the Irish gentlewoman receives a valuable lesson in the politics of fashion.

By making Emily Merton the standard bearer of republican virtue, Selden revised older conceptions of republicanism and republican womanhood.[15] In the wake of the Revolution, American writers and thinkers tended to look askance at the practices of gentility—practices that had originated in European courts and undermined the austere simplicity demanded by citizens of a republic. Judith Sargent Murray, Charles Brockden Brown, and Benjamin Rush had emphasized self-reliance, reason, and industry as the qualities that best enabled women to serve the republic, if only as wives and mothers. Selden maintained the tension between republican simplicity and aristocratic elegance by altering the meanings of both to fit them with nineteenth-century sensibilities. Judging by Miss Armyne, aristocratic corruption had less to do with gentility per se than with artificial social distinctions—distinctions that might banish a young woman as gracious and lovely as Emily Merton from the realm of polite sociability. And however Emily Merton appears when compared with Miss Armyne, she hardly embodies the eighteenth-century ideal. Although she avoids the worst excesses of fashion, her education has most notably provided her with a smattering of poetry and the classics: precisely the sort of education deplored by eighteenth-century thinkers. Through Emily Merton, Almira Selden condemns fashion and crowns republicanism with refinement.[16]

Despite provincial New Englanders' growing refinement, aristocracy was slow to lose its power as a check against fashionable excess. Although aristocratic pretensions rarely received the thoroughgoing critique that Selden had leveled, they continued to figure as a trope in provincial discourses of social emulation and fashionable consump-

[14]Ibid., 152, 139.

[15]On the ideology of women's role in the early republic, see especially Linda K. Kerber, *Women of the Republic: Intellect and Ideology in the American Revolution* (Chapel Hill: University of North Carolina Press, 1980) and Mary Beth Norton, *Liberty's Daughters: The Revolutionary Experience of American Women, 1750–1800* (Boston: Little, Brown, 1980). On the connections between republican and domestic ideologies, see Nancy F. Cott, *The Bonds of Womanhood: "Woman's Sphere" in New England, 1780–1835* (New Haven, Conn.: Yale University Press, 1977), 94–96; and Ruth H. Bloch, "American Feminine Ideals in Transition: The Rise of the Moral Mother, 1785–1815," *Feminist Studies* 4 (1978): 100–126.

[16]On the tensions between republicanism and refinement, see Bushman, *Refinement of America*, 199–200.

tion through the 1840s. Provincial newspapers regularly printed essays and stories that accused urban elites, in particular, of aping the habits of European nobility. Indeed, reportage, short stories, and stray comments that cast city residents as ersatz aristocrats appeared so frequently that editors and readers alike must have taken real pleasure in them. Stories such as an 1835 piece condemning New York City's "fashionables" for "following in the wake of European nobility" by engraving armorial crests on their calling cards must have generated more than a few self-righteous smiles among Greenfield, Massachusetts, readers.[17] The ascension of Queen Victoria to the British throne briefly breathed new life to the twin threats of aristocracy and fashion. In 1840, William Hawley, editor of the *Hampshire Gazette*, wrote that he was appalled by the American fascination with the young queen, who had managed to attain far greater popularity in rural Massachusetts than she ever enjoyed at home. To his dismay, New England women found Queen Victoria more intriguing than a "plain republican lady, of ten times the talents, ability and moral worth." In their race to "ap[e] foreign notions and manners as fast as possible," women lost all reason. He pointed out than when certain straw bonnets had been touted as London imports, they sold for fifteen dollars. But when they were revealed as the products of Roxbury, Massachusetts, "they were decreed to be a vulgar article," worth only four dollars. In language drawn from the eighteenth century, Hawley used fashion to mark the boundaries between Republicanism, rationality, and simplicity, on the one hand, and nobility, irrationality, and pretentiousness on the other.[18]

Yoked to republican ideology, the problems posed by fashion and social emulation served as barometers of civic virtue and as metaphors for political relations. Seen this way, fashion bore little tangible connection to the acquisition and display of commodities, much less to the constellation of changes, large and small, that accompanied and accelerated the development of rural capitalism. Even William Hawley was less concerned about the price or quality of bonnets than with the ways those bonnets demonstrated Americans' idealization of European styles. After around 1830, however, the increasing density of market relations, the erosion of the household economy, and the emergence of a middle class prompted provincial writers to consider fashion in more concrete terms. Reducing their emphasis on the inverse relation be-

[17]"Very Republican," *Greenfield Gazette and Franklin Herald*, 13 January 1835.
[18]"Queen Victoria," *Hampshire Gazette*, 6 May 1840. On the American middle class's rehabilitation of aristocracy, see Gillian Brown, *Domestic Individualism: Imagining Self in Nineteenth-Century America* (Berkeley: University of California Press, 1990).

tween fashion and republicanism, writers focused instead on fashion's power to mediate relations between households and markets. They recast their discussions of fashionable consumption as discourses of domestic economy.

Until the 1830s, the domestic literature available in the countryside had been largely confined to almanacs, a few instructional manuals, and a handful of newspaper stories that stressed both the need for economy and the productive importance of the household. These early treatises on domestic economy frequently linked agricultural and household labor. For example, Thomas Fessenden's *Husbandman and Housewife*, published in 1820, offered Vermont's prosperous yeomen and their wives "recipes and directions" for success in the fields and in the home.[19] He included extensive and specific instructions on the cultivation of potatoes, the uses of manure, and the best ways to preserve meat, along with recipes for beer, butter, and soap and instructions for making cheese and dyeing linen. Despite his attention to the productive work of Vermont's yeomen, Fessenden understood that they were not, and had no desire to be, completely isolated from regional and even international markets. His readers regularly purchased the necessities that neither they nor their neighbors could make. They also imported such luxuries as they could afford, and were careful to preserve these treasured symbols of status and success. When they were unable or unwilling to purchase fashionable clothing and furnishings, they remained interested in using the materials at hand to approximate cosmopolitan styles. Accordingly, alongside advice on getting rid of bedbugs and conserving flour during bread-baking, Fessenden provided provincial women with instructions for laundering chintz "so as to preserve its beauty," a technique for dressing flax to make it look like silk, and a recipe for cosmetics drawn from a "London Publication." Fessenden never questioned the motivations behind these small, scattered attempts at refinement, nor did he doubt that the yeomanry's participation in the market would be governed by the strictest principles of economy.

Similar advice reached an even wider audience via regional newspapers. Anxious to capitalize on the growing number of female readers, newspaper editors began to court women with stories related to their domestic duties. Along with fiction, poetry, and advertisements for products aimed at women, newspapers regularly published excerpts from a variety of domestic manuals. Like Fessenden's *Hus-*

[19]Thomas G. Fessenden, *The Husbandman and Housewife: A Collection of Valuable Recipes and Directions, Relating to Agriculture and Domestic Economy* (Bellows Falls, Vt.: Bill Blake & Co., 1820).

bandman and Housewife, these stories emphasized the importance of doing for oneself and keeping a careful eye on expenditures.[20]

This conception of a relatively self-sufficient household, which anchored not only the agricultural economy but the republic itself, gave way to cautionary images of a home held hostage to the fluctuations of the market. Where earlier writers had taken for granted industry and frugality, the twin pillars of domestic virtue, writers of the mid-1830s and the 1840s struggled to convince provincial women of the value of economy. Fessenden, Child, and like-minded writers insisted that if thrift did not always lead to wealth, it might at least ensure financial stability, whereas lavish spending could only lead to ruin. But as the market economy and the cash nexus took root in the region's larger towns, writers pointed out that *any* degree of carelessness could lead to ruin. In 1836, the editor of Northampton's *Hampshire Gazette* wrote that high prices and climbing interest rates, compounded by drought, were making for hard times. The difficulties families faced were further exacerbated by the market economy, for "with most of society living in large towns, there is a misapprehension as to what part of our living costs the dearest."[21] In such a context, the pursuit of fashion was especially treacherous.

Alarmed by the growing difficulty of securing a "modest competency," some writers began to consider fashion in the context of market relations, as an unsettling indicator of economic dislocation. These writers increasingly invoked the relation between production and consumption, between saving and spending, and, by extension, between household and market. Provincial newspapers frequently featured original and reprinted essays warning against excessive consumption. Story after story drove home both the dangers that attended fashionable consumption and the moral and monetary rewards of thrift. The editor of the *Hampshire Gazette* took special pains to single out families who spent their entire annual income merely "for the sake of

---

[20]Especially popular was Lydia Maria Child's *Frugal Housewife* (Boston: Carter, Hendee, & Co., 1832), which showed women "how money can be *saved*, not how it can be *enjoyed*" (6). Child's book remained enormously popular with rural and small-town readers. As late as 1847, the *Cultivator Almanac* included an essay entitled "Household Economy," in which an experienced housekeeper offered a list of the most valuable of Child's rules for housewives. See Luther Tucker, *The Cultivator Almanac for the Year 1847* (Rutland, Vt.: W. E. C. Stoddard, 1847). On the efforts of regional newspapers to cultivate a female readership, see William J. Gilmore, *Reading Becomes a Necessity of Life: Material and Cultural Life in Rural New England, 1780–1835* (Knoxville: University of Tennessee Press, 1989), 221.

[21]"Hints on Economy," *Hampshire Gazette*, 9 November 1836. For a useful description and analysis of this economic transformation in Northampton, see Clark, *Roots of Rural Capitalism*.

appearing with the more wealthy and fashionable," for even slight fluctuations in the market would give them "abundant cause to regret such an unthrifty course." By 1840, according to Catharine Sedgwick, emulative consumption had created a new category of unfortunates, "the fashionable expense poor," which included "all those, whether merchants, farmers, mechanics, day laborers, &c., that live in the imitation of expensive fashions."[22]

This message extended from essays on domestic economy and brief "hints to families" to imaginative literature. "The Old Bonnet," which appeared in the *Hampshire Gazette* in 1855, championed economy through the characters of Sallie Curtis and her mother, two women who resolutely resisted the pull of fashion. Indeed, the two women created such a spectacle in their old-fashioned gowns and bonnets that they became a source of humor among their fellow boarders. When asked why she wore her old bonnet when her father could surely afford to spend ten dollars on a new one, Sallie responded that "the consciousness that I am trying to lighten his cares is a great deal to me; and mother says that the feeling of independence, which we call forth by our self-denial will be of lasting benefit to me." These values paid off. Sallie married a man wealthy enough to invest $30,000 in a partnership with her father, a man who admitted to choosing Sallie precisely because of her economical spirit. "I wanted a *companion* in a wife not a mere doll to please my fancy by her pretty face and costly dress," he explained. After all, "a girl who can reason thus correctly about economy, and who has independence enough to carry out that reasoning by wearing an old bonnet, has a mind above the ordinary stamp."[23]

Certainly, provincial writers were not alone in exposing the dangers of consumption and the value of thrift. But writers addressing the wives of urban clerks and tradesmen emphasized the importance of budgets for wage earners, for families whose dependence on the market was taken for granted. Provincial writers frequently emphasized both saving and household production to guarantee some measure of independence from the market. Sophia Hewes, who edited the *Mother's Book and Lady's Companion* in the 1830s and 1840s, offers a case in point. Like domestic writers on both sides of the Atlantic, she tirelessly attacked fashion as the antithesis of both middle-class moderation and womanly virtue, for it primed young women for the plea-

---

[22] "'Fashionable Expense Poor,' from Sedgwick's Public and Private Economy," Greenfield *Gazette and Mercury*, 21 January 1840; "Hints to Families," *Hampshire Gazette*, 1 January 1834. See also "Hints on Economy," *Hampshire Gazette*, 9 November 1836; "On the Changes of Fashion," *Hampshire Gazette*, 12 July 1837.

[23] Harriet Babb, "The Old Bonnet," *Hampshire Gazette*, 16 October 1855.

sures of courtship and ruined them for the duties of wife- and motherhood. But fashion's destructive power reached beyond individual
lives. Bad for women, bad for families, fashion was also bad for New
England's towns and villages. Socially ambitious, idle women hastened market penetration, driving up the prices of "life's necessaries"
and leaving even the thrifty in the thrall of merchants. Registering her
distaste for "young ladies," Hewes also registered her alarm at the
growing power that merchants wielded within provincial communities, imagined as a collection of independent households.[24]

The significance of household production in an unstable economy
was most often imagined as a conflict between past and present, a conflict created by women's failure to match their grandmothers' resolve
in the face of fashion's temptations. For example, during the hard times
that followed the depression of 1837, several Connecticut River Valley
newspapers reprinted "An Address to the Ladies," an 1808 poem written to encourage the domestic manufacture of textiles. Observing that
"money's so scarce, and times growing worse," the poet urged young
women to "throw aside [their] high top knot[s] of pride" and "wear
none but [their] own country's linen."[25] Without considering whether
a return to the age of homespun was a viable or desirable option for
rural families in 1840, the editor of the *Hampshire Gazette* prefaced the
poem with the observation that it might "not be wholly inapplicable to
the present time." To find a satisfactory standard of female behavior,
provincial thinkers looked back to the early republic, to women whose
fathers and husbands had fought in the Revolution. The same essay
that warned New Englanders against the woman of fashion looked to
the daughters of Columbia for a remedy. *Those* brave and industrious
women were accustomed to hard work and were loved for it by their
beaux:

.The damsel who understood most thoroughly and economically the
management of domestic affairs, and was not afraid to put her hands
into the wash tub, or to "lay hold of the distaff," for fear of destroy-

[24]For examples of Hewes's critique, see "Female Education—Address to Mothers," *The
Mother's Book and Young Lady's Companion*, April 1838; "Address to the Patrons of the
Book," *The Mother's Book and Young Lady's Companion*, November 1838; "Tight Dressing—Corsets," *The Mother's Book and Young Lady's Companion*, August 1838. For
accounts of the growing power of merchants in rural New England during the 1830s and
1840s, see Clark, *Roots of Rural Capitalism*, and Roth, *Democratic Dilemma*.

[25]"An Address to the Ladies," *Hampshire Gazette*, 29 June 1840; the editor noted that the
poem had recently appeared "in the *Hampden Post*, where [it was] creditted to the *Republican Spy*, a paper printed in this town in 1808."

ing their elasticity, and dimming their snowy whiteness, was sought by the young men of those days as a fit companion for life, but in modern times to learn the mysteries of the household would make our fair ones faint away; and to labor comes not into the modern code of gentility.[26]

Certainly, this association with the past lent encomiums to thrift and simplicity the air of time-tested gravity. But it also gave them an air of unreality. By 1840, the spindles and looms on which feminine virtue was woven were relics of a household economy that was more the stuff of memory than lived experience. Still, stories making the "daughters of Columbia" out as exemplars of industry were not simply pro forma exercises in nostalgia, although nostalgia certainly permeates the descriptions of back-breaking household labor. The point of this litera-ture was not simply that the past was more virtuous than the present, or that women ought to keep busy. What is so striking is the kind of pro-ductive labor that provincial writers and editors singled out for praise.

Time and again, they returned to the image of the woman at the spin-ning wheel as *the* embodiment of feminine virtue. This image owed much to New Englanders' republican heritage. The efforts of patriot women during the American Revolution and the Federalist emphasis on domestic manufactures during the early republic established close connections between republican ideology and practice, domestic man-ufactures, and women's work. But the image of the woman seated duti-fully at the wheel also recalled the household economy of the late eigh-teenth and early nineteenth centuries. The woman at the wheel labored not only to secure the political independence of her nation but also, and more immediately, to maintain the economic independence of her household and her men. Like her mate, the mythic yeoman, she per-sonified one strand of republican political economy, the strand that linked household independence to a healthy suspicion of the market. The lady of fashion, the woman who refused to "lay hold of the

[26]"Can She Spin." Complaints about the poor housekeeping skills of young women, espe-cially compared with the skills of earlier generations of women, were common throughout the 1830s and 1840s. See, for example, an 1838 story in the Greenfield *Gazette and Mer-cury* that define "housewifery" as "an ancient art, said to have been fashionable among young girls and young wives; now entirely out of use, or practiced only by the lower orders" ("Witty Definitions for Common Things," *Gazette and Mercury*, 25 December 1838). On provincial New Englanders' nostalgia for the "age of homespun" and the role that nostalgia played in the creation of middle-class culture, see my " 'The Consummation of Rural Prosperity and Happiness': New England Agricultural Fairs and the Construction of Class and Gender, 1810–1860," *American Quarterly* 49 (1997): 574–602.

distaff," severed the ties that bound political culture, household economy, and gender role together into a seamless whole. Laying bare the contradictions between the political economy of eighteenth-century republicanism and the political economy of liberal capitalism, she also gave familiar shape to the constellation of social, cultural, and economic forces that were gradually undermining the household economy. The chief danger of emulative consumption, embodied as a socially ambitious lady, was less a leveling of the social hierarchies separating rich and poor or an erasure of the boundaries separating city and country than the dissolution of an older social structure.

By figuring the problems that fashion created, along with the problems that fashions represented, as a contest between two poles of womanhood, provincial writers obscured the social, the cultural, and especially the economic processes that undergirded this transformation. If writers such as Sophia Hewes and William Hawley associated fashionable consumption with the increasing variety of commodities that filled New England's towns and villages, they divorced it from changing class relations, particularly the emergence of a middle class. As we have seen, women who sought their places as members of an emerging middle class had come to depend far more heavily on the performance of fashion than on productive labor for their self-representation. Although painstaking economy allowed families to join the ranks of the middle class, their arrival could only be announced by a certain amount of display. Fashionable clothing, elaborate furnishings, and the performance of gentility set middle-class families apart from their poorer neighbors. Moreover, the economic transformation that gave rise to this provincial middle class—with its teas, its literary societies, and its balls—was itself dependent on the expansion of commercial relations throughout the region's towns and villages.

Urban Fashion and Rural Style

While some writers discussed fashion's influence on the rural economy, others depicted a sentimentalized countryside, immune to fashion's corruptions. In their telling, the distinction between fashion and social emulation on the one hand and simplicity and sincerity on the other collapsed into the distance between city and country. The hinterland's geographic and cultural distance from the fashionable center was proof enough of its superiority. Rural New Englanders had always been quick to twit the pretensions of their urban cousins: From the eighteenth century, snide jokes about dandies and ladies countered equally snide jokes about rustic clods.[27] By the 1830s, however, the defensiveness that lent those jokes their edge gave way to complacent self-assurance. Editors and writers rarely missed an opportunity to point out the differences between city and country; almost any item could be grist for the mill. One writer offered a scathing review of "ungrateful" Fanny Kemble's travel narrative, which was "highly spiced . . . with ridicule of persons and things in America." But if the book as a whole was "coarse and vulgar," it nevertheless "contain[ed] some rather cutting truths, which will no doubt edify certain city fashionables who have idolized her." When an observer as clumsy as Kemble could find evidence of the folly of city fashionables, that was good evidence, indeed. And following the panic of 1837, the editor of the *Hampshire Gazette* predicted, erroneously as it turned out, that the "distress of the times" was an urban phenomenon. Disaster might befall urban speculators, who undoubtedly deserved it, but, he wrote, "the business man of the country, who was satisfied with a small but safe business, is still on sure ground, and is saved all the misery of the state of bankrupcy." From the safety of the countryside, the panic offered provincial men "at least one good lesson . . . and that is, to be contented with their lot." Speculation was a moral lapse, and a peculiarly urban lapse at that.[28]

Given the gendered nature of fashion, is not surprising that the distance between city and country, like the difference between fashion and simplicity, often figured as a comparison between two women. Generally, the comparisons were earnestly conventional: While women in towns and cities became "almost universally extravagant, foolish and fashionable," country girls maintained their "truth, household knowledge and economy, health (and consequently beauty), simplicity, affection, and freshness of impulse and thought."[29] Other times, the comparison took the shape of outright humor: While city belles squandered their families' resources on expensive and exotic skin creams, such as "the grand imperial *double and twisted* perfume of Allah Fad Laddem Mahommed's distilled essence of Rain bows," "us farmers and our daughters" attained "smooth and healthy skin" with a cornmeal paste mask. Still, when a Northampton poet compared the " 'gay belles of fashion' " whose days were spent rolling through city streets with their "coaches and six" with the "neat village school

[27]Lawrence Buell describes this dialectic in *New England Literary Culture: From Revolution through Renaissance* (New York: Cambridge University Press, 1986), 335–50.

[28]"A Good Lesson to Be Learned," *Hampshire Gazette*, 31 May 1837; "Miss Kemble's Journal," *Greenfield Gazette and Franklin Herald*, 12 May 1835.

[29]"Country Girls," *Hampshire Gazette*, 15 July 1856.

ma'am," with her "eyes bright and shining," no sensible reader doubted who was "the finest, the best, the most useful of girls."[30]

In the 1838 short story "Ernestine Campbell," a Plainfield, Massachusetts, writer took aim at those foolish enough to abandon rural simplicity for urban fashion. Edward Forsyth, the promising son of a local yeoman and a Harvard man to boot, was engaged to marry a distant, impoverished relation, Ernestine Campbell. Ernestine was pretty enough, but she also possessed "all that strength of feeling and vigor of mind that is thought to constitute genius." Unfortunately, Edward's time in Boston and Cambridge had sowed the seeds of social ambition; he began to imagine a grander future than his village could offer. When Ernestine refused to broaden her horizons beyond the worlds of family, village, and productive labor, he broke off the engagement. Back in Boston, Edward became obsessed with a mysterious young lady in a carriage who embodied all that was fine and fashionable. After months of foolish and futile pursuit (including a memorable carriage chase through Mount Auburn Cemetery), he learned from a mutual acquaintance that

> the object of his desire was not all that he had imagined. She was "uncultivated, . . . cold and unfeeling," for her feminine sensibilities had been eroded by fashion. Worse, she was neither wealthy nor cosmopolitan. In fact, she was the daughter of an illiterate if successful country peddler, whose own social ambition led him to hire a carriage so that his wife and daughter might catch a "glimpse of the wonders of the metropolis." Having learned "the folly of ambition and the vanity of display," Edward decided to marry Ernestine after all.[31]

Edward Forsyth's brief obsession with fashion threatened to undermine his future happiness, but it was a limited threat, private and individual. Forsyth discovered the truth about the peddler's daughter before they could be introduced, much less court. And she remained confined within the city. The mysterious young woman never encroached on Edward's life or on village life. The caprices of fashionable consumption, embodied in the peddler's daughter, never seriously threatened the economic security of Edward Forsyth's household,

[30]J. G. H., "The Neat Village School-Ma'am," *Hampshire Gazette*, 27 June 1838. "Cheap Cosmetic," *Hampshire Gazette*, 16 March 1836.

[31]F. H. of Plainfield, "Ernestine Campbell," *Hampshire Gazette*, 19 December 1838. The story does not include any mention of Ernestine's response to Edward's change of heart; for all Ernestine's virtues, apparently neither Edward nor F. H. of Plainfield considered her worth consulting.

much less the social structure of his village. Indeed, far from threatening provincial society, fashion was defeated by it. The old-fashioned values of the household economy offered the best protection against the caprices of fashion. Like Dorothy in *The Wizard of Oz*, Edward discovered that his heart's desire had been in his own back yard all along.

Holding up the countryside as the antithesis of fashion, provincial writers continued to deplore the excessive consumption born of social emulation. But the logic of their critique was mired in fashion itself. The difference between city and country was increasingly imagined as a difference in manners and style. Cast as a conflict between urban splendor and rural simplicity, discourses about fashion, consumption, and social emulation spoke less to the transformation of social relations and economic structures than to the tension between two bourgeois styles. Discussions about fashion provoked questions about the boundaries of good taste, about the precise point where gentility collapsed into ostentation.

Seen this way, the chief virtue of the country was simply that it was in better taste than the city. F. H. of Plainfield championed the same values in "Ernestine Campbell" that Francis Underwood would later praise in his tale about the "pyanner's triumph," the story that pitted the cosmopolitan, piano-playing Misses Grant against the small-minded, small-town prejudices of a rustic deacon and his wife. Whatever Underwood's story reveals about the hierarchies of village life, it also reveals his unyielding faith in the power of good taste. Indeed, it is the appallingly bad taste of the deacon and his wife, who possessed neither graceful prose nor elegant clothes, that immediately undermines their pretension to moral authority. The author of "Ernestine Campbell" simply inverts the dichotomy that structures Underwood's tale and countless earlier screeds against rural backwardness. According to "F. H. of Plainfield," true taste resides in the country; it does not careen through the streets of Cambridge in hired carriages. But if "Ernestine Campbell" inverts the values assigned to city and country, the story also accepts the categories that structure that dichotomy— categories that pit city against country and that serve to underscore the signal importance of taste as an indicator of virtue.[32] By extracting fashion from the tangle of commodity production and market relations, provincial writers contributed to the bourgeois vision of the countryside as landscape—a landscape composed not of independent households but of pretty cottages. As ubiquitous descriptions of "sweet

[32]The ease with which these pastoral critiques could be adopted to a bourgeois, urban vision was demonstrated in the number of stories that began to appear in *Godey's Lady's Book* by the 1840s.

country home[s]" trellised with "roses and honeysuckle" suggest, country had dissolved into fashion—a morally and aesthetically superior form of fashion, to be sure, but fashion nevertheless.

Writers who deplored fashion's grip on the countryside and those who reduced the countryside to fashion stopped short of recapitulating the bourgeois depiction of fashion as an exclusively female vice. Certainly, provincial writers drew on Western literary conventions that deployed women as symbolic representations of both fashion and its negation. In large measure, the struggle between republican and patrician polities, between household economy and market society, between country and city was engaged through the bodies of women. And provincial writers clearly associated women with consumption. Acknowledging shopping as an increasingly important and increasingly feminized activity, writers directed a good deal of criticism and advice at female consumers. Some, like Sophia Hewes, attributed excessive consumption to women's vanity and voracious appetite for fashion. Others assumed that women's foibles in the market derived from ignorance or lapses in judgment rather than the desire for personal display. Accordingly, the pages of provincial newspapers regularly featured stories urging women to buy in bulk, not to prepare a new dish until the last had been consumed, to dress well on a budget, and to conserve fuel grates. Such stories aimed to educate sensible women about changing economic contexts, not to shame them into conquering their passion for finery. From this perspective, buying too many dresses was no different from squandering fuel grates.[33]

But men were hardly immune to the lure of fashion. In "Ernestine Campbell," it is Edward, not Ernestine, who aspires to cosmopolitan elegance. And even Sophia Hewes conceded that women put on style partly to attract husbands, who were all too often taken in by soft hands, pretty dresses, and a smattering of French. More to the point, men were not merely susceptible to fashionable women; they were susceptible to fashion itself. An 1835 article denouncing the duplicity of "fashionable conversation" condemned women's parlor sociability for nurturing false friendships. Yet the author also took aim at the "man of business" who showered the innocent with fake hospitality in the hope of "accruing patronage and gain." Men did more—and worse—than play the game of fashion to advance careers; just like women, they lost their reason in the face of fashion's temptations. In a short story by Connecticut River Valley writer H. A. Dwight, the reckless pursuit of

[33]These examples are drawn from "Hints on Economy," *Hampshire Gazette*, 9 November 1836.

fashion plunged a young married couple into poverty. They quickly amassed so many debts that they could no longer answer the door for fear of confronting hostile creditors. In Dwight's telling, however, it is the young *man* who exhausts the family resources to "keep up with the fashions"; despite regular visits from creditors, the wife never realized that her family was sinking into debt. At the story's conclusion, the couple agree to share information about and responsibility for the family's accounts, an arrangement that allowed the young woman to act as a check on her husband's extravagant impulses.[34]

Several writers accused men of a weakness for personal display, a weakness typically attributed to women. When a Massachusetts writer condemned the "custom of wearing a superfluity of *gew gaw* trinkets" in 1840, he was thinking not of fancy ladies but of men who were "slave[s] of six by four inch breastpins, watch chains like the tiller rope of a Mississippi steamboat or finger rings that would enchain a culprit." Indeed, men had greater difficulty than women in mastering simple attire. A Greenfield, Massachusetts, writer pointed out that women were always "either dirty or slovenly in the extreme, or neat and respectable, however poverty stricken in appearance." But the desire to maintain the veneer of fashion polish condemned "poor men" who had "seen better days" to an especially "strange compound of dirty slovenliness and wretched attempts at a kind of faded smartness." As shoppers and lovers of fashion, provincial women bore some resemblance to their urban sisters, but provincial men had their difficulties mastering the subdued fashions and the restrained manners demanded of the bourgeois businessman.[35]

Provincial Women and the Languages of Fashion

When writers as different as Sophia Hewes and the author of "Ernestine Campbell" invoked "fashion," they called to mind the growing variety of commodities that filled the shelves of provincial stores and the parlors of provincial homes as well as elaborate entertainments whose success depended on delicate confections, tasteful decorations, and fancy gowns. In their texts, however, those commodi-

---

[34]H. A. Dwight, "The Door Bell, or Keeping up with the Fashions," *Hampshire Gazette*, 4 May 1858; "Things by Their Wrong Names," *Hampshire Gazette*, 18 November 1835.

[35]"Shabby Genteel," *Greenfield Gazette and Franklin Herald*, 20 January 1835; "Useless Ornaments," *Hampshire Gazette*, 8 January 1840. On nineteenth-century male fashion and bourgeois culture, see Elizabeth Wilson, *Adorned in Dreams: Fashion and Modernity* (Berkeley: University of California Press, 1985).

ties and practices serve only as a prism through which to explore the tensions between household economy and bourgeois culture or the tensions between the provincial and urban middle classes. Drawing on conventions that described fashion through a series of binary oppositions, they narrowed the range of meanings that might apply to any particular commodity or to consumption in general. As historian Amanda Vickery has made clear, these conventions eclipsed the complex and often contradictory meanings that ordinary women and men ascribed to consumption, imposing a sense of order that was artificial at best.[36]

In general, women were disinclined to imagine their kin, their neighbors, or themselves in the terms set by discourses of fashion and social emulation. This divergence between public and private discourse should not be attributed to the tired gap between prescription and practice, or worse, dismissed as evidence of cynical hypocrisy. Provincial women seem to have shared writers' concerns about the dangers that social emulation posed for provincial communities, but they simultaneously reserved for themselves a different understanding of consumption, one that recalled the mutual obligation of the household economy. No less than exchanges of labor, exchanges centering on consumption and the elaboration of fashion structured the relations between kin, friends, and households. Women's consumption and their shared interest in fashion merged with other forms of female reciprocity.

Provincial women routinely shopped not only for themselves but for their extended families, keeping an eye out for bargains or rare items. Women who lived in cities or visited them combed shops and markets for goods that were unavailable in the hinterland. Amelia Peabody, for example, formed part of a kin-based shopping network that extended from Salem, Massachusetts, inland to Springfield and north to rural New Hampshire. Her Salem cousins shopped with Amelia in mind; for her part, she sent pins, patterns, trimmings, and fabrics to sisters who remained in rustic Lancaster, New Hampshire. When she traveled from Springfield to visit kin in the Boston vicinity, shopping for New Hampshire relatives formed a good part of her itinerary. On an 1829 trip to Boston, she bought "ornaments" for her father to give to her sisters. "Jewelry having fallen in value," she wrote, "instead of rings I bought pins, finding I could get very handsome ones for even less than the sum

[36]Amanda Vickery, "Women and the World of Goods: A Lancashire Consumer and Her Possessions, 1751–81," in *Consumption and the World of Goods,* 274–304.

you mentioned."[37] The next year, Peabody's sister Mary Jane White traveled from Lancaster to Springfield to visit, help with the children, and shop. She shared her access to new goods and new styles with her other sister, Charlotte, who had remained in Lancaster. Citing Amelia Peabody as the arbiter of fashion, Mary Jane reported that "Amelia says silk pelisses were more fashionable last winter, and there is a splendid kind of silk for them and also for dresses, which I can send to New York for." On Amelia's advice, Mary Jane had decided to "send for a dress for myself, and you must let me know if you will venture other people's taste so far as to send in the same way."[38] When they shopped for their kin, women put their good taste and good sense to the service of others.

Throughout New England's hinterland, women created similar networks to obtain information about fashion. Over the course of the antebellum period, several of the women's magazines that included fashion plates gradually worked their way into countryside, where they undoubtedly educated and entertained some readers. And when women traveled to Boston or New York, they took care to notice new trimmings and modifications in the cut and drape of clothing; in other words, they kept an eye out for relatively easy and inexpensive ways to update the clothes they already owned. Still, most of the information that provincial women gathered about style came from one another. More important, their gleaned their definition of tasteful style from one another. Hungry as they were for information about fashion, provincial women looked to one another rather than to city fashionables or the cosmopolitan press to set the standards of style.

Mary Hooker of Springfield, Massachusetts, turned to her friend Weltha Brown in Hartford, Connecticut, for trimmings and advice in 1822. When she asked Brown to "procure . . . plush the color of the pattern enclosed . . . to trim the collar and sleeves of a coat" for herself and her sister in 1822, Hooker solicited Brown's own thoughts on the merits of plush. Although Hooker had been given to understand that "plush was more worn than velvet," if it was "not as fashionable as velvet or any other trimming" that Brown found "handsome," then she should send what was "most suitable and fashionable with directions about putting it on." Weltha Brown was instructed to trim Mary Hooker and her sister as she would trim herself. If she did, Hooker wrote, "I shall not only be perfectly satisfied but much obliged to

[37]Amelia White Peabody to Moses White, 13 May 1829, Everett-Peabody Family Papers, MHS.

[38]Mary Jane White to Charlotte White, 4 July 1830, Everett-Peabody Family Papers, MHS.

you."[39] These exchanges could begin quite early in a girl's life. While attending boarding school in Claremont, New Hampshire, Maria Clark wrote that "the little girls all have their hair cut off a little below their ears and so I have got mine cut off." When her Claremont kin agreed that the new style made her "look a great deal better," Maria Clark decided that her younger sister must have the same hairstyle. "I want Emily to [get] hers cut off too have it cut off about an inch below her ears just the way we always wanted it," she instructed her mother. "Then let her knit her a net out of black silk and oil her hair with bears oil and it will grow much faster and don't you let her wet it any if you do it will make it coarse."[40]

Looking good mattered. Looking stylish mattered. But for young Maria Clark, as for Mary Hooker some twenty years earlier, looking good had little to do with meeting the distant, cosmopolitan standards set by *Godey's Lady's Book*, purchasing the latest finery displayed in the stores of urban retailers, or matching the elegant ladies who promenaded through the parks of Boston, New York, and Philadelphia. Instead, the standards of fashion, and appearance generally, were set by provincial friends and relatives. This is not to deny the significance of urban culture, in either its genteel or rowdy variants, in determining the props of fashion. Nor is it to deny the close association that nineteenth-century observers drew between city life and fashionable life. But it is to suggest that the spread of fashion, like the elaboration of new codes of genteel behavior, did not progress in a straight line from city to country. On the contrary. Provincial New Englanders' participation in the culture of fashion, like their participation in the culture of gentility, was mediated by village culture, by standards and practices that had obtained in the household economy.

Despite this, the unpublished writings of provincial women and men also reveal the influence of public, published discourses on consumption. The conventional critiques of fashion, which associated it with social climbing, with dissipation, and with femininity were reproduced well beyond the pages of domestic manuals and the provincial press. New Hampshire schoolgirl Martha Stone mastered these conventions at an early age. "Fashion is an ornament to the body, pride an injury to the soul; fashion tends to excite pride, & pride fashion; these follow one another and destroy the happiness of many," she wrote. She also understood the gendered dimensions of fashionable display: "Levity of manner, I think very unbecoming in a young lady, but much more

[39]Mary Hooker to Weltha Brown, 6 November 1822, Hooker Collection, SL.
[40]Maria Clark to Morris Clark and Lucy Fisher Clark, 12 August 1846, Morris Clark Papers, NHHS, 1991–030.

so in a young gentleman." After all, people expected "females to be vain and thoughtless." Then, perhaps measuring that stereotype against her own vision of femininity, she crossed out those lines to conclude simply that people expected "to see more wisdom in and sedateness in a gentleman, as they are called the wiser sex."[41] Another New Hampshire writer tied the story of New England town-building to a critique of women's weakness for fashion. In a poem produced for a Concord literary society, "Mathetes" recounted the history of Concord Village from uninhabited wilderness through Native American settlement and the arrival of the first European Americans and then into the antebellum era. But rather than tracing a whiggish trajectory of progress, culminating in the triumph of the republic or even the sentimentalization of the New England village, Mathetes's story ended on a sour note. Fashionable women had corrupted the village center:

> If e'er you wish to pass along this street
> A dozen Ladies you are sure to meet.
> They've left their knitting work at home to go
> To see forsooth how all the neighbors do.
> Many there are who every day are found
> In ruffles, silk, & flounces, gadding round
> Joining anon in fashions noisy din
> To tell the news and webs of scandal spin.[42]

Elements of this discourse also found their way into private writings, providing many New Englanders with a language through which to judge themselves and, more often, to judge others. For many women, fashion provided the terrain on which to fight the battle with pride. Describing the many tests of faith that confronted her, the deeply religious Sophronia Grout found the temptations of fashion, and especially social emulation, especially bedeviling. After enduring one particularly acute struggle, she recalled that "situated as I am, often in the society of well dressed people, I was sometimes tempted to believe it

[41]Martha Stone, "Tower of Fashion," n.d. [ca. 1830s], Letters from Mrs. Roland Beers Records, Stone Family Papers, DCL MS. 831104.

[42]"Mathetes," "For the Oasis: Concord Village," Concord Public Library Materials Collection, NHHS, Box 14, Folder 11, 1983–84. Not surprisingly, sermons drove home similar messages. Elizabeth Phelps Huntington reported hearing a Northampton sermon on why home "so often fails of being what the Author of our nature designed that it should be." The Reverend Dwight pointed to families who "tho' suitable desirous of advancing themselves, and providing for their families the means of education and refined enjoyments, were still destitute of that which constitutes a happy home, And this one thing is religion." Elizabeth Phelps Huntington to Frederic Dan Huntington, 23 September 1840, PPHFP, Box 12, Folder 8.

rather my duty to purchase some article of clothing to dress more decently to appear among those whose presence I could not well avoid." She was saved by her faith. "But the debt I could not forget. I owed my Maker," she wrote; the money she would have spent on dresses and trimmings went to her church and to a variety of missionary societies.[43] Sophronia Grout's pride was vanquished by faith; young Fanny Negus's pride was checked by her mother. Away at school following the death of her father, Fanny found her wardrobe sadly lacking. Her request for new or better gowns provoked a sharp reproof from her mother. "You rote you wish'd to dress as well as any of the Ladies, you must not take them for a patron, recollect you situation, dress decently and that will satisfy a mind that is rightly improved." Although Fanny needed to conquer her pride, Arethusa Negus sympathized with her daughter's situation. A new dress was out of the question, for "at present you know I have ways for all I can earn." Still, mother and sisters were happy to sacrifice their own gowns to ease Fanny's situation. "If my stript muslin will do you any good you may use it this summer, to ware to school if you dress in white. Rosanna says she don't know how to spare her coarse cambric, but will send you her white spencer." Arethusa Negus's criticism of her daughter's desires was framed by discursive conventions emphasizing women's struggle with vanity, while her solution to the girl's problem was prompted by standards of provincial reciprocity.[44]

If discourses that tied fashionable dress and genteel behavior to social emulation colored women's description of those they loved, it is not surprising that those same discourses colored their accounts of those they disdained. Amelia Peabody echoed the words of Sophia Hewes in condemning the fashionable education offered to Springfield's young ladies at Miss Hawkes's popular school. Young girls were better off "laying up a stock of useful qualities . . . according to my old-fashioned notions" than spending time at Miss Hawkes's, where they wasted their time on "geology, algebra and a dozen other abstruse sciences, the very names of which I should be afraid to write, lest I should not know how to spell them." "I have got out of patience with the modern fooleries of female education," she wrote, for "it fits [young women] for no earthly purpose and makes them nothing but upstarts."[45]

And when they described the airs of their social inferiors, provincial

[43]Sophronia Grout Diary, n.d., PVMA.

[44]Arethusa Negus to Fanny Negus, 19 May 1816, Fuller-Higginson Papers, PVMA.

[45]Amelia Peabody to Mary Jane White, 16 January 1830, Everett-Peabody Family Papers, MHS.

women looked first to the language of fashion and social emulation. When Katherine Hodges, attending boarding school in Greenfield, asked for a hat similar to her old one, her mother replied that the hats in question were "decidedly ugly" and were no longer carried by any of the "first class establishments." More to the point, the style had trickled down and out, to include members of the laboring classes. "All say [the hats] will be worn only by common bold faced girls," she explained.[46] Indeed, fashion's power lay less in its capacity to elicit a precise portrait of the middle class than in its power to graphically distinguish that class from the region's poorer farmers and laborers, to highlight the divisions riddling an increasingly stratified society.

Provincial women called on the discursive conventions of fashion, consumption, and social emulation to draw boundaries, to delineate distinctions of wealth between classes and distinctions of refinement and virtue within the middle class. And the convention they invoked most frequently was the juxtaposition between city and country. We have seen the ways in which provincial women and men condemned the perceived pretensions of city fashionables. Marianne Cochran registered her disapproval when some Boston acquaintances gave "parties innumerable each vying for the other in extravagance." She concluded that "much offense is given by these . . . nobility.[47] And Theodore Huntington recalled that when his Boston-bred aunt first appeared in a South Hadley, Massachusetts, church, "she was very much dressed indeed, her costume was so altogether beyond that of our people, that to my youthful eyes it was very near the grotesque." Her appearance was explained by her origins, for she was a "Boston Lady." For Huntington and Cochran, city style spelled bad taste.[48] Country style spelled virtue and simplicity. It was not only that provincial women and men took the superiority of rural style and rural life as an article of faith, although they often did. But by the 1840s, provincials self-consciously put on "rural style" in order to signal their virtue. When Joseph Bartlett, a minister, decided to marry, he planned his wedding to accord with provincial standards and to represent rural virtues. He

[46]Mrs. S. E. Hodges to Katherine Craddoc Hodges, 17 October 1861, Hodges Family Papers, SL. See also Henry Hills to [Mary] Adelaide Spencer, 12 January 1855, Hills Family Papers, ACASC; Hattie Fuller to George Fuller, 30 January 1853, Fuller-Higginson Family Papers, PVMA.

[47]Marianne Cochran to Agnes Cochran Higginson, 10 February 1839, Fuller-Higginson Papers, PVMA.

[48]Huntington's aunt must have seen her gaffe, or been made to see it, for he concluded that eventually "she took kindly to country life and made a very affectionate wife and mother." Theodore Huntington, "Sketches by Theodore G. Huntington of the Family and Life in Hadley Written in Letters to H. F. Quincy," 24, PPHFP, Box 21, Folder 7.

explained that "we have endeavored to make all things suitable for a country parson's bridal in regard to dress & c. There will be no wedding party—not even the indispensable cake."[49]

As signifiers of style, "city" and "country" were remarkably elastic terms. Used this way, they referred less to specific locales than to relative degrees of pretension or refinement. Abstracted from material geography, "city" and "country" could map the hierarchies within provincial society and even within the provincial middle class. Any number of slights and pretensions could be attributed to the cultural distance between city and country. When Georgianna Drake, a girl from rural New Hampshire, visited kin in Pembroke, she felt snubbed when her cousin failed to invite her to socialize with callers. She gave voice to her hurt and her indignation through the juxtaposition between city and country. "Cousin Ellen has callers & I ('the country cousin') have not been invited into the room," Georgianna complained to her mother. "But if I am but a 'country cousin' I think I should have sufficient politeness to ask a friend who might be visiting at my home, into the room when I had callers & that is an act of politeness of which my 'city cousin' is destitute."[50] Sarah Olcott of Hanover, New Hampshire, sent out invitations for an 8 P.M. wedding, all "nicely sealed with a white Ribbon" and "with her card 'at home' " included. But not all of her guests appreciated these pains. "Such things I think are rather ridiculous in a small country village," concluded one woman. This lapse in taste and judgment was all the worse considering that bride was moving from a "small country village" to someplace even more rustic. "It is said Candia is to be her place of residence. What can she show off to show off to there"? the disapproving guest wondered.[51] The distance between city and country was not simply the distance between Boston and Northampton but also the distance between Hanover and Candia.

This contrast between city and country proved compelling in large measure because it spoke to provincial women's experiences. The city *was* different from the country. And Candia *was* different than Hanover. This juxtaposition also resonated with New Englanders' attempts to

[49]Joseph Bartlett to Samuel C. Bartlett and Mary Bartlett, 11 October 1847, Bartlett Family Papers, DCL. Middle-class provincials of the nineteenth century were not alone in their enthusiasm for simplicity; city residents idealized simplicity without yoking it to a rural landscape. See David E. Shi, *The Simple Life: Plain Living and High Thinking in American Culture* (New York: Oxford University Press, 1985), 100–124; Halttunen, *Confidence Men and Painted Women*, 56–91.

[50]Georgianna Drake to Betsy Drake, n.d. [ca. 1850], Drake Family Papers, DCL.

[51]M. C. Hale to Rev. Bingham Hale, 24 June 1834, DCL.

maintain some vestige of the household economy, if only as a sensibility, style, or rural landscape. But this juxtaposition was also central to the creation of the provincial middle class. From the 1820s, provincial New Englanders manipulated an increasingly hollow notion of the household economy to position themselves uneasily between their poorer neighbors and their urban counterparts. Men and women whose lives were shaped by the imperatives of a market society continued to hold the homely virtues of their households and towns against the fashion and show they associated with bourgeois society. In the process, they obscured the growing distance that separated even members of a provincial middle class from their poorer farming and laboring neighbors. They also obscured their deepening commitment to bourgeois culture and bourgeois social relations.

9

"An elevated tone to the whole town"

In October 1864, Arethusa Hall began to write her life story.[1] She cast her life as a novel, told in the third person, whose central character was Sauthera—an anagram of her own name.[2] Her life's narrative, "Sautherea: The Story of a Life," points both to the capitalist transformation of the New England countryside and to the ways in which that process was sentimentalized by members of the provincial middle class. In her account, the process of self-realization merged with the movement from country to city, the evolution from rusticity to refinement, and, more obliquely, the transition from household economy to bourgeois society. The story she tells, and the language she uses to tell that story, show how deeply intertwined the discourses of gentility and rural life had become for members of the provincial middle class by the end of the antebellum period.

Like Arethusa Hall, Sautherea was born into a farm family in one of New England's hill towns, which provided the "first influences upon her character." She grew up beneath "pure clean skies," breathing

[1]Arethusa Hall, "Sautherea: The Story of a Life," Judd Papers, HCL, 55M-1, Box 2. I am indebted to Christopher Clark for alerting me to this source.

[2]Because no autobiography (perhaps least of all a woman's) constitutes an unmediated reflection of its author, and because Hall herself chose to rename her fictionalized self, I use "Arethusa Hall" to mean the writer of the narrative and "Sautherea" to mean the heroine of that narrative. On women's autobiographical writing, see especially Shari Binstock, ed., *The Private Self: Theory and Practice of Women's Autobiographical Writings* (Chapel Hill: University of North Carolina Press, 1988).

"fresh animating air." She attended the district school, taught by "maiden twin sisters." And she walked to worship at an "old fashioned meeting-house, which on Sunday Mornings, especially, seemed surrounded by a sacred halo." Reared in such an environment, Sautherea was all that a country girl ought to be. Even as a child, she was "kind, loving, and truthful, desiring peace and harmony above all things." Her character was reflected in her beauty, her "fair complexion, blue eyes, [and] brown hair flecked with gold with a tendency to curl."

Her childhood was measured in the seasonal rhythms of the countryside: At harvesttime, she gathered chestnuts, picked apples, and played on hay carts. But her life was also marked by the rhythms of household production. She helped make butter, bread, and cheese ("an intricate process"). And she spent a great deal of time spinning and winding spools, for "all of the clothing of the family was homemade, in the strictest sense, the wool and flax being raised upon the farm, and the carding, spinning, dyeing and weaving all being done by the household." Sautherea participated in household manufacture alongside her mother and sisters. But Hall was careful to point out that Sautherea's labor was not merely productive; it was also a badge of refined sensibility and intellectual ambition. "There was to her a sort of poetry in all these homely operations," Hall wrote, "also a kind of philosophical interest, a strong tendency to inform herself of the course of things, to seek the whys and the wherefores."

Although they were hardly wealthy, Sautherea's family nevertheless lived in a kind of rustic gentility. Her mother, father, and seven brothers and sisters crowded into a house consisting of two downstairs rooms and several "low chambers" under the roof. The parents and youngest children slept in the kitchen; the older children found places upstairs. At night, the house was lit by firelight and the occasional pine knot torch, for candles were luxuries to be conserved. Still, there were touches of refinement. The pewter was "not the adulterated kind of after days." Instead, it was "almost white as silver . . . kept bright by nice washing" and "lustrous from frequent hand rubbing with rushes." And the family benefited from "quite a number of valuable books." Her father epitomized the republican yeoman. A Harvard student, he had "quitted the peaceful seclusion of college walls and marched to the fight for liberty and freedom." At the war's end, when he found himself too old for college and too poor for the "more cultivated parts of Eastern Massachusetts," he settled in the poor, rocky hills of western New England. Sautherea's mother lacked the "few advantages of even common school education." But her "natural insight, strong reasoning power, and quick perceptions supplied the deficiency." Together, these two created a family life in which the routines of farm labor and household production were punctuated by social visits, political debates, reading, and family worship.

This tranquil life was interrupted when Sautherea, at age ten, was sent to help a married sister keep house. The move marked a "great change" not because it separated Sautherea from her family but because it introduced her to hitherto unimagined levels of refinement. Her new home was "nearer to the shire town of the county, which held the relation of city to its suburbs."[3] Most of the residents were farmers, but, Hall explained, "this sort of metropolis had early been settled by some of the old aristocracy of New England," and the town was still "in some measure peopled from it." In her new home, "frequent intercourse was kept up, as well as communication with the outside world." There was an "elevated tone to the whole town." And for the first time, Sautherea began to encounter "something . . . of the refinements and manners of more cultivated society."

Moving down from the hills toward the shire town also introduced Sautherea to new patterns of work. She was no longer occupied with the "busy and varied labors" of the farm. Instead, she and her sister spent their time washing, ironing, cooking, cleaning, and, above all, caring for a rapidly growing "flock of little ones." The care of her nieces and nephews placed an especially "heavy tax" on Sautherea's "patience and good nature." "When the number [of children] came to be reckoned up by the half dozen or more, it must be allowed that the prospect of a new accession was more than she could sustain with becoming complacency," Hall wryly observed. Like many provincial women, Sautherea and her sister found that even when they left weaving, churning, and cheese-making behind, they remained burdened by housework. Still, by rising early and working hard, the two women managed to complete their work, "and in no half finished, slatternly way, either." By the late afternoon, the two women were ready for "a neat change of clothes" and a stream of visitors.

The frustrations of child care and the drudgery of housework were balanced by the educational opportunities that her new life afforded. Her brother-in-law, "more interested in the pursuit of knowledge than money," encouraged Sautherea's intellectual development, teaching her French and introducing her to the poetry of Milton and Cowper, to the

[3]For Arethusa Hall, this move was from Norwich, Massachusetts, to Westhampton, Massachusetts, to live with her sister Apphia Hall Judd and her brother-in-law, Sylvester Judd. For biographical information on Sylvester Judd, see Christopher Clark, *The Roots of Rural Capitalism: Western Massachusetts, 1780–1860* (Ithaca, N.Y.: Cornell University Press, 1990), 3–7.

sermons of Solomon Stoddard, and to novels like *Clarissa Harlowe* and *Eliza Wharton*. Sautherea taught her sister's children to entertain themselves so that she could study. She taught herself to knit and read at the same time so that she could study some more. When a college student opened an academy nearby, Sautherea "availed herself of it with avidity," advancing in several subjects in only a quarter. "It was a period of great delight to her, and its close brought tears of regret," Hall wrote.

With the end of this magical quarter, Sautherea faced an uncertain future. She "found books and study most satisfying," but provincial New England offered little nourishment to her inchoate intellectual ambitions, nor did marriage offer a resolution. After spending several years among town folk, the courtship rituals she had observed as a child seemed faintly ridiculous. The hapless suitor's "awkward" calls, conducted under the eyes of the entire "titter[ing]" family, provided a "scene worth witnessing." Hardly the stuff of romance. Possessed by the "idealizations of love," Sautherea offered her heart to a town man, a college man, who showered her with "many nameless attentions, . . . moonlit walks, and so on." For her part, she was "entirely permeated by his image and invested him with a brilliant halo of beauty and attractiveness." When she learned that he had never intended any lasting attachment, the "blow came with almost annihilating force." As time passed, she received marriage proposals from other men, but none she could accept. Without a vocation, without a husband, without options beyond her sister's household, Sautherea began to doubt herself. Although she was "naturally self-distrustful" she began to "carry that feeling entirely too far."

Things got worse when her brother-in-law moved the family into the shire town, a "metropolis" that bore an uncanny resemblance to Northampton.[4] Before the move, Sautherea was marginalized by the constraints that bound all provincial women. After the move, she was marginalized by the divisions that had grown up between them. It would be difficult to overstate the difference between the two communities. Sautherea had become accustomed to a "community of farmers, all nearly on an equality as to property and standing." For all their cultivation, these "working people" paid "little regard to dress, fashion, furniture, or equipage." But in the "shire-town," she found herself living amid "an old aristocracy of wealth and culture."

Here, "men whose livelihood was obtained not by labor of the hands but by that of the brain" and women "whose garments were rich and

---

[4]For Arethusa Hall, this constituted a move to Northampton, less than ten miles east of Westhampton, in 1822.

fashionable" lived in "handsomely built and elegantly furnished houses." The ladies of the town presided over a fashionable sociability, one that demanded pretty gowns, elegant furniture, graceful manners, cultured speech, and an abundance of hired help. The town's brilliance threw new light on the sisters' lives. For the first time, Sautherea noticed that she was living in a house bereft of woven carpets, nice furniture, and pictures to decorate the walls. Worse, she realized that their country backgrounds had never provided "intercourse with polished society." Sautherea and her sister were completely out of place. After a few formal calls, "social intercourse was almost completely given up." Abandoned by the ladies, Sautherea could have enjoyed "free and unembarrassed access" to "families of lower rank." But that would never do. Her "choice was for the most refined and cultured or none at all." Local hierarchies being what they were, Sautherea was left with none at all.[5]

"Lonely and desolate," aware that she needed a change, Sautherea decided to "fit herself for a teacher in a private school or academy." After earning a portion of the tuition and borrowing the balance, she entered an academy where she found "happiness greater than she had ever before enjoyed." She was "entirely at leisure" to study, respected among her peers, and voted second in beauty among all the pupils. After completing her education, she waited two years to secure a position; the competition was fierce, and women without experience were the last to be hired. After a brief stint teaching among strangers in a small town far from her home, Sautherea moved to Providence to bolster her credentials by improving her French.

The time spent in Providence marked an "important epoch in the life our heroine," Hall wrote. Sautherea boarded with a family who moved in the "best society," despite their reduced circumstances. The family treated her as kin, introducing her to "the most accomplished society in the country." The woman who had been snubbed by provincial ladies found herself learning to mingle with members of Congress, judges, army officers, clergymen, and the British consul. Indeed, by the end of her stay, Sautherea had become so refined that she briefly flirted with Episocpalianism, attracted by its "poetic, devotional, and aes-

[5]Arethusa Hall's depiction of Northampton society might seem to contradict the recollections of Theodore Bliss or Caroline Clapp Briggs, who emphasized its inclusive, even egalitarian, dimensions. But Hall and her sister were not shut out of genteel society. They received calls from the women of Northampton's better families when they arrived in town and were invited to make calls in return. Yet the two sisters were put off by the unarticulated markers of social distance that characterized provincial sociability—markers that Bliss and Briggs either failed to notice or chose to ignore.

thetic elements." On leaving Providence, she secured a position not as a teacher but as a principal. She boarded with a trustee, a man of "high culture and literary taste" whose "large and stately" house was filled with "brass andirons, mahogany furniture, and silver polished like mirrors." Withal, the polish Sautherea picked up in Providence was probably more valuable than the French.

Arethusa Hall never finished writing her "story of a life." The narrative ends in mid-paragraph. But in a deeper sense, Sautherea's life story was complete. Recapitulating the trajectory of many nineteenth-century fictional heroines, Sautherea moved from rusticity to refinement, from obscurity to visibility.[6] Her self is fashioned, her progress concluded. But if Hall yoked the elements of Sautherea's life to the conventions of sentimental fiction, she also cataloged the dilemmas that provincial women confronted in the decades before the Civil War. Sautherea could measure the demands of domestic manufactures against the toil of middle-class housework. Along with her sister, she understood the value of household help and the difficulty of going without it. And as an unmarried woman, she faced all the predicaments that provincial society could serve up. There were chances to marry, but none that proved satisfactory, none that met the standards of romantic love. The autonomy and individual attainment promised by learning was checked by the many constraints within provincial households and the pronounced lack of opportunity beyond them. Sautherea experienced both the pleasure and the slights afforded by provincial sociability. She witnessed the growing importance of fashion and consumption in marking the subtle divisions within the middle class. Finally, by casting her life as a novel that conformed to the conventions of sentimental literature, Hall testified to the connections between literary culture and female self-fashioning. The story of Sautherea's life speaks to the opportunities, hierarchies and tensions that accompanied the creation of a provincial middle class.[7]

Although Arethusa Hall detailed the ways in which the transition to capitalism and the emergence of a provincial middle class changed

---

[6]This trajectory is described by Richard Bushman, *The Refinement of America: Persons, Houses, Cities* (New York: Vintage Books, 1993), 308–12.

[7]This reading is similar to Lawrence Buell's approach to literary depictions of the New England village. He suggests that "we understand literary depictions of the New England village best if we approach them at once semiologically, as a codification of a repertoire of motifs built up over time, and mimetically, as referring to historical reality, however transmuted that reality may have been in the process of literary embodiment." (*New England Literary Culture: From Revolution to Renaissance* [New York: Cambridge University Press, 1986], 305).

women's lives, she stopped short of addressing the transition itself. All the markers are there: the movement away from domestic manufactures, the growing urgency of women's claims to liberal individualism, the rise of fashion and consumption. But those markers don't occur over time; instead, they are arrayed over space. In Hall's narrative, the distance between household economy and market society becomes the difference between the New England hill country and Northampton. From Hall's perspective, the development of rural capitalism is not a historic process but a movement from periphery to center. In part, her account reflected material reality. Rural New England was not a monolithic whole. Historians have long recognized it as a region riddled by economic, religious, political, and even topographical differences; they have also recognized the ways in which the development of capitalism might erase or reinforce those differences.[8] Provincials themselves were keenly aware of these differences. They well understood the distinction between working the soil on a hardscrabble farm and earning a living in one of the prosperous commercial villages along the Connecticut River. They also understood and elaborated subtler distinctions—distinctions of refinement and gentility that drew impenetrable boundaries between towns such as Hanover and Candia.

But Hall's preoccupation with geography also provided a way of writing about the effects of change while denying the processes that created it. In Hall's telling, the provincial landscape is fixed. All that changes is Sautherea's position in it. Change over time collapses into change over terrain. And in the process, the agency, the struggle, and the contingency that fueled the creation of the provincial middle class disappears. But as we have seen, this narrative strategy was not limited to purely literary endeavors. On the contrary. There is a marked continuity not only between the experiences of Sautherea and provincial women but also between the ideological dimensions of Hall's fictionalized narrative and everyday narratives of provincial women. All of these narratives distance provincial women, men, and communities from the processes of social and economic change and from the market society born of that change. If Arethusa Hall cast Northampton as a mean-spirited "metropolis" and Caroline Clapp Briggs cast it as an

[8]For examples of historians' attempts to trace regions within rural New England, see, among many, Clark, *Roots of Rural Capitalism*; William J. Gilmore, *Reading Becomes a Necessity of Life: Material and Cultural Life in Rural New England, 1780–1835* (Knoxville: University of Tennessee Press, 1989); Stephen Nissenbaum, "New England as Region and Nation," in *All over the Map: Rethinking American Regions*, ed. Edward L. Ayers, et al. (Baltimore: Johns Hopkins University Press, 1996).

idyllic village, both women displaced the contested process of historical change onto the tranquil, timeless opposition of town and country. These discourses, like the social and cultural practices that undergirded them, contributed much to the creation of the mythic New England village, a place free from change, free from the taint of bourgeois social relations, and, eventually, free from the forces of production and labor itself.

Toward the New England Village

By the end of the antebellum era, this mythic village assumed physical shape, taking on new reality with the transformation of town geography. The quickening pace of trade and manufactures during the Federalist era had exerted a centralizing force on the region's geography, redrawing the contours of towns and villages. Residences and shops that had followed the scattered placement of farms across the landscape for two hundred years began to cluster around town centers. Spacious homes, busy shops, tall churches and dignified public buildings formed a white-painted, green-shuttered circle around the town commons. For Timothy Dwight and countless other like-minded men and women, this ordered village stood at the heart of the New England myth, offering proof enough of the region's moral and cultural superiority.[9]

Eventually, even the commons themselves succumbed to the myth. Once muddy, unkempt, public squares, they were appropriated and improved by the middle class beginning in the 1850s. Improvement required planting trees, hiring landscape architects, and restricting the flow of traffic across the commons. Improvement also demanded that the commons become pastoral greens, scenes of genteel leisure. In 1859, for example, a group of Amherst businessmen that included Edward Dickinson succeeded in banishing both the town's agricultural fair and the college commencement from the commons. The fair moved several miles outside of town; the commencement retreated to the Amherst College campus, making a private ritual out of what had once been a public celebration. As Christopher Clark has observed, by relocating these public celebrations, members of the provincial middle class erased all evidence of labor in general and agricultural labor in

[9]See Joseph S. Wood, with a contribution by Michael P. Steinetz, *The New England Village* (Baltimore: Johns Hopkins University Press, 1997); and Nissenbaum, "New England as Region and Nation."

particular from the town center.[10] Ignoring recent history, the same provincials who had busied themselves beautifying their towns drew direct connections between the recently refurbished towns and the distant colonial past. In their eyes, the New England town remained aloof from history; its virtue lay precisely in its timelessness.

Over the course of the nineteenth century, New Englanders carried this invented tradition well beyond the confines of the countryside. Moving west, they reproduced both their tidy villages and their social and cultural institutions. As the careers of Lyman Beecher and Catharine Beecher suggest, this was not simply a matter of finding comfort in the familiar but of bringing New England's special brand of civilization to the savage wilderness and beyond.[11] By 1850, Daniel Webster could fantasize about the day when the influence of the New England "race" would spread over the continent, across the Pacific, and to the "three hundred millions of people in China."[12] At the same time that provincials carried their vision west, they carried it to eastern cities. These men and women hardly aspired to make the metropolis over in the image of the village; they had the suburbs for that.[13] But even from the heart of cities such as Boston and New York, New Englanders used the growing culture industry, especially its lyceums and its literary culture, to extend and elaborate the myth of the New England village. As Stephen Nissenbaum has observed, nineteenth-century literary elites like Emerson, Stowe, Hawthorne, and Whittier became national writers by cultivating a regional perspective, by memorializing not simply the village geography but social relations that obtained within it.[14]

Thus was provincial New England inscribed in the heart of national identity. But this pastoral village center, abstracted from the worlds of farming and manufactures, was the culmination of a larger sentimentalizing process—a process that originated not simply in the minds of Federalist elites, the agendas of Whig politicians, or the imaginations of Romantic writers, but also in the experiences and imaginations of

[10]Clark, *Roots of Rural Capitalism*, 311–12. See also Wood, *New England Village*; Randolph A. Roth, *The Democratic Dilemma: Religion, Reform and the Social Order in the Connecticut River Valley of Vermont, 1750–1850* (New York: Cambridge University Press, 1987), 265; Nissenbaum, "New England as Region and Nation"; and Wood, *The New England Village*.

[11]See Kathryn Kish Sklar, *Catharine Beecher: A Study in American Domesticity* (New York: Norton, 1976), 107–21, 168–83; Joan D. Hedrick, *Harriet Beecher Stowe: A Life* (New York: Oxford University Press, 1994), 67–69.

[12]Quoted in Nissenbaum, "New England as Region and Nation," 51.

[13]John R. Stilgoe, *Borderland: Origins of the American Suburb, 1820–1939* (New Haven, Conn.: Yale University Press, 1988).

[14]Nissenbaum, "New England as Region and Nation."

more ordinary women and men. New England's sanitized greens and idealized village life owed as much to an Elizabeth Phelps Huntington or a Fanny Fuller as to a Timothy Dwight or an Edward Dickinson, for the sentimentalization of New England was not simply a matter of literature or landscape architecture. As Arethusa Hall's "Sautherea: The Story of a Life" suggests, it was forged in the nexus of experience and imagination. It derived from women's and men's daily efforts to understand and manipulate the development of rural capitalism and the transformation of the New England countryside. More to the point, it was rooted in the connections that members of an emerging provincial middle class drew between past and present, between household economy and market society.

Provincial women's lives and the stories they told about their lives reveal attempts to master change, to secure a place within an emerging middle class, and to define new gender roles and identities within that class. In the process, these women helped to shape a distinctive, rural middle class. In the face of all this change, provincial women and men looked to their pasts—however fictionalized, however constructed— for guidance. Their stories help us to understand the development of rural capitalism. But those stories also help us to understand the ways in which the past survives into the present. New Englanders looked to their pasts for many things: reassurance, legitimation, power. Once imagined as a bulwark against the encroachments of a market society, their collective past ultimately became a convention of that market society. Above all, their stories demonstrate the folly of holding up the fictions of the past as a talisman against the dilemmas of the present— both in their day and in our own.

Index

Numbers in italic refer to illustrations.

Academies and seminaries, 70–71, 72, 246; curriculum, 70–72; examinations, 206–207. *See also* education; *individual schools*
Adams, Eliza. *See* Young, Eliza Adams
Adams, Harriet. *See* Aiken, Harriet Adams
Aiken, Harriet Adams, 24, 29; education, 86–88
Aiken, John, 86
Amherst, Mass., 1–2, 152
anti-slavery societies, 199–200, 201–202, 203
associations: maternal, 200, 201; voluntary, 191n, 195–199, 203. *See also* benevolent associations

Bartlett, Joseph, 239
Beecher, Catharine, 197, 250
Beecher, Lyman, 250
benevolent associations, 14–15, 199–203; in community life, 203–204; women's identities and, 199–203; women's participation in, 117, 121, 200–203, 208
benevolent fairs, 204–205
Bliss, Abigail Rowland, 162
Bliss, George, 162–163
Bliss, Theodore, 176, 180–181, 188–189, 213
Blumin, Stuart, 177n, 191n
Bodman, Angelina, 197, 202
Boydston, Jeanne, 44

Bradford, Vt., 183
Bradlee, Louisa, 23, 46
Bradley, Elizabeth, 136
Bradley, Emily 49
Bradley, Mehab Ann, 49, 75, 182
Bradley, William Czar, 32, 129–130
Brattleboro, Vt., 43, 117, 168, 169
Briggs, Caroline Clapp: household of, 22, 34, 52–53; marriage of, 109–110; and Northampton social networks, 180–181
Brown, Charles Brockden, 221
Brown, Weltha, 76, 235–236; friendship with Eliza Perkins, 82–84
Buckland, Mass., 85
Bushman, Richard L., 143

Candia, N.H., 240, 248
capitalism, 216–217, 228; rural, 11–14, 23–24
cash exchange, 4, 23, 41–43, 44–47, 224. *See also* debt; market society
cattle shows, 205–206
Chambers-Schiller, Lee, 117, 204n
Cheney, Nathaniel, 134–135
Chicopee, Mass., 27
Child, Lydia Maria, 224
city, contrasted with country, 2–3, 7–8, 10, 15–16, 175–178, 184–187, 228–233, 239–241
civic rituals, 207–212, 220–221

Clark, Asel, 107, 140–142
Clark, Christopher, 23, 40, 54, 177–178, 249
Clark, Clarissa Warner, 107, 140–142
Clarke, Anne Laura, 42–43, 118
Clarke, Elizabeth, 43
class: distinctions, 152–161, 157–158, 178–181, 183, 238–239, 245–246; structure, 177–178. *See also* middle class; working class
clothing, 237–238. *See also* Fashion
Cochran, Lizzie, 30, 131, 201
Cochran, Marianne, 185, 239
Cochran, Martha, 173–174; friendship with Judge Lyman, 193–195; Northampton social networks, 180–181; as single woman, 120–122
Cochran, Mary, 25
Coleman, Maria Flynt, 104, 108
Coleman, Lyman, 103–104, 105
Concord, N.H., 237
Connecticut River Valley, 40, 82, 140
consumer revolution, 215–216
consumption, 214–218, 223–228, 236; production and, 4, 224–228; women and, 223–225, 232. *See also* fashion; emulation, social
Cott, Nancy, 20, 74, 76, 108–109
Coult, Mary Giddings, 61
country, contrasted with city, 2–3, 7–8, 10, 15–16, 175–178, 184–187, 221–222, 228–233, 239–241
courtship, 134–135, 157–159, 180–181, 196; community involvment in, 102–104, 152–156; growing privacy of, 156–157. *See also* heterosociability; love; marriage
Cowles, Elijah, 153–156
Crossman, Susan Mina, 68–69
cultural studies, 17
culture
    literary, 6–7, 148–149, 196, 197–199, 247; and provincial women's writing, 2, 176, 232. *See also* self-fashioning, Village Enlightenment
    public, 191–192, 195, 204–212

de Tocqueville, Alexis, 108–109
debt, 38–39; women's efforts to relieve, 41–43, 44–46. *See also* cash exchange; market society
Deerfield Academy, 81, 207
Deerfield, Mass., 32, 49, 69, 95–96 168
Denison, Madame, 49, 193–195
Dickinson, Edward, 132, 205, 249, 251;

courtship of, 103–107, 110–112, 130, 160
Dickinson, Emily Norcross: courtship of, 103–107, 108, 110–112, 130, 160; and women's authority, 142
Dillingham, Lucinda, 45
Dorr, Elizabeth Bradley, 30
Drake, Georgianna, 240
Durham, N.H., *26*
Dutton, Julia, 62–63
Dwight, H. A., 232
Dwight, Margaretta, 71
Dwight, Timothy, 249, 251

economy
    domestic, 27, 223–228. *See also* ideology, domestic; labor, women's; spheres, separate
    household, 3–5, 8–10, 13, 243; and domesticity, 9–11, 206; representations of, 206, 224–228. *See also* household production; labor, women's; rural capitalism
education, 65–66, 73–75, 221, 238; and household economy, 85–92. *See also* academies and seminaries; friendship, female; Village Enlightenment
emulation, social, 216, 218, 219, 221, 228, 237–239. *See also* consumption; fashion
"Ernestine Campbell" (1838), 230–231

fashion, 214–215, 219–223, 228, 245–248; extracted from market relations, 231–232; gender and, 229–230, 232–233; provincial, 235–36, 239–241. *See also* consumption; emulation, social; gentility
Fessenden, Thomas, 134, 160, 223–224
Fisher, Elizabeth Huntington, 19–22, 24, 57
Fiske, Catharine, 70, 73
Fiske, Fidelia, 117–118
Flynt, Olivia, 133
Forbes, Catherine White, 203
Freeman, Abigail Alden, 30
friendship
    books, 77–79, *78*
    female, 65–69, 79–84, 194, 220; and academies, 65–66; and bourgeois culture, 66–67; and household economy, 91–92; and literary conventions, 68–69, 77–81; religious devotion and, 67–68, 78–79
    between women and men, 193–195

Fuller, Aaron, 73; marriage of, 93–97
Fuller, Aaron Jr., 124–125
Fuller, Augustus, *96*
Fuller, Elizabeth, 51, 58, 73
Fuller, Fanny Negus, *96*, 251, 238; court-
    ship of, 134–135; education of, 73;
    marriage of, 93–97; work and family, 30,
    37, 49–50, 50–51, 58–59
Fuller, Harriet (Hattie), 73, 131, 157–158,
    160, 193

gender, and division of labor, 35–40
generations, 9, 127–128
gentility, 74, 157–160, 164, *167*, *168*,
    243–246; Protestantism and, 143–144,
    220–221, 231. *See also* class, distinc-
    tions; gentility
Gilmanton, N.H., 184
Ginzberg, Lori D., 210–211
Goodell, Esther, 57
Goodell, Harriett, 1, 147
Goodell, Marcus, 130
Goodman, Dena, 190
gossip, 100–101, 102, 135, 160
Gothic Seminary, 71–73
Great Transformation, 5
Greenfield, Mass., 222, 239
Grout, Sophronia, 69, 81, 182–183,
    237–238
Guilford, Vt., 124, 169
Gunnell Eliza Perkins, 76; friendship with
    Weltha Brown, 82–84
Habermas, Jürgen, 190
Hadley, Mass., 19
Hall, Arethusa, 242–249, 251
Hanover, N.H., 86, 198–199, 240, 248
Harrison, William Henry, 210–211
Hawley, William, 222, 228
Hawthorne, Nathaniel, 15
Hedrick, Joan, 198
Henretta, James, 54
heterosociability, 150, 191–199, 207,
    212–213; and middle-class formation,
    190. *See also* courtship, sociability
Hewes, Sophia, 116, 232; on domestic
    economy, 214, 215, 225–226, 228;
    *Mother's Book and Young Lady's
    Companion*, 225
Hidden, Elizabeth Parsons, 53
Higginson, Agnes Cochran, 32–33, 121, 122
Higginson, Agnes Gordon, 62, 167–168,
    172
Higginson, Annie Storrow, 150, 167–168
Higginson, Frances, 44–45
Hills, Henry, 151, 152, 160

history, rural, 11–12; intellectual, 6–7,
    16–17
Hitchcock, Edward, 75
Hitchcock, Orra White, 139
Hodges, Katherine, 152–153, 239
Hodges, Mrs. S. E., 152–153, 171, 239
Hooker, Mary, 235–236
Hopkins Academy, 76
Hopkins, Marion, 23
Hopkins, Mary, 196
household production, 4, 13, 23–25,
    243–244, 247
Howard, Leora, 152
Howe, Arethusa, 29
Howe, Joel, 38–39
Huntington, Bethia Throop, 19–22, 58,
    207; as single woman, 118–120
Huntington, Dan, 22, 24, 52, 58, 123,
    192–193
Huntington, Elizabeth Phelps, 119, 172,
    193, 251; marriage of, 123; religious
    faith and practice of, 169–170; work and
    family, 19–22, 24, 28–29, 34, 52, 57,
    58
Huntington, Elizabeth Sumner, 19–22, 24
Huntington, Frederic Dan, 50
Huntington, Helen Mills, 192
Huntington, Mary Dwight, 57, 74
Huntington, Theodore, 19–22, 119–120,
    196, 239
Husbandman and Housewife (1820),
    223–224
husbands, 99, 128–132, 137–142. *See also*
    marriage
Hutchinson, Mary, *78*

ideology
    domestic, 9, 15, 20, 47–51; female
        friendships and, 67; women's labor
        and, 40–41, 50–51. *See also* economy,
        domestic; spheres, separate
    republican, 140–143, 219–223, 227–228
individualism, 97–98, 109, 125, 248
industrial revolution, 215–216
Irish Exiles in America (1820), 219–221

Jaffee, David, 195n, 218
Judd, Apphia, 71
July Fourth, celebrations of, 208–209,
    220–221
Juster, Susan, 143

Keene, N.H., 70
Kelsey, H. S., 144, 145–147
Kemble, Fanny, 229

kin: emotional ties, 19–22, 57–58; and
  exchange, 53–58, 58–62, 234–235;
  networks, 125–126, 159n, 203; and
  women's labor, 19–23, 48–52
Kingsbury, Hannah, 29, 34
Kulikoff, Alan, 216–217

labor, women's
  paid, 23–24, 35–41, 43–44; rural capitalism and, 39–40. *See also* cash exchange; debt; economy, household;
  ideology, domestic
  unpaid, 19–23, 47–52, 58–62, 226–228;
  and domestic ideology, 20, 47–48;
  housework, 24–25, 29–31, 83. *See also*
  economy, domestic; ideology, domestic
Ladies' Monitor, The (1818), 134 160
Lancaster, N.H., 183, 234
literary culture, 6–7, 148–149, 196,
  197–199, 247; and provincial women's
  writing, 2, 176, 232. *See also* self-fashioning; Village Enlightenment
literary societies and reading clubs, 196,
  197–199; women's participation in,
  198–199
literature, didactic, 223–227
localism, 181–184
love
  reciprocal, 129–132
  romantic, 128–130, 145–148, 150, 151,
  157; gradual acceptance of, 142–144;
  and selfhood, 128–129, 148–149;
  women's critique of, 132–137
  See also courtship, marriage
lyceums, 196–197
Lyman, Amelia, 81
Lyman, Judge, 193–195
Lyon, Mary, 85
Lystra, Karen, 147n

manners, 166, 173–174, 178–179, 240. *See
  also* gentility; sociability
market society, 5, 8–10, 62–63. *See also*
  cash exchange; debt
marriage: bourgeois ideal of, 93–97; de
  Tocqueville's analysis, of 108–109;
  female identity and, 109–114, 122,
  123–125, 148–149; provincial ideal of,
  93–102; women's reluctance to marry,
  107–109. *See also* courtship; husbands;
  love; wives
Massachusetts, 17

Mathews, Mary, 153–156
Mayo, Sarah Edgarton, 149
Merrill, Michael, 54
middle class, 14, 16–17; family strategies
  and, 58–63; provincial, 5–6, 9–10, 13,
  15–16, 52, 58, 151–152, 177–178, 190,
  211–213, 228, 238–239. *See also* class
Millbury, Mass., 200
Mills, Sally, 29
Mirick, Mrs., 45
Mt. Holyoke Seminary, 64, 72
Murray, Judith Sargent, 221

Negus, Arethusa, 238
Negus, Caroline, 58
Negus, Luthera, 115
networks, social, 117–181
New England, representations of, 1–3, 15,
  26, 185–187, 249–251
New Hampshire, 17, 196
newspapers, 222, 224, 229, 232
Nissenbaum, Stephen, 250
Norcross, Emily. *See* Dickinson, Emily
  Norcross
North Hadley, Mass., 156
Northampton, Mass., 25, 42, 117, 121, 156,
  176–177, 180–181, 198, 208, 209, 217,
  248

Odell, Sarah, *26*
Olcott, Sarah, 240
"The Old Bonnet" (1855), 225
Olcutt, Sarah Jane, 127 148–150
Osterud, Nancy Grey, 166n, 203

Parsons, Hannah, 53
Parsons, Sarah, 53, 61, 184
particularism, 181–184
partisanship, women's, 210–212
*Pastor's Offering on Courtship and Mar-
  riage*, 98–102
Peabody, Amelia White, 123, 166, 173,
  181, 234–235, 238; and benevolent work,
  183–184, 201–202, 204; and kin net-
  works, 53–55; marriage of, 113–114;
  work and family, 27, 29, 30, 33
Peabody, William Bourn Oliver, 113–114
Pelham, Mass., 156
Penaimen, Julietta, 173
Princeton, Mass., 25, 37
Prude, Jonathan, 177

Queen Victoria, 222

Reed, Milton, 196
religious faith and practice, 67–68, 75,
    78–79, 82, 118–119, 140–141, 143–144,
    169–73, 220–221, 231, 237–238; and
    love, 137–145; and women's identities,
    142–143, 169–170
Rothman, Ellen, 129
Rush, Benjamin 221
Russell, Charles, 37–39, 115
Russell, Persis Hastings, 37–39
Russell Sarah, 41
Russell, Maria Wiswell, 25
Russell, Mary Elizabeth, 153–156
Russell, Theodore, 40
Ryan, Mary P., 205, 208

Salem, Mass., 173
Sanborn, Mary Ann Webster, 30
"Sautherea: The Story of a Life" (1864),
    242–249, 251
schools: dancing, 196; singing, 195–196
Scott, Anne Firor, 74
Second Great Awakening, 67, 137
Sedgwick, Catharine, 15, 225
Selden, Almira, 219–221
self-fashioning, 165, 195, 247. See also
    literary culture
sentimentality, 2, 7, 69–70, 148,
servants, 25–35, 155–156; social distance
    from employers, 32–35
sewing circles, 199–203, 201, 202
Shields, David S., 190
shopping, 232, 234–236
Skinner, Francis, 131
Smith, Sophia, 124–125
Snell, Ebenezar Strong, 103, 130–131,
    145–147, 146, 167, 217–218
Snell, Martha, 144, 145–147
Snell, Sabra Clark, 1, 103, 130–131, 146,
    217–218
sociability, 151, 157–159, 165–168,
    173–175; and class, 164, 165, 173,
    178–179; distinctiveness of provincial,
    175–181; informality of, 173–175; and
    women's identities, 169–173. See also
    heterosociability; visiting
South Hadley, Mass., 239
speculation, 229
spheres: public, 188–192, 195, 212–
    213; separate, 15, 20–21, 36, 40–41,
    161, 189–190, 210. See also
    economy, domestic; ideology,
    domestic

spinning, 4, 24, 243, 226–228. See also
    household production
Springfield, Mass., 166, 183, 201–202, 238
Stone, Martha, 236
Stowe, Harriet Beecher, 15, 197
Strong, Rachel, 76, 78–79, 80
"Susan Burnett—a true sketch" (1838),
    138–139

Tarble, Polly Flint, 54–55
temperance societies, 199–200, 203, 208
Tenney, Thomas, 198
textile production, 4, 24, 226
Thistle, Theophilus, 158–9, 160
Troy Seminary, 72, 74, 75
Tyler, Amelia, 131, 192
Tyler, Mary Palmer: financial struggles of,
    45, 124; marriage of, 123–124; religious
    faith and practice of, 169; and sociabil-
    ity, 174–175, 181, 192, 197, 208–209;
    work and family, 31, 35–36, 45, 48–49
Tyler, Mary W., 59
Tyler, Royall, 35–36, 174–175, 193–195
Tyler, William, 45, 131

Ulrich, Laurel Thatcher Ulrich, 39
Underwood, Frances H., 5, 178–179, 231
urbanization, 11–12, 14–15

Varon, Elizabeth R., 210–211
Veblen, Thorstein, 215
Vermont, 17, 173
Vickery, Amanda, 234
Village Enlightenment, 65, 195, 197. See
    also education; literary culture
visiting, 59–60, 173–174, 190, 192–193,
    240. See also sociability
voluntary associations, 191n, 195–199, 203

Warner, Clarissa. See Clark, Clarissa
    Warner
Warriner, Soloman, 133
weddings, 150, 175
White, Amelia. See Peabody, Amelia
    White
White, Eliza, 55
White, Mary Jane 55, 235
White, Moses, 56
Willard, Samuel, 131
Wilson, Mary Hoyt, 69, 81, 207
Withersby, Leander, 62
wives, 99–101, 128–130, 137–142. See also
    marriage

women
  authority of, 106–107, 140–143,
    157–161, 201–203, 211–212
  economic dependence of, 45–46, 116,
    132–133, 158
  labor of. *See* labor, women's
  occupations of, 23, 37–39, 43–44,
    117–118. *See also* labor, women's, paid
  single, 60–61, 115, 116–122, 158, 160;
    economic dependence of, 16, 117; and
    selfhood, 118–122

Wood, Gordon, 216–217
work: fancy, 204, 206; women's. *See* labor,
  women's
working class 13, 177–178
Wright, Mary, 180–181

yeoman, representations of, 10, 206, 227
Young, Adaline, 54, 171
Young, Eliza Adams, 60, *90*, *168*;
  education of, 86–89, 170–171
Young, Ira, 89, *168*